British Poetry

of the

Long Nineteenth Century

A Selection for College Students

Edited by

Beverley Park Rilett, PhD.

University of Nebraska–Lincoln

Zea Books
Lincoln, Nebraska

ISBN: 978-1-60962-163-6
doi 10.32873/unl.dc.zea.1096

Cover image: *The Lady of Shalott* by John William Waterhouse, 1888

Zea Books are published by the University of Nebraska–Lincoln Libraries.

Electronic (pdf) ebook edition available online at
https://digitalcommons.unl.edu/zeabook/

Print edition available from
http://www.lulu.com/spotlight/unllib

UNL does not discriminate based upon any protected status.
Please go to http://www.unl.edu/equity/notice-nondiscrimination

CONTENTS

PREFACE

British Poetry of the Long Nineteenth Century was created specifically for a university English course that introduces students to influential texts of nineteenth-century British literature. While there are suitable anthologies available, they are either inconveniently divided into separate volumes for "Romantic" and "Victorian" poets, or far more comprehensive (and expensive) than necessary for the relatively short span of time my students study the poetry of the period. Furthermore, though these poems have long been in the public domain and are readily available online, having a common print text to refer to during our class discussions of the works is more efficient. For these reasons, I decided to curate my own edition of representative poets and poetry of the long nineteenth century.

Scholars usually refer to the "long" nineteenth century because the significant literary movements of the period do not correspond neatly with the beginning and ending of the 1800s. The Romantic Movement in British poetry is usually said to begin either with Charlotte Smith or William Blake in the late 1700s. Similarly, late Victorian authors such as Oscar Wilde, whose work ushered in modernist aesthetics, continued to publish into the early 1900s. The title of this anthology is an attempt to more accurately categorize the poets I believe should be part of a course in nineteenth-century British literature.

In any collection, an editor must make choices about what to keep and what to leave out. My students and I debate these selections, sometimes vigorously. We ultimately cut some excellent poems in an attempt to balance, more or less, the number of pages devoted to each poet. Limiting our number of different authors to eighteen also allows an average class of students to pair up or work individually to introduce each one, which is a teaching strategy I have found effective. The poet's gender was another important factor in our selection process, and we included several women poets who are often overlooked in nineteenth century studies. Furthermore, readers may be surprised to see the poetry of some British authors whose fiction usually garners more recognition than their verse. Many of these poems, however, are among my own and my students' favorites.

Several exceptional features of this anthology make it a useful classroom text, such as the addition of line numbers to all the poems. By numbering every fifth line, we balanced the need for simple referencing with the need to reduce clutter on the designed page. Each poet's section also opens with a brief biographical sketch and an image of the poet from the public domain—a taste that may cultivate the desire to learn more about the person behind the poetry.

After surveying what other professors are teaching in comparable courses; revisiting what I was taught as an undergraduate; poring through the anthologies available for adoption; and taking into consideration my own and my students' intellectual and emotional responses, I created this edition of British poetry from the long nineteenth century. I am eager to use it with my future students and if you teach a similar unit or course, I hope you will consider using it too. Enjoy!

Dr. Beverley Park Rilett
University of Nebraska-Lincoln

CHARLOTTE SMITH (1749-1806)

Charlotte Smith, born Charlotte Turner, suffered difficulties in her life that leave their trace on her poetry. Smith's father married her off at the age of fifteen to Benjamin Smith. She bore twelve children, three of whom died in infancy. She wrote *Elegiac Sonnets* in 1783 while in debtor's prison with her husband and children. Smith expanded *Elegiac Sonnets* over the next nine years. The family later had to flee to France to escape debt. After leaving her abusive husband in 1787, Smith returned to England and was able to support their children as an author of novels and poetry. In 1788, Smith published a successful novel, *Emmeline*. Smith's writing typically addresses issues of social injustice and the class system. She helped to remake the sonnet form as an expression of mournful feeling and of natural detail. Smith's most famous long poem, "Beachy Head", was published posthumously, in 1807.

WRITTEN AT THE CLOSE OF SPRING

Charlotte Smith

1   The garlands fade that Spring so lately wove,
      Each simple flower, which she had nursed in dew,
Anemonies, that spangled every grove,
      The primrose wan, and hare-bell mildly blue.
5   No more shall violets linger in the dell,
      Or purple orchis variegate the plain,
Till Spring again shall call forth every bell,
      And dress with humid hands her wreaths again. —
Ah! poor humanity! so frail, so fair,
10   Are the fond visions of thy early day,
Till tyrant passion and corrosive care
      Bid all thy fairy colours fade away!
Another May new buds and flowers shall bring;
Ah! why has happiness—no second spring?

TO SLEEP

Charlotte Smith

1   Come, balmy Sleep! tired nature's soft resort!
      On these sad temples all thy poppies shed;
And bid gay dreams, from Morpheus' airy court,
      Float in light vision round my aching head!
5   Secure of all thy blessings, partial Power!
      On his hard bed the peasant throws him down;
And the poor sea-boy, in the rudest hour,
      Enjoys thee more than he who wears a crown.
Clasp'd in her faithful shepherd's guardian arms,
10   Well may the village girl sweet slumbers prove;
And they, O gentle Sleep! still taste thy charms,
      Who wake to labour, liberty, and love.
But still thy opiate aid dost thou deny
To calm the anxious breast; to close the streaming eye.

TO NIGHT

Charlotte Smith

1   I love thee, mournful, sober-suited Night!
      When the faint moon, yet lingering in her wane,
    And veil'd in clouds, with pale uncertain light
      Hangs o'er the waters of the restless main.
5   In deep depression sunk, the enfeebled mind
      Will to the deaf cold elements complain,
      And tell the embosom'd grief, however vain,
    To sullen surges and the viewless wind.
    Though no repose on thy dark breast I find,
10   I still enjoy thee—cheerless as thou art;
      For in thy quiet gloom the exhausted heart
    Is calm, though wretched; hopeless, yet resigned.
    While to the winds and waves its sorrows given,
    May reach--though lost on earth--the ear of Heaven!

WRITTEN IN THE CHURCH-YARD AT MIDDLETON, IN SUSSEX.

Charlotte Smith

1   Press'd by the moon, mute arbitress of tides,
      While the loud equinox its power combines,
      The sea no more its swelling surge confines,
    But o'er the shrinking land sublimely rides.
5   The wild blast, rising from the western cave,
      Drives the huge billows from their heaving bed;
      Tears from their grassy tombs the village dead,
    And breaks the silent sabbath of the grave!
    With shells and sea-weed mingled, on the shore,
10   Lo! their bones whiten in the frequent wave;
      But vain to them the winds and waters rave;
    They hear the warring elements no more:
    While I am doom'd—by life's long storm opprest,
    To gaze with envy on their gloomy rest.

ON BEING CAUTIONED AGAINST WALKING OVER A HEADLAND OVERLOOKING THE SEA, BECAUSE IT WAS FREQUENTED BY A LUNATIC.

Charlotte Smith

1 Is there a solitary wretch who hies
  To the tall cliff, with starting pace or slow,
 And, measuring, views with wild and hollow eyes
  Its distance from the waves that chide below;
5 Who, as the sea-born gale with frequent sighs
  Chills his cold bed upon the mountain turf,
 With hoarse, half utter'd lamentation, lies
  Murmuring responses to the dashing surf?
 In moody sadness, on the giddy brink,
10 I see him more with envy than with fear;
 He has no *nice felicities* that shrink
  From giant horrors; wildly wandering here,
 He seems (uncursed with reason) not to know
 The depth or the duration of his woe.

THE SEA VIEW

Charlotte Smith

1   The upland shepherd, as reclined he lies
    On the soft turf that clothes the mountain brow,
Marks the bright sea-line mingling with the skies;
    Or from his course celestial, sinking slow,
5   The summer-sun in purple radiance low,
Blaze on the western waters; the wide scene
    Magnificent, and tranquil, seems to spread
Even o'er the rustic's breast a joy serene,
    When, like dark plague-spots by the demons shed,
10   Charged deep with death, upon the waves, far seen,
    Move the war-freighted ships; and fierce and red,
    Flash their destructive fires—The mangled dead
And dying victims then pollute the flood.
Ah, thus man spoils Heaven's glorious works with blood!

HUGE VAPOURS BROOD ABOVE THE CLIFTED SHORE

Charlotte Smith

1   Huge vapours brood above the clifted shore,
     Night o'er the ocean settles, dark and mute,
     Save where is heard the repercussive roar
     Of drowsy billows, on the rugged foot
5   Of rocks remote; or still more distant tone
     Of seamen, in the anchored bark, that tell
     The watch relieved; or one deep voice alone,
     Singing the hour, and bidding "strike the bell."
     All is black shadow, but the lucid line
10   Marked by the light surf on the level sand,
     Or where afar, the ship-lights faintly shine
     Like wandering fairy fires, that oft on land
     Mislead the pilgrim; such the dubious ray
     That wavering reason lends, in life's long darkling way.

TO HOPE

Charlotte Smith

1   Oh, Hope! thou soother sweet of human woes!
      How shall I lure thee to my haunts forlorn!
For me wilt thou renew the withered rose,
      And clear my painful path of pointed thorn?
5   Ah come, sweet nymph! in smiles and softness drest,
      Like the young hours that lead the tender year
Enchantress come! and charm my cares to rest:
      Alas! the flatterer flies, and will not hear!
A prey to fear, anxiety, and pain,
10   Must I a sad existence still deplore?
Lo! the flowers fade, but all the thorns remain,
      "For me the vernal garland blooms no more."
Come then, "pale Misery's love!" be thou my cure,
And I will bless thee, who though slow art sure.

ON THE DEPARTURE OF THE NIGHTINGALE

Charlotte Smith

1   Sweet poet of the woods, a long adieu!
      Farewell soft mistrel of the early year!
    Ah! 't will be long ere thou shalt sing anew,
      And pour thy music on the "night's dull ear."
5   Whether on spring thy wandering flights await,
      Or whether silent in our groves you dwell,
    The pensive muse shall own thee for her mate,
      And still protect the song she loves so well.
    With cautious step the love-lorn youth shall glide
10   Through the lone brake that shades thy mossy nest;
    And shepherd girls from eyes profane shall hide
      The gentle bird who sings of pity best:
    For still thy voice shall soft affections move,
    And still be dear to sorrow and to love!

TO THE SHADE OF BURNS

Charlotte Smith

1 Mute is thy wild harp, now, O Bard sublime!
   Who, amid Scotia's mountain solitude,
  Great Nature taught to "build the lofty rhyme,"
   And even beneath the daily pressure, rude,
5 Of laboring Poverty, thy generous blood,
  Fired with the love of freedom—Not subdued
   Wert thou by thy low fortune: But a time
   Like this we live in, when the abject chime
  Of echoing Parasite is best approved,
10   Was not for thee—Indignantly is fled
  Thy noble Spirit; and no longer moved
   By all the ills o'er which thine heart has bled,
   Associate worthy of the illustrious dead,
  Enjoys with them "the Liberty it loved."

THIRTY-EIGHT. TO MRS ___ Y

Charlotte Smith

1   In early youth's unclouded scene,
      The brilliant morning of eighteen,
      With health and sprightly joy elate,
      We gazed on youth's enchanting spring,
5   Nor thought how quickly time would bring
               The mournful period — thirty-eight!

      Then the starch maid, or matron sage,
      Already of the sober age,
      We viewed with mingled scorn and hate;
10   In whose sharp words, or sharper face,
               With thoughtless mirth, we loved to trace
               The sad effects of — thirty-eight!

      Till, saddening, sickening at the view,
      We learned to dread what time might do;
15   And then preferred a prayer to Fate
      To end our days ere that arrived,
               When (power and pleasure long survived)
               We meet neglect, and — thirty-eight!

      But Time, in spite of wishes, flies;
20   And Fate our simple prayer denies,
      And bids us Death's own hour await!
      The auburn locks are mixed with grey,
               The transient roses fade away,
               But reason comes at — thirty-eight!

25   Her voice the anguish contradicts
      That dying vanity inflicts;
      Her hand new pleasures can create,
      For us she opens to the view
               Prospects less bright — but far more true,

30   And bids us smile at — thirty-eight!

No more shall Scandal's breath destroy
The social converse we enjoy
With bard or critic, tête à tête —
O'er youth's bright blooms her blight shall pour,
35   But spare the improving, friendly hour
        Which Science gives at — thirty-eight!

Stripped of their gaudy hues by Truth,
We view the glittering toys of youth,
And blush to think how poor the bait
40 For which to public scenes we ran,
        And scorned of sober sense the plan
        Which gives content at — thirty-eight!

O may her blessings now arise,
Like stars that mildly light the skies,
45 When the sun's ardent rays abate!
And in the luxuries of mind —
        In friendship, science — may we find
        Increasing joys at — thirty-eight!

Though Time's inexorable sway
50 Has torn the myrtle bands away,
For other wreaths — 'tis not too late:
The amaranth's purple glow survives,
        And still Minerva's olive thrives
        On the calm brow of — thirty-eight!

55 With eye more steady, we engage
To contemplate approaching age,
And life more justly estimate;
With firmer souls and stronger powers,
With reason, faith, and friendship ours,
        We'll not regret the stealing hours
60   That lead from thirty- e'en to forty-eight!

from *BEACHY HEAD*

Charlotte Smith

1   On thy stupendous summit, rock sublime!
     That o'er the channel reared, half way at sea
     The mariner at early morning hails,
     I would recline; while Fancy should go forth,
5   And represent the strange and awful hour
     Of vast concussion; when the Omnipotent
     Stretched forth his arm, and rent the solid hills,
     Bidding the impetuous main flood rush between
     The rifted shores, and from the continent
10   Eternally divided this green isle.
     Imperial lord of the high southern coast!
     From thy projecting head-land I would mark
     Far in the east the shades of night disperse,
     Melting and thinned, as from the dark blue wave
15   Emerging, brilliant rays of arrowy light
     Dart from the horizon; when the glorious sun
     Just lifts above it his resplendent orb.
     Advances now, with feathery silver touched,
     The rippling tide of flood; glisten the sands,
20   While, inmates of the chalky clefts that scar
     Thy sides precipitous, with shrill harsh cry,
     Their white wings glancing in the level beam,
     The terns, and gulls, and tarrocks, seek their food,
     And thy rough hollows echo to the voice
25   Of the gray choughs, and ever restless daws,
     With clamor, not unlike the chiding hounds,
     While the lone shepherd, and his baying dog,
     Drive to thy turfy crest his bleating flock.

     The high meridian of the day is past,
30   And Ocean now, reflecting the calm Heaven,

Is of cerulean hue; and murmurs low
The tide of ebb, upon the level sands.
The sloop, her angular canvas shifting still,
Catches the light and variable airs
35   That but a little crisp the summer sea,
Dimpling its tranquil surface.

Afar off,
And just emerging from the arch immense
Where seem to part the elements, a fleet
Of fishing vessels stretch their lesser sails;
40   While more remote, and like a dubious spot
Just hanging in the horizon, laden deep,
The ship of commerce richly freighted, makes
Her slower progress, on her distant voyage,
Bound to the orient climates, where the sun
45   Matures the spice within its odorous shell,
And, rivalling the gray worm's filmy toil,
Bursts from its pod the vegetable down;
Which in long turban'd wreaths, from torrid heat
Defends the brows of Asia's countless casts.
50   There the Earth hides within her glowing breast
The beamy adamant, and the round pearl
Enchased in rugged covering; which the slave,
With perilous and breathless toil, tears off
From the rough sea-rock, deep beneath the waves.
55   These are the toys of Nature; and her sport
Of little estimate in Reason's eye:
And they who reason, with abhorrence see
Man, for such gaudes and baubles, violate
The sacred freedom of his fellow man
60   Erroneous estimate ! As Heaven's pure air,
Fresh as it blows on this aërial height,
Or sound of seas upon the stony strand,
Or inland, the gay harmony of birds,
And winds that wander in the leafy woods;
65   Are to the unadulterate taste more worth

Than the elaborate harmony, brought out
From fretted stop, or modulated airs
Of vocal science. So the brightest gems,
Glancing resplendent on the regal crown,
70 Or trembling in the high born beauty's ear,
Are poor and paltry, to the lovely light
Of the fair star, that as the day declines,
Attendant on her queen, the crescent moon,
75 Bathes her bright tresses in the eastern wave.
For now the sun is verging to the sea,
And as he westward sinks, the floating clouds
Suspended, move upon the evening gale,
And gathering round his orb, as if to shade
80 The insufferable brightness, they resign
Their gauzy whiteness; and more warm'd, assume
All hues of purple. There, transparent gold
Mingles with ruby tints, and sapphire gleams,
And colours, such as Nature through her works
85 Shews only in the ethereal canopy.
Thither aspiring Fancy fondly soars,
Wandering sublime thro' visionary vales,
Where bright pavilions rise, and trophies, fann'd
By airs celestial; and adorn'd with wreaths
90 Of flowers that bloom amid elysian bowers.
Now bright, and brighter still the colours glow,
Till half the lustrous orb within the flood
Seems to retire: the flood reflecting still
Its splendor, and in mimic glory drest;
95 Till the last ray shot upward, fires the clouds
With blazing crimson; then in paler light,
Long lines of tenderer radiance, lingering yield
To partial darkness; and on the opposing side
The early moon distinctly rising, throws
100 Her pearly brilliance on the trembling tide.
The fishermen, who at set seasons pass
Many a league off at sea their toiling night,
Now hail their comrades, from their daily task

Returning; and make ready for their own,
105 With the night tide commencing: The night tide
Bears a dark vessel on, whose hull and sails
Mark her a coaster from the north. Her keel
Now ploughs the sand; and sidelong now she leans,
While with loud clamours her athletic crew
110 Unload her; and resounds the busy hum
Along the wave-worn rocks. Yet more remote,
Where the rough cliff hangs beetling o'er its base,
All breathes repose; the water's rippling sound
Scarce heard; but now and then the sea-snipe's cry
115 Just tells that something living is abroad;
And sometimes crossing on the moonbright line,
Glimmers the skiff, faintly discern'd awhile,
Then lost in shadow.

WILLIAM BLAKE (1757–1827)

Blake was not only an English poet; he was also a printmaker and a painter who remains nearly as famous for his art as for his poetry. He began art school at age ten, and wrote his first poems at twelve. After a short four years of art school, Blake became apprenticed to a carver for the next seven and thereafter worked as an engraver and illustrator. He depicted visions he claimed to have from childhood and throughout his life; for example, Blake believed he saw the spirit of his brother after he died. Consequently, many of Blake's peers thought he was insane. In 1782, Blake married Catherine Boucher. They appeared to be an excellent team; he taught her to read, while she helped him to print his illuminated poetry, for which he is best known today. Blake's poems espoused freedom of the body and soul, and he famously championed imagination over reason.

THE ECCHOING GREEN

from Songs of Innocence
William Blake

1   The sun does arise,
    And make happy the skies.
    The merry bells ring
    To welcome the Spring.
5   The sky-lark and thrush,
    The birds of the bush,
    Sing louder around,
    To the bells' cheerful sound.
    While our sports shall be seen
10 On the Ecchoing Green.

    Old John, with white hair
    Does laugh away care,
    Sitting under the oak,
    Among the old folk,
15 They laugh at our play,
    And soon they all say.
    "Such, such were the joys.
    When we all girls & boys,
    In our youth-time were seen,
20 On the Ecchoing Green."

    Till the little ones weary
    No more can be merry
    The sun does descend,
    And our sports have an end.
25 Round the laps of their mothers,
    Many sisters and brothers,
    Like birds in their nest,
    Are ready for rest;
    And sport no more seen,
    On the darkening Green.

THE LAMB

from Songs of Innocence
William Blake

1   Little Lamb, who made thee
   Dost thou know who made thee
 Gave thee life & bid thee feed.
 By the stream & o'er the mead;
5   Gave thee clothing of delight,
 Softest clothing wooly bright;
 Gave thee such a tender voice,
 Making all the vales rejoice!
   Little Lamb, who made thee
10   Dost thou know who made thee

   Little Lamb, I'll tell thee,
   Little Lamb, I'll tell thee!
 He is called by thy name,
 For he calls himself a Lamb:
15 He is meek & he is mild,
 He became a little child:
 I a child & thou a lamb,
 We are called by his name.
   Little Lamb, God bless thee.
20   Little Lamb, God bless thee.

THE LITTLE BLACK BOY

from Songs of Innocence
William Blake

1   My mother bore me in the southern wild,
And I am black, but O! my soul is white;
White as an angel is the English child:
But I am black as if bereav'd of light.

5   My mother taught me underneath a tree
And sitting down before the heat of day,
She took me on her lap and kissed me,
And pointing to the east began to say:

"Look on the rising sun: there God does live
10   And gives his light, and gives his heat away.
And flowers and trees and beasts and men receive
Comfort in morning, joy in the noonday.

"And we are put on earth a little space,
That we may learn to bear the beams of love,
15   And these black bodies and this sun-burnt face
Is but a cloud, and like a shady grove."

"For when our souls have learn'd the heat to bear
The cloud will vanish; we shall hear his voice.
Saying: 'come out from the grove my love & care,
20   And round my golden tent like lambs rejoice.'

Thus did my mother say and kissed me,
And thus I say to little English boy.
When I from black and he from white cloud free,
And round the tent of God like lambs we joy:

25   I'll shade him from the heat till he can bear,
To lean in joy upon our father's knee.
And then I'll stand and stroke his silver hair,
And be like him and he will then love me.

THE CHIMNEY SWEEPER

from Songs of Innocence
William Blake

1   When my mother died I was very young,
And my father sold me while yet my tongue
Could scarcely cry "'weep! 'weep! 'weep! 'weep!"
So your chimneys I sweep and in soot I sleep.

5   There's little Tom Dacre, who cried when his head
That curled like a lamb's back, was shaved, so I said,
"Hush, Tom! never mind it, for when your head's bare,
You know that the soot cannot spoil your white hair."

And so he was quiet, and that very night,
10   As Tom was a-sleeping he had such a sight!
That thousands of sweepers, Dick, Joe, Ned, and Jack,
Were all of them locked up in coffins of black;

And by came an Angel who had a bright key,
And he opened the coffins and set them all free;
15   Then down a green plain, leaping, laughing they run,
And wash in a river and shine in the Sun.

Then naked and white, all their bags left behind,
They rise upon clouds, and sport in the wind.
And the Angel told Tom, if he'd be a good boy,
20   He'd have God for his father and never want joy.

And so Tom awoke; and we rose in the dark
And got with our bags and our brushes to work.
Though the morning was cold, Tom was happy and warm;
So if all do their duty, they need not fear harm.

THE DIVINE IMAGE

from Songs of Innocence
William Blake

1 To Mercy, Pity, Peace, and Love
 All pray in their distress;
 And to these virtues of delight
 Return their thankfulness.

5 For Mercy, Pity, Peace, and Love
 Is God, our father dear,
 And Mercy, Pity, Peace, and Love
 Is Man, his child and care.

 For Mercy has a human heart,
10 Pity a human face,
 And Love, the human form divine,
 And Peace, the human dress.

 Then every man, of every clime,
 That prays in his distress,
15 Prays to the human form divine,
 Love, Mercy, Pity, Peace.

 And all must love the human form,
 In heathen, Turk, or Jew;
 Where Mercy, Love, and Pity dwell
20 There God is dwelling too.

HOLY THURSDAY

from Songs of Innocence
William Blake

1   'Twas on a Holy Thursday, their innocent faces clean,
     The children walking two & two, in red & blue & green,
     Grey-headed beadles walk'd before, with wands as white as snow,
     Till into the high dome of Paul's they like Thames' waters flow.

5   O what a multitude they seem'd, these flowers of London town!
     Seated in companies they sit with radiance all their own.
     The hum of multitudes was there, but multitudes of lambs,
     Thousands of little boys & girls raising their innocent hands.

     Now like a mighty wind they raise to heaven the voice of song,
10   Or like harmonious thunderings the seats of Heaven among.
     Beneath them sit the aged men, wise guardians of the poor;
     Then cherish pity, lest you drive an angel from your door.

NURSE'S SONG

from Songs of Innocence
William Blake

1   When voices of children are heard on the green
And laughing is heard on the hill,
My heart is at rest within my breast
And everything else is still.

5   "Then come home my children the sun is gone down
And the dews of night arise;
Come come leave off play, and let us away
Till the morning appears in the skies."

"No no let us play, for it is yet day
10   And we cannot go to sleep.
Besides in the sky, the little birds fly
And the hills are all covered with sheep."

"Well, well, go & play till the light fades away,
And then go home to bed."
15   The little ones leaped & shouted & laugh'd
And all the hills echoed.

INFANT JOY

from Songs of Innocence
William Blake

1   "I have no name;
     I am but two days old."
     What shall I call thee?
     "I happy am;
5   Joy is my name."
     Sweet joy befall thee!

     Pretty joy!
     Sweet joy, but two days old.
     Sweet Joy I call thee;
10   Thou dost smile,
     I sing the while;
     Sweet joy befall thee!

THE SHEPHERD

from Songs of Innocence
William Blake

1   How sweet is the Shepherd's sweet lot!
     From the morn to the evening he strays;
     He shall follow his sheep all the day,
     And his tongue shall be filled with praise.

5   For he hears the lamb's innocent call,
     And he hears the ewe's tender reply;
     He is watchful while they are in peace,
     For they know when their Shepherd is nigh.

EARTH'S ANSWER

from Songs of Experience
William Blake

1   Earth rais'd up her head,
     From the darkness dread & drear.
     Her light fled:
     Stony dread!
5   And her locks cover'd with grey despair.

     Prison'd on wat'ry shore
     Starry Jealousy does keep my den
     Cold and hoar
     Weeping o'er
10   I hear the Father of the ancient men

     Selfish father of men!
     Cruel, jealous, selfish fear!
     Can delight
     Chain'd in night
15   The virgins of youth and morning bear?

     Does spring hide its joy
     When buds and blossoms grow?
     Does the sower
     Sow by night?
20   Or the plowman in darkness plow?

     Break this heavy chain,
     That does freeze my bones around.
     Selfish! vain!
     Eternal bane!
25   That free Love with bondage bound.

THE CLOD AND THE PEBBLE

from Songs of Experience
William Blake

1   "Love seeketh not itself to please,
Nor for itself hath any care,
But for another gives its ease,
And builds a Heaven in Hell's despair."

5   So sung a little Clod of Clay
Trodden with the cattle's feet,
But a Pebble of the brook
Warbled out these metres meet:

     "Love seeketh only self to please,
10   To bind another to its delight,
Joys in another's loss of ease,
And builds a Hell in Heaven's despite."

HOLY THURSDAY

from Songs of Experience
William Blake

1   Is this a holy thing to see,
In a rich and fruitful land,
Babes reducd to misery,
Fed with cold and usurous hand?

5   Is that trembling cry a song?
Can it be a song of joy?
And so many children poor?
It is a land of poverty!

And their sun does never shine,
10   And their fields are bleak & bare,
And their ways are fill'd with thorns:
It is eternal winter there.

For where-e'er the sun does shine,
And where-e'er the rain does fall:
15   Babe can never hunger there,
Nor poverty the mind appall.

THE CHIMNEY SWEEPER

from Songs of Experience
William Blake

1   A little black thing among the snow,
Crying "weep! 'weep!" in notes of woe!
"Where are thy father and mother? say?"
"They are both gone up to the church to pray.

5   "Because I was happy upon the heath,
And smil'd among the winter's snow,
They clothed me in the clothes of death,
And taught me to sing the notes of woe.

"And because I am happy and dance and sing,
10   They think they have done me no injury,
And are gone to praise God and his Priest and King,
Who make up a heaven of our misery."

NURSE'S SONG

from Songs of Experience
William Blake

1   When the voices of children are heard on the green,
And whisperings are in the dale,
The days of my youth rise fresh in my mind,
My face turns green and pale.

5   Then come home, my children, the sun is gone down,
And the dews of night arise;
Your spring and your day are wasted in play,
And your winter and night in disguise.

THE SICK ROSE

from Songs of Experience
William Blake

1   O Rose, thou art sick.
The invisible worm
That flies in the night,
In the howling storm,

5   Has found out thy bed
Of crimson joy:
And his dark secret love
Does thy life destroy.

THE TYGER

from Songs of Experience
William Blake

1 Tyger, Tyger, burning bright
  In the forests of the night;
  What immortal hand or eye,
  Could frame thy fearful symmetry?

5 In what distant deeps or skies
  Burnt the fire of thine eyes?
  On what wings dare he aspire?
  What the hand, dare seize the fire?

  And what shoulder, & what art,
10 Could twist the sinews of thy heart?
  And when thy heart began to beat,
  What dread hand? & what dread feet?

  What the hammer? what the chain,
  In what furnace was thy brain?
15 What the anvil? what dread grasp,
  Dare its deadly terrors clasp?

  When the stars threw down their spears
  And water'd heaven with their tears:
  Did he smile his work to see?
20 Did he who made the Lamb make thee?

  Tyger, Tyger, burning bright
  In the forests of the night:
  What immortal hand or eye,
  Dare frame thy fearful symmetry?

LONDON

from Songs of Experience
William Blake

1   I wander thro' each charter'd street,
       Near where the charter'd Thames does flow,
       And mark in every face I meet
       Marks of weakness, marks of woe.

5   In every cry of every Man,
       In every Infant's cry of fear,
       In every voice, in every ban,
       The mind-forg'd manacles I hear

       How the Chimney-sweeper's cry
10   Every black'ning Church appalls,
       And the hapless Soldier's sigh
       Runs in blood down Palace walls

       But most thro' midnight streets I hear
       How the youthful Harlot's curse
15   Blasts the new-born Infant's tear
       And blights with plagues the Marriage hearse.

A POISON TREE

from Songs of Experience
William Blake

1   I was angry with my friend:
I told my wrath, my wrath did end.
I was angry with my foe:
I told it not, my wrath did grow.

5   And I water'd it in fears,
Night & morning with my tears;
And I sunned it with smiles,
And with soft deceitful wiles.

And it grew both day and night,
10   Till it bore an apple bright.
And my foe beheld it shine,
And he knew that it was mine.

And into my garden stole,
When the night had veil'd the pole;
15   In the morning glad I see;
My foe outstretched beneath the tree.

A DIVINE IMAGE

from Songs of Experience
William Blake

1 Cruelty has a Human Heart,
And Jealousy a Human Face,
Terror, the Human Form Divine,
And Secrecy, the Human Dress.

5 The Human Dress, is forged Iron
The Human Form, a fiery Forge.
The Human Face, a Furnace seal'd
The Human Heart, its hungry Gorge.

LOVE'S SECRET

William Blake

1 Never seek to tell thy love,
  Love that never told can be;
For the gentle wind doth move
  Silently, invisibly.

5 I told my love, I told my love,
  I told her all my heart,
Trembling, cold, in ghastly fears.
  Ah! she did depart!

Soon after she was gone from me,
10   A traveller came by,
Silently, invisibly:
  He took her with a sigh.

AUGURIES OF INNOCENCE

William Blake

1   To see a world in a grain of sand,
      And a heaven in a wild flower,
    Hold infinity in the palm of your hand,
      And eternity in an hour.

5   A robin redbreast in a cage
    Puts all heaven in a rage.
    A dove-house fill'd with doves and pigeons
    Shudders hell thro' all its regions.
    A dog starv'd at his master's gate
10   Predicts the ruin of the state.
    A horse misused upon the road
    Calls to heaven for human blood.
    Each outcry of the hunted hare
    A fibre from the brain does tear.
15   A skylark wounded in the wing,
    A cherubim does cease to sing.
    The game-cock clipt and arm'd for fight
    Does the rising sun affright.

    Every wolf's and lion's howl
20   Raises from hell a human soul.
    The wild deer, wand'ring here and there,
    Keeps the human soul from care.
    The lamb misus'd breeds public strife,
    And yet forgives the butcher's knife.
25   The bat that flits at close of eve
    Has left the brain that won't believe.
    The owl that calls upon the night
    Speaks the unbeliever's fright.
    He who shall hurt the little wren

30   Shall never be belov'd by men.
      He who the ox to wrath has mov'd
      Shall never be by woman lov'd.
      The wanton boy that kills the fly
      Shall feel the spider's enmity.
35   He who torments the chafer's sprite
      Weaves a bower in endless night.
      The caterpillar on the leaf
      Repeats to thee thy mother's grief.
      Kill not the moth nor butterfly,
40   For the last judgment draweth nigh.
      He who shall train the horse to war
      Shall never pass the polar bar.
      The beggar's dog and widow's cat,
      Feed them and thou wilt grow fat.
45   The gnat that sings his summer's song
      Poison gets from slander's tongue.
      The poison of the snake and newt
      Is the sweat of envy's foot.
      The poison of the honey bee
50   Is the artist's jealousy.

      The prince's robes and beggar's rags
      Are toadstools on the miser's bags.
      A truth that's told with bad intent
      Beats all the lies you can invent.
55   It is right it should be so;
      Man was made for joy and woe;
      And when this we rightly know,
      Thro' the world we safely go.
      Joy and woe are woven fine,
60   A clothing for the soul divine.
      Under every grief and pine
      Runs a joy with silken twine.
      The babe is more than swaddling bands;
      Throughout all these human lands
65   Tools were made, and born were hands,

Every farmer understands.
Every tear from every eye
Becomes a babe in eternity;
This is caught by females bright,
70 And return'd to its own delight.
The bleat, the bark, bellow, and roar,
Are waves that beat on heaven's shore.
The babe that weeps the rod beneath
Writes revenge in realms of death.
75 The beggar's rags, fluttering in air,
Does to rags the heavens tear.
The soldier, arm'd with sword and gun,
Palsied strikes the summer's sun.
The poor man's farthing is worth more
80 Than all the gold on Afric's shore.
One mite wrung from the lab'rer's hands
Shall buy and sell the miser's lands;
Or, if protected from on high,
Does that whole nation sell and buy.
85 He who mocks the infant's faith
Shall be mock'd in age and death.
He who shall teach the child to doubt
The rotting grave shall ne'er get out.
He who respects the infant's faith
90 Triumphs over hell and death.
The child's toys and the old man's reasons
Are the fruits of the two seasons.
The questioner, who sits so sly,
Shall never know how to reply.
95 He who replies to words of doubt
Doth put the light of knowledge out.
The strongest poison ever known
Came from Caesar's laurel crown.
Nought can deform the human race
100 Like to the armour's iron brace.
When gold and gems adorn the plow,
To peaceful arts shall envy bow.

A riddle, or the cricket's cry,
Is to doubt a fit reply.
105 The emmet's inch and eagle's mile
Make lame philosophy to smile.
He who doubts from what he sees
Will ne'er believe, do what you please.
If the sun and moon should doubt,
110 They'd immediately go out.
To be in a passion you good may do,
But no good if a passion is in you.
The whore and gambler, by the state
Licensed, build that nation's fate.
115 The harlot's cry from street to street
Shall weave old England's winding-sheet.
The winner's shout, the loser's curse,
Dance before dead England's hearse.
Every night and every morn
120 Some to misery are born,
Every morn and every night
Some are born to sweet delight.
Some are born to sweet delight,
Some are born to endless night.
125 We are led to believe a lie
When we see not thro' the eye,
Which was born in a night to perish in a night,
When the soul slept in beams of light.
God appears, and God is light,
130 To those poor souls who dwell in night;
But does a human form display
To those who dwell in realms of day.

WILLIAM
WORDSWORTH
(1770-1850)

Wordsworth is known for his poetry of remembrance, which celebrates in particular England's rural Lake District, the land of his childhood. At the age of eight, Wordsworth was orphaned, along with his four young siblings. In 1795, he began living with his younger sister, Dorothy, who was a poet in her own right. After studying at the University of Cambridge (where he met and collaborated with Samuel Taylor Coleridge on *Lyrical Ballads*), Wordsworth spent a year in France, hoping to witness in person the "glorious renovation" and social transformation wrought by the French Revolution. He felt a bond of sympathy with the "common man," a strong theme throughout his works. In 1802, Wordsworth married his childhood friend, Mary Hutchinson, and had five children with her. The loss of two of their children in 1812 inspired powerful poems of mourning; when their daughter Dora died in 1847, however, Wordsworth was so distraught that he lost his will to write. He was England's Poet Laureate from 1843 until his death in 1850.

WE ARE SEVEN

William Wordsworth

1 ————A simple Child,
That lightly draws its breath,
And feels its life in every limb,
What should it know of death?

5 I met a little cottage Girl:
She was eight years old, she said;
Her hair was thick with many a curl
That clustered round her head.

She had a rustic, woodland air,
10 And she was wildly clad:
Her eyes were fair, and very fair;
—Her beauty made me glad.

"Sisters and brothers, little Maid,
How many may you be?"
15 "How many? Seven in all," she said,
And wondering looked at me.

"And where are they? I pray you tell."
She answered, "Seven are we;
And two of us at Conway dwell,
20 And two are gone to sea.

"Two of us in the church-yard lie,
My sister and my brother;
And, in the church-yard cottage, I
Dwell near them with my mother."

25   "You say that two at Conway dwell,
   And two are gone to sea,
   Yet ye are seven! I pray you tell,
   Sweet Maid, how this may be."

   Then did the little Maid reply,
30   "Seven boys and girls are we;
   Two of us in the church-yard lie,
   Beneath the church-yard tree."

   "You run about, my little Maid,
   Your limbs they are alive;
35   If two are in the church-yard laid,
   Then ye are only five."

   "Their graves are green, they may be seen,"
   The little Maid replied,
   "Twelve steps or more from my mother's door,
40   And they are side by side.

   "My stockings there I often knit,
   My kerchief there I hem;
   And there upon the ground I sit,
   And sing a song to them.

45   "And often after sun-set, Sir,
   When it is light and fair,
   I take my little porringer,
   And eat my supper there.

   "The first that died was sister Jane;
50   In bed she moaning lay,
   Till God released her of her pain;
   And then she went away.

   "So in the church-yard she was laid;
   And, when the grass was dry,

55   Together round her grave we played,
My brother John and I.

"And when the ground was white with snow,
And I could run and slide,
My brother John was forced to go,
60   And he lies by her side."

"How many are you, then," said I,
"If they two are in heaven?"
Quick was the little Maid's reply,
"O Master! we are seven."

65   "But they are dead; those two are dead!
Their spirits are in heaven!"
'Twas throwing words away; for still
The little Maid would have her will,
"Nay, we are seven!"

LINES COMPOSED A FEW MILES ABOVE TINTERN ABBEY

William Wordsworth

1   Five years have past; five summers, with the length
Of five long winters! and again I hear
These waters, rolling from their mountain-springs
With a soft inland murmur.—Once again
5   Do I behold these steep and lofty cliffs,
That on a wild secluded scene impress
Thoughts of more deep seclusion; and connect
The landscape with the quiet of the sky.
The day is come when I again repose
10   Here, under this dark sycamore, and view
These plots of cottage-ground, these orchard-tufts,
Which at this season, with their unripe fruits,
Are clad in one green hue, and lose themselves
'Mid groves and copses. Once again I see
15   These hedge-rows, hardly hedge-rows, little lines
Of sportive wood run wild: these pastoral farms,
Green to the very door; and wreaths of smoke
Sent up, in silence, from among the trees!
With some uncertain notice, as might seem
20   Of vagrant dwellers in the houseless woods,
Or of some Hermit's cave, where by his fire
The Hermit sits alone.

                        These beauteous forms,
Through a long absence, have not been to me
As is a landscape to a blind man's eye:
25   But oft, in lonely rooms, and 'mid the din
Of towns and cities, I have owed to them,
In hours of weariness, sensations sweet,
Felt in the blood, and felt along the heart;

And passing even into my purer mind
30 With tranquil restoration:—feelings too
Of unremembered pleasure: such, perhaps,
As have no slight or trivial influence
On that best portion of a good man's life,
His little, nameless, unremembered, acts
35 Of kindness and of love. Nor less, I trust,
To them I may have owed another gift,
Of aspect more sublime; that blessed mood,
In which the burthen of the mystery,
In which the heavy and the weary weight
40 Of all this unintelligible world,
Is lightened:—that serene and blessed mood,
In which the affections gently lead us on,—
Until, the breath of this corporeal frame
And even the motion of our human blood
45 Almost suspended, we are laid asleep
In body, and become a living soul:
While with an eye made quiet by the power
Of harmony, and the deep power of joy,
We see into the life of things.

                                        If this
50 Be but a vain belief, yet, oh! how oft—
In darkness and amid the many shapes
Of joyless daylight; when the fretful stir
Unprofitable, and the fever of the world,
Have hung upon the beatings of my heart—
How oft, in spirit, have I turned to thee,
55 O sylvan Wye! thou wanderer thro' the woods,
        How often has my spirit turned to thee!

    And now, with gleams of half-extinguished thought,
With many recognitions dim and faint,
And somewhat of a sad perplexity,
60 The picture of the mind revives again:
While here I stand, not only with the sense

Of present pleasure, but with pleasing thoughts
That in this moment there is life and food
For future years. And so I dare to hope,
65 Though changed, no doubt, from what I was when first
I came among these hills; when like a roe
I bounded o'er the mountains, by the sides
Of the deep rivers, and the lonely streams,
Wherever nature led: more like a man
70 Flying from something that he dreads, than one
Who sought the thing he loved. For nature then
(The coarser pleasures of my boyish days
And their glad animal movements all gone by)
To me was all in all.—I cannot paint
75 What then I was. The sounding cataract
Haunted me like a passion: the tall rock,
The mountain, and the deep and gloomy wood,
Their colours and their forms, were then to me
An appetite; a feeling and a love,
80 That had no need of a remoter charm,
By thought supplied, not any interest
Unborrowed from the eye.—That time is past,
And all its aching joys are now no more,
And all its dizzy raptures. Not for this
85 Faint I, nor mourn nor murmur; other gifts
Have followed; for such loss, I would believe,
Abundant recompense. For I have learned
To look on nature, not as in the hour
Of thoughtless youth; but hearing oftentimes
90 The still sad music of humanity,
Nor harsh nor grating, though of ample power
To chasten and subdue.—And I have felt
A presence that disturbs me with the joy
Of elevated thoughts; a sense sublime
95 Of something far more deeply interfused,
Whose dwelling is the light of setting suns,
And the round ocean and the living air,
And the blue sky, and in the mind of man:

A motion and a spirit, that impels
100 All thinking things, all objects of all thought,
And rolls through all things. Therefore am I still
A lover of the meadows and the woods
And mountains; and of all that we behold
From this green earth; of all the mighty world
105 Of eye, and ear,—both what they half create,
And what perceive; well pleased to recognise
In nature and the language of the sense
The anchor of my purest thoughts, the nurse,
The guide, the guardian of my heart, and soul
110 Of all my moral being.

                        Nor perchance,
If I were not thus taught, should I the more
Suffer my genial spirits to decay:
For thou art with me here upon the banks
Of this fair river; thou my dearest Friend,
115 My dear, dear Friend; and in thy voice I catch
The language of my former heart, and read
My former pleasures in the shooting lights
Of thy wild eyes. Oh! yet a little while
May I behold in thee what I was once,
120 My dear, dear Sister! and this prayer I make,
Knowing that Nature never did betray
The heart that loved her; 'tis her privilege,
Through all the years of this our life, to lead
From joy to joy: for she can so inform
125 The mind that is within us, so impress
With quietness and beauty, and so feed
With lofty thoughts, that neither evil tongues,
Rash judgments, nor the sneers of selfish men,
Nor greetings where no kindness is, nor all
130 The dreary intercourse of daily life,
Shall e'er prevail against us, or disturb
Our cheerful faith, that all which we behold
Is full of blessings. Therefore let the moon

Shine on thee in thy solitary walk;
135   And let the misty mountain-winds be free
To blow against thee: and, in after years,
When these wild ecstasies shall be matured
Into a sober pleasure; when thy mind
Shall be a mansion for all lovely forms,
140   Thy memory be as a dwelling-place
For all sweet sounds and harmonies; oh! then,
If solitude, or fear, or pain, or grief,
Should be thy portion, with what healing thoughts
Of tender joy wilt thou remember me,
145   And these my exhortations! Nor, perchance—
If I should be where I no more can hear
Thy voice, nor catch from thy wild eyes these gleams
Of past existence—wilt thou then forget
That on the banks of this delightful stream
150   We stood together; and that I, so long
A worshipper of Nature, hither came
Unwearied in that service: rather say
With warmer love—oh! with far deeper zeal
Of holier love. Nor wilt thou then forget,
155   That after many wanderings, many years
Of absence, these steep woods and lofty cliffs,
And this green pastoral landscape, were to me
More dear, both for themselves and for thy sake!

STRANGE FITS OF PASSION I HAVE KNOWN

William Wordsworth

1 Strange fits of passion have I known:
  And I will dare to tell,
  But in the lover's ear alone,
  What once to me befell.

5 When she I loved looked every day
  Fresh as a rose in June,
  I to her cottage bent my way,
  Beneath an evening-moon.

  Upon the moon I fixed my eye,
10 All over the wide lea;
  With quickening pace my horse drew nigh
  Those paths so dear to me.

  And now we reached the orchard-plot;
  And, as we climbed the hill,
15 The sinking moon to Lucy's cot
  Came near, and nearer still.

  In one of those sweet dreams I slept,
  Kind Nature's gentlest boon!
  And all the while my eye I kept
20 On the descending moon.

  My horse moved on; hoof after hoof
  He raised, and never stopped:
  When down behind the cottage roof,
  At once, the bright moon dropped.

25 What fond and wayward thoughts will slide
  Into a Lover's head!
  'O mercy!' to myself I cried,
  'If Lucy hould be dead!'

SHE DWELT AMONG THE UNTRODDEN WAYS

William Wordsworth

1   She dwelt among the untrodden ways
      Beside the springs of Dove,
    A Maid whom there were none to praise
      And very few to love:

5   A violet by a mossy stone
      Half hidden from the eye!
    —Fair as a star, when only one
      Is shining in the sky.

    She lived unknown, and few could know
10   When Lucy ceased to be;
    But she is in her grave, and, oh,
      The difference to me!

MY HEART LEAPS UP

William Wordsworth

1   My heart leaps up when I behold
    A rainbow in the sky:
    So was it when my life began;
    So is it now I am a man;
5   So be it when I shall grow old,
    Or let me die!
    The Child is father of the Man;
    And I could wish my days to be
    Bound each to each by natural piety.

A SLUMBER DID MY SPIRIT SEAL

William Wordsworth

1   A slumber did my spirit seal;
I had no human fears:
She seemed a thing that could not feel
The touch of earthly years.

5   No motion has she now, no force;
She neither hears nor sees;
Rolled round in earth's diurnal course,
With rocks, and stones, and trees.

LUCY GRAY

William Wordsworth

1   Oft I had heard of Lucy Gray:
And, when I crossed the wild,
I chanced to see at break of day
The solitary child.

5   No mate, no comrade Lucy knew;
She dwelt on a wide moor,
- The sweetest thing that ever grew
Beside a human door!

You yet may spy the fawn at play,
10   The hare upon the green;
But the sweet face of Lucy Gray

Will never more be seen.

"To-night will be a stormy night-
You to the town must go;
15 And take a lantern, Child, to light
Your mother through the snow."

"That, Father! will I gladly do:
'Tis scarcely afternoon-
The minster-clock has just struck two,
20 And yonder is the moon!"

At this the Father raised his hook,
And snapped a faggot-band;
He plied his work; - and Lucy took
The lantern in her hand.

25 Not blither is the mountain roe:
With many a wanton stroke
Her feet disperse the powdery snow,
That rises up like smoke.

The storm came on before its time:
30 She wandered up and down;
And many a hill did Lucy climb:
But never reached the town.

The wretched parents all that night
Went shouting far and wide;
35 But there was neither sound nor sight
To serve them for a guide.

At day-break on a hill they stood
That overlooked the moor;
And thence they saw the bridge of wood,
40 A furlong from their door.

They wept- and, turning homeward, cried,
'In heaven we all shall meet; '
- When in the snow the mother spied
The print of Lucy's feet.

45   Then downwards from the steep hill's edge
They tracked the footmarks small;
And through the broken hawthorn hedge,
And by the long stone-wall;

And then an open field they crossed:
50   The marks were still the same;
They tracked them on, nor ever lost;
And to the bridge they came.

They followed from the snowy bank
Those footmarks, one by one,
55   Into the middle of the plank;
And further there were none!

- Yet some maintain that to this day
She is a living child;
That you may see sweet Lucy Gray
60   Upon the lonesome wild.

O'er rough and smooth she trips along,
And never looks behind;
And sings a solitary song
That whistles in the wind.

I TRAVELLED AMONG UNKNOWN MEN

William Wordsworth

1   I travelled among unknown men,
In lands beyond the sea;
Nor, England! did I know till then
What love I bore to thee.

5   'Tis past, that melancholy dream!
Nor will I quit thy shore
A second time; for still I seem
To love thee more and more.

Among thy mountains did I feel
10   The joy of my desire;
And she I cherished turned her wheel
Beside an English fire.

Thy mornings showed, thy nights concealed,
The bowers where Lucy played;
15   And thine too is the last green field
That Lucy's eyes surveyed.

I WANDERED LONELY AS A CLOUD

William Wordsworth

1   I wandered lonely as a cloud
     That floats on high o'er vales and hills,
     When all at once I saw a crowd,
     A host, of golden daffodils;
5   Beside the lake, beneath the trees,
     Fluttering and dancing in the breeze.

     Continuous as the stars that shine
     And twinkle on the milky way,
     They stretched in never-ending line
10   Along the margin of a bay:
     Ten thousand saw I at a glance,
     Tossing their heads in sprightly dance.

     The waves beside them danced; but they
     Out-did the sparkling waves in glee:
15   A poet could not but be gay,
     In such a jocund company:
     I gazed—and gazed—but little thought
     What wealth the show to me had brought:

     For oft, when on my couch I lie
20   In vacant or in pensive mood,
     They flash upon that inward eye
     Which is the bliss of solitude;
     And then my heart with pleasure fills,
     And dances with the daffodils.

ODE TO DUTY

William Wordsworth

> *"Jam non consilio bonus, sed more eo perductus, ut non tantum recte facere tpossim, sed nisi recte facere non possim."*

> *"I am no longer good through deliberate intent, but by long habit have reached a point where I am not only able to do right, but am unable to do anything but what is right."*
> (*Seneca, Letters* 120.10)

1 Stern Daughter of the Voice of God!
 O Duty! if that name thou love
 Who art a light to guide, a rod
 To check the erring, and reprove;
5 Thou, who art victory and law
 When empty terrors overawe;
 From vain temptations dost set free;
 And calm'st the weary strife of frail humanity!

 There are who ask not if thine eye
10 Be on them; who, in love and truth,
 Where no misgiving is, rely
 Upon the genial sense of youth:
 Glad Hearts! without reproach or blot;
 Who do thy work, and know it not:
15 Oh! if through confidence misplaced
 They fail, thy saving arms, dread Power! around them cast.

 Serene will be our days and bright,
 And happy will our nature be,
 When love is an unerring light,
20 And joy its own security.
 And they a blissful course may hold

Even now, who, not unwisely bold,
Live in the spirit of this creed;
Yet seek thy firm support, according to their need.

25 I, loving freedom, and untried;
No sport of every random gust,
Yet being to myself a guide,
Too blindly have reposed my trust:
And oft, when in my heart was heard
30 Thy timely mandate, I deferred
The task, in smoother walks to stray;
But thee I now would serve more strictly, if I may.

Through no disturbance of my soul,
Or strong compunction in me wrought,
35 I supplicate for thy control;
But in the quietness of thought:
Me this unchartered freedom tires;
I feel the weight of chance-desires:
My hopes no more must change their name,
40 I long for a repose that ever is the same.

Stern Lawgiver! yet thou dost wear
The Godhead's most benignant grace;
Nor know we anything so fair
As is the smile upon thy face:
45 Flowers laugh before thee on their beds
And fragrance in thy footing treads;
Thou dost preserve the stars from wrong;
And the most ancient heavens, through Thee, are fresh and strong.

To humbler functions, awful Power!
50 I call thee: I myself commend
Unto thy guidance from this hour;
Oh, let my weakness have an end!
Give unto me, made lowly wise,
The spirit of self-sacrifice;
55 The confidence of reason give;
And in the light of truth thy Bondman let me live!

CHARACTER OF THE HAPPY WARRIOR

William Wordsworth

1   Who is the happy Warrior? Who is he
That every man in arms should wish to be?
—It is the generous Spirit, who, when brought
Among the tasks of real life, hath wrought
5   Upon the plan that pleased his boyish thought:
Whose high endeavours are an inward light
That makes the path before him always bright;
Who, with a natural instinct to discern
What knowledge can perform, is diligent to learn;
10   Abides by this resolve, and stops not there,
But makes his moral being his prime care;
Who, doomed to go in company with Pain,
And Fear, and Bloodshed, miserable train!
Turns his necessity to glorious gain;
15   In face of these doth exercise a power
Which is our human nature's highest dower:
Controls them and subdues, transmutes, bereaves
Of their bad influence, and their good receives:
By objects, which might force the soul to abate
20   Her feeling, rendered more compassionate;
Is placable—because occasions rise
So often that demand such sacrifice;
More skilful in self-knowledge, even more pure,
As tempted more; more able to endure,
25   As more exposed to suffering and distress;
Thence, also, more alive to tenderness.
—'Tis he whose law is reason; who depends
Upon that law as on the best of friends;
Whence, in a state where men are tempted still
30   To evil for a guard against worse ill,
And what in quality or act is best
Doth seldom on a right foundation rest,

He labours good on good to fix, and owes
To virtue every triumph that he knows:
35 —Who, if he rise to station of command,
Rises by open means; and there will stand
On honourable terms, or else retire,
And in himself possess his own desire;
Who comprehends his trust, and to the same
40 Keeps faithful with a singleness of aim;
And therefore does not stoop, nor lie in wait
For wealth, or honours, or for worldly state;
Whom they must follow; on whose head must fall,
Like showers of manna, if they come at all:
45 Whose powers shed round him in the common strife,
Or mild concerns of ordinary life,
A constant influence, a peculiar grace;
But who, if he be called upon to face
Some awful moment to which Heaven has joined
50 Great issues, good or bad for human kind,
Is happy as a Lover; and attired
With sudden brightness, like a Man inspired;
And, through the heat of conflict, keeps the law
In calmness made, and sees what he foresaw;
55 Or if an unexpected call succeed,
Come when it will, is equal to the need:
—He who, though thus endued as with a sense
And faculty for storm and turbulence,
Is yet a Soul whose master-bias leans
60 To homefelt pleasures and to gentle scenes;
Sweet images! which, wheresoe'er he be,
Are at his heart; and such fidelity
It is his darling passion to approve;
More brave for this, that he hath much to love:—
65 'Tis, finally, the Man, who, lifted high,
Conspicuous object in a Nation's eye,
Or left unthought-of in obscurity,—
Who, with a toward or untoward lot,
Prosperous or adverse, to his wish or not—

70 Plays, in the many games of life, that one
    Where what he most doth value must be won:
    Whom neither shape or danger can dismay,
    Nor thought of tender happiness betray;
    Who, not content that former worth stand fast,
75 Looks forward, persevering to the last,
    From well to better, daily self-surpast:
    Who, whether praise of him must walk the earth
    For ever, and to noble deeds give birth,
    Or he must fall, to sleep without his fame,
80 And leave a dead unprofitable name—
    Finds comfort in himself and in his cause;
    And, while the mortal mist is gathering, draws
    His breath in confidence of Heaven's applause:
    This is the happy Warrior; this is he
85 That every man in arms should wish to be.

THE WORLD IS TOO MUCH WITH US

William Wordsworth

1   The world is too much with us; late and soon,
       Getting and spending, we lay waste our powers;—
       Little we see in Nature that is ours;
       We have given our hearts away, a sordid boon!
5   This Sea that bares her bosom to the moon;
       The winds that will be howling at all hours,
       And are up-gathered now like sleeping flowers;
       For this, for everything, we are out of tune;
       It moves us not. Great God! I'd rather be
10   A Pagan suckled in a creed outworn;
       So might I, standing on this pleasant lea,
       Have glimpses that would make me less forlorn;
       Have sight of Proteus rising from the sea;
       Or hear old Triton blow his wreathèd horn.

MUTABILITY

William Wordsworth

1 From low to high doth dissolution climb,
 And sink from high to low, along a scale
 Of awful notes, whose concord shall not fail;
 A musical but melancholy chime,
5 Which they can hear who meddle not with crime,
 Nor avarice, nor over-anxious care.
 Truth fails not; but her outward forms that bear
 The longest date do melt like frosty rime,
 That in the morning whitened hill and plain
10 And is no more; drop like the tower sublime
 Of yesterday, which royally did wear
 His crown of weeds, but could not even sustain
 Some casual shout that broke the silent air,
 Or the unimaginable touch of Time.

SCORN NOT THE SONNET

William Wordsworth

1 Scorn not the Sonnet; Critic, you have frowned,
 Mindless of its just honours; with this key
 Shakespeare unlocked his heart; the melody
 Of this small lute gave ease to Petrarch's wound;
5 A thousand times this pipe did Tasso sound;
 With it Camöens soothed an exile's grief;
 The Sonnet glittered a gay myrtle leaf
 Amid the cypress with which Dante crowned
 His visionary brow: a glow-worm lamp,
10 It cheered mild Spenser, called from Faery-land
 To struggle through dark ways; and, when a damp
 Fell round the path of Milton, in his hand
 The Thing became a trumpet; whence he blew
 Soul-animating strains—alas, too few!

SAMUEL TAYLOR COLERIDGE (1772-1834)

Coleridge is best remembered for his haunting and strikingly original poems, "The Rime of the Ancient Mariner," "Kubla Khan," and "Christabel." He also wrote influential literary criticism and theory, including "Hints towards the Formation of a More Comprehensive Theory of Life" and *Biographia Literaria*. As a student at the University of Cambridge, Coleridge accumulated debt and an opium addiction; both problems plagued him for the rest of his life. He never graduated, but the friendship he developed there with William Wordsworth resulted in the collaborative *Lyrical Ballads* (1798), a major influence in the Romantic poetry movement. Coleridge's personal life was full of challenges. He fell in love and was spurned by his best friend's sister, Mary Evans, planned and failed to establish a socialist commune in Pennsylvania with Robert Southey, and later married Southey's wife's sister—an unhappy marriage, according to biographers.

THIS LIME-TREE BOWER MY PRISON

Samuel Taylor Coleridge

[Addressed to Charles Lamb, of the India House, London]

1   Well, they are gone, and here must I remain,
     This lime-tree bower my prison! I have lost
     Beauties and feelings, such as would have been
     Most sweet to my remembrance even when age
5   Had dimm'd mine eyes to blindness! They, meanwhile,
     Friends, whom I never more may meet again,
     On springy heath, along the hill-top edge,
     Wander in gladness, and wind down, perchance,
     To that still roaring dell, of which I told;
10   The roaring dell, o'erwooded, narrow, deep,
     And only speckled by the mid-day sun;
     Where its slim trunk the ash from rock to rock
     Flings arching like a bridge;—that branchless ash,
     Unsunn'd and damp, whose few poor yellow leaves
15   Ne'er tremble in the gale, yet tremble still,
     Fann'd by the water-fall! and there my friends
     Behold the dark green file of long lank weeds,
     That all at once (a most fantastic sight!)
     Still nod and drip beneath the dripping edge
20   Of the blue clay-stone.

     Now, my friends emerge
     Beneath the wide wide Heaven—and view again
     The many-steepled tract magnificent
     Of hilly fields and meadows, and the sea,
25   With some fair bark, perhaps, whose sails light up
     The slip of smooth clear blue betwixt two Isles
     Of purple shadow! Yes! they wander on
     In gladness all; but thou, methinks, most glad,

My gentle-hearted Charles! for thou hast pined
30   And hunger'd after Nature, many a year,
In the great City pent, winning thy way
With sad yet patient soul, through evil and pain
And strange calamity! Ah! slowly sink
Behind the western ridge, thou glorious Sun!
35   Shine in the slant beams of the sinking orb,
Ye purple heath-flowers! richlier burn, ye clouds!
Live in the yellow light, ye distant groves!
And kindle, thou blue Ocean! So my friend
Struck with deep joy may stand, as I have stood,
40   Silent with swimming sense; yea, gazing round
On the wide landscape, gaze till all doth seem
Less gross than bodily; and of such hues
As veil the Almighty Spirit, when yet he makes
Spirits perceive his presence.

45   A delight
Comes sudden on my heart, and I am glad
As I myself were there! Nor in this bower,
This little lime-tree bower, have I not mark'd
Much that has sooth'd me. Pale beneath the blaze
50   Hung the transparent foliage; and I watch'd
Some broad and sunny leaf, and lov'd to see
The shadow of the leaf and stem above
Dappling its sunshine! And that walnut-tree
Was richly ting'd, and a deep radiance lay
55   Full on the ancient ivy, which usurps
Those fronting elms, and now, with blackest mass
Makes their dark branches gleam a lighter hue
Through the late twilight: and though now the bat
Wheels silent by, and not a swallow twitters,
60   Yet still the solitary humble-bee
Sings in the bean-flower! Henceforth I shall know
That Nature ne'er deserts the wise and pure;
No plot so narrow, be but Nature there,
No waste so vacant, but may well employ

65   Each faculty of sense, and keep the heart
     Awake to Love and Beauty! and sometimes
     'Tis well to be bereft of promis'd good,
     That we may lift the soul, and contemplate
     With lively joy the joys we cannot share.
70   My gentle-hearted Charles! when the last rook
     Beat its straight path along the dusky air
     Homewards, I blest it! deeming its black wing
     (Now a dim speck, now vanishing in light)
     Had cross'd the mighty Orb's dilated glory,
75   While thou stood'st gazing; or, when all was still,
     Flew creeking o'er thy head, and had a charm
     For thee, my gentle-hearted Charles, to whom
     No sound is dissonant which tells of Life.

THE RIME OF THE ANCIENT MARINER

Samuel Taylor Coleridge

Argument
How a Ship having passed the Line was driven by
storms to the cold Country towards the South Pole; and how
from thence she made her course to the tropical Latitude of the
Great Pacific Ocean; and of the strange things that befell; and in
what manner the Ancyent Marinere came back to his own
Country.

PART I

1 It is an ancient Mariner,
And he stoppeth one of three.
'By thy long grey beard and glittering eye,
Now wherefore stopp'st thou me?

5 The Bridegroom's doors are opened wide,
And I am next of kin;
The guests are met, the feast is set:
May'st hear the merry din.'

He holds him with his skinny hand,
10 'There was a ship,' quoth he.
'Hold off! unhand me, grey-beard loon!'
Eftsoons his hand dropt he.

He holds him with his glittering eye—
The Wedding-Guest stood still,
15 And listens like a three years' child:
The Mariner hath his will.

The Wedding-Guest sat on a stone:
He cannot choose but hear;
And thus spake on that ancient man,

20   The bright-eyed Mariner.

'The ship was cheered, the harbour cleared,
Merrily did we drop
Below the kirk, below the hill,
Below the lighthouse top.

25   The Sun came up upon the left,
Out of the sea came he!
And he shone bright, and on the right
Went down into the sea.

Higher and higher every day,
30   Till over the mast at noon—'
The Wedding-Guest here beat his breast,
For he heard the loud bassoon.

The bride hath paced into the hall,
Red as a rose is she;
35   Nodding their heads before her goes
The merry minstrelsy.

The Wedding-Guest he beat his breast,
Yet he cannot choose but hear;
And thus spake on that ancient man,
40   The bright-eyed Mariner.

And now the STORM-BLAST came, and he
Was tyrannous and strong:
He struck with his o'ertaking wings,
And chased us south along.

45   With sloping masts and dipping prow,
As who pursued with yell and blow
Still treads the shadow of his foe,
And forward bends his head,
The ship drove fast, loud roared the blast,
50   And southward aye we fled.

And now there came both mist and snow,
And it grew wondrous cold:
And ice, mast-high, came floating by,
As green as emerald.

55 And through the drifts the snowy clifts
Did send a dismal sheen:
Nor shapes of men nor beasts we ken—
The ice was all between.

The ice was here, the ice was there,
60 The ice was all around:
It cracked and growled, and roared and howled,
Like noises in a swound!

At length did cross an Albatross,
Thorough the fog it came;
65 As if it had been a Christian soul,
We hailed it in God's name.

It ate the food it ne'er had eat,
And round and round it flew.
The ice did split with a thunder-fit;
70 The helmsman steered us through!

And a good south wind sprung up behind;
The Albatross did follow,
And every day, for food or play,
Came to the mariner's hollo!

75 In mist or cloud, on mast or shroud,
It perched for vespers nine;
Whiles all the night, through fog-smoke white,
Glimmered the white Moon-shine.'

'God save thee, ancient Mariner!
80 From the fiends, that plague thee thus!—
Why look'st thou so?'—With my cross-bow
I shot the ALBATROSS.

PART II
The Sun now rose upon the right:
Out of the sea came he,
85   Still hid in mist, and on the left
Went down into the sea.

And the good south wind still blew behind,
But no sweet bird did follow,
Nor any day for food or play
90   Came to the mariner's hollo!

And I had done a hellish thing,
And it would work 'em woe:
For all averred, I had killed the bird
That made the breeze to blow.
95   Ah wretch! said they, the bird to slay,
That made the breeze to blow!

Nor dim nor red, like God's own head,
The glorious Sun uprist:
Then all averred, I had killed the bird
100   That brought the fog and mist.
'Twas right, said they, such birds to slay,
That bring the fog and mist.

The fair breeze blew, the white foam flew,
The furrow followed free;
105   We were the first that ever burst
Into that silent sea.

Down dropt the breeze, the sails dropt down,
'Twas sad as sad could be;
And we did speak only to break
110   The silence of the sea!

All in a hot and copper sky,
The bloody Sun, at noon,
Right up above the mast did stand,
No bigger than the Moon.

115   Day after day, day after day,
    We stuck, nor breath nor motion;
    As idle as a painted ship
    Upon a painted ocean.

    Water, water, every where,
120   And all the boards did shrink;
    Water, water, every where,
    Nor any drop to drink.

    The very deep did rot: O Christ!
    That ever this should be!
125   Yea, slimy things did crawl with legs
    Upon the slimy sea.

    About, about, in reel and rout
    The death-fires danced at night;
    The water, like a witch's oils,
130   Burnt green, and blue and white.

    And some in dreams assurèd were
    Of the Spirit that plagued us so;
    Nine fathom deep he had followed us
    From the land of mist and snow.

135   And every tongue, through utter drought,
    Was withered at the root;
    We could not speak, no more than if
    We had been choked with soot.

    Ah! well a-day! what evil looks
140   Had I from old and young!
    Instead of the cross, the Albatross
    About my neck was hung.

PART III
There passed a weary time. Each throat
Was parched, and glazed each eye.
145   A weary time! a weary time!
How glazed each weary eye,
When looking westward, I beheld
A something in the sky.

At first it seemed a little speck,
150   And then it seemed a mist;
It moved and moved, and took at last
A certain shape, I wist.

A speck, a mist, a shape, I wist!
And still it neared and neared:
155   As if it dodged a water-sprite,
It plunged and tacked and veered.

With throats unslaked, with black lips baked,
We could nor laugh nor wail;
Through utter drought all dumb we stood!
160   I bit my arm, I sucked the blood,
And cried, A sail! a sail!

With throats unslaked, with black lips baked,
Agape they heard me call:
Gramercy! they for joy did grin,
165   And all at once their breath drew in.
As they were drinking all.

See! see! (I cried) she tacks no more!
Hither to work us weal;
Without a breeze, without a tide,
170   She steadies with upright keel!

The western wave was all a-flame.
The day was well nigh done!
Almost upon the western wave
Rested the broad bright Sun;

175   When that strange shape drove suddenly
    Betwixt us and the Sun.

    And straight the Sun was flecked with bars,
    (Heaven's Mother send us grace!)
    As if through a dungeon-grate he peered
180   With broad and burning face.

    Alas! (thought I, and my heart beat loud)
    How fast she nears and nears!
    Are those her sails that glance in the Sun,
    Like restless gossameres?

185   Are those her ribs through which the Sun
    Did peer, as through a grate?
    And is that Woman all her crew?
    Is that a DEATH? and are there two?
    Is DEATH that woman's mate?

190   Her lips were red, her looks were free,
    Her locks were yellow as gold:
    Her skin was as white as leprosy,
    The Night-mare LIFE-IN-DEATH was she,
    Who thicks man's blood with cold.

195   The naked hulk alongside came,
    And the twain were casting dice;
    'The game is done! I've won! I've won!'
    Quoth she, and whistles thrice.

    The Sun's rim dips; the stars rush out;
200   At one stride comes the dark;
    With far-heard whisper, o'er the sea,
    Off shot the spectre-bark.

    We listened and looked sideways up!
    Fear at my heart, as at a cup,
205   My life-blood seemed to sip!
    The stars were dim, and thick the night,

The steersman's face by his lamp gleamed white;
From the sails the dew did drip—
Till clomb above the eastern bar
210 The hornèd Moon, with one bright star
Within the nether tip.

One after one, by the star-dogged Moon,
Too quick for groan or sigh,
Each turned his face with a ghastly pang,
215 And cursed me with his eye.

Four times fifty living men,
(And I heard nor sigh nor groan)
With heavy thump, a lifeless lump,
They dropped down one by one.

220 The souls did from their bodies fly,—
They fled to bliss or woe!
And every soul, it passed me by,
Like the whizz of my cross-bow!

PART IV
'I fear thee, ancient Mariner!
225 I fear thy skinny hand!
And thou art long, and lank, and brown,
As is the ribbed sea-sand.

I fear thee and thy glittering eye,
And thy skinny hand, so brown.'—
230 Fear not, fear not, thou Wedding-Guest!
This body dropt not down.

Alone, alone, all, all alone,
Alone on a wide wide sea!
And never a saint took pity on
235 My soul in agony.

The many men, so beautiful!

And they all dead did lie:
And a thousand thousand slimy things
Lived on; and so did I.

240   I looked upon the rotting sea,
And drew my eyes away;
I looked upon the rotting deck,
And there the dead men lay.

I looked to heaven, and tried to pray;
245   But or ever a prayer had gusht,
A wicked whisper came, and made
My heart as dry as dust.

I closed my lids, and kept them close,
And the balls like pulses beat;
250   For the sky and the sea, and the sea and the sky
Lay dead like a load on my weary eye,
And the dead were at my feet.

The cold sweat melted from their limbs,
Nor rot nor reek did they:
255   The look with which they looked on me
Had never passed away.

An orphan's curse would drag to hell
A spirit from on high;
But oh! more horrible than that
260   Is the curse in a dead man's eye!
Seven days, seven nights, I saw that curse,
And yet I could not die.

The moving Moon went up the sky,
And no where did abide:
265   Softly she was going up,
And a star or two beside—

Her beams bemocked the sultry main,
Like April hoar-frost spread;

But where the ship's huge shadow lay,
270 The charmèd water burnt alway
A still and awful red.

Beyond the shadow of the ship,
I watched the water-snakes:
275 They moved in tracks of shining white,
And when they reared, the elfish light
Fell off in hoary flakes.

Within the shadow of the ship
I watched their rich attire:
280 Blue, glossy green, and velvet black,
They coiled and swam; and every track
Was a flash of golden fire.

O happy living things! no tongue
Their beauty might declare:
285 A spring of love gushed from my heart,
And I blessed them unaware:
Sure my kind saint took pity on me,
And I blessed them unaware.

The self-same moment I could pray;
290 And from my neck so free
The Albatross fell off, and sank
Like lead into the sea.

PART V
Oh sleep! it is a gentle thing,
Beloved from pole to pole!
295 To Mary Queen the praise be given!
She sent the gentle sleep from Heaven,
That slid into my soul.

The silly buckets on the deck,
That had so long remained,
300 I dreamt that they were filled with dew;
And when I awoke, it rained.

My lips were wet, my throat was cold,
My garments all were dank;
Sure I had drunken in my dreams,
305   And still my body drank.

I moved, and could not feel my limbs:
I was so light—almost
I thought that I had died in sleep,
And was a blessed ghost.

310   And soon I heard a roaring wind:
It did not come anear;
But with its sound it shook the sails,
That were so thin and sere.

The upper air burst into life!
315   And a hundred fire-flags sheen,
To and fro they were hurried about!
And to and fro, and in and out,
The wan stars danced between.

And the coming wind did roar more loud,
320   And the sails did sigh like sedge,
And the rain poured down from one black cloud;
The Moon was at its edge.

The thick black cloud was cleft, and still
The Moon was at its side:
325   Like waters shot from some high crag,
The lightning fell with never a jag,
A river steep and wide.

The loud wind never reached the ship,
Yet now the ship moved on!
330   Beneath the lightning and the Moon
The dead men gave a groan.

They groaned, they stirred, they all uprose,

Nor spake, nor moved their eyes;
It had been strange, even in a dream,
335   To have seen those dead men rise.

The helmsman steered, the ship moved on;
Yet never a breeze up-blew;
The mariners all 'gan work the ropes,
Where they were wont to do;
340   They raised their limbs like lifeless tools—
We were a ghastly crew.

The body of my brother's son
Stood by me, knee to knee:
The body and I pulled at one rope,
345   But he said nought to me.

'I fear thee, ancient Mariner!'
Be calm, thou Wedding-Guest!
'Twas not those souls that fled in pain,
Which to their corses came again,
350   But a troop of spirits blest:

For when it dawned—they dropped their arms,
And clustered round the mast;
Sweet sounds rose slowly through their mouths,
And from their bodies passed.

355   Around, around, flew each sweet sound,
Then darted to the Sun;
Slowly the sounds came back again,
Now mixed, now one by one.

Sometimes a-dropping from the sky
360   I heard the sky-lark sing;
Sometimes all little birds that are,
How they seemed to fill the sea and air
With their sweet jargoning!

And now 'twas like all instruments,

365   Now like a lonely flute;
And now it is an angel's song,
That makes the heavens be mute.

It ceased; yet still the sails made on
A pleasant noise till noon,
370   A noise like of a hidden brook
In the leafy month of June,
That to the sleeping woods all night
Singeth a quiet tune.

375   Till noon we quietly sailed on,
Yet never a breeze did breathe:
Slowly and smoothly went the ship,
Moved onward from beneath.

Under the keel nine fathom deep,
380   From the land of mist and snow,
The spirit slid: and it was he
That made the ship to go.
The sails at noon left off their tune,
And the ship stood still also.

385   The Sun, right up above the mast,
Had fixed her to the ocean:
But in a minute she 'gan stir,
With a short uneasy motion—
Backwards and forwards half her length
390   With a short uneasy motion.

Then like a pawing horse let go,
She made a sudden bound:
It flung the blood into my head,
And I fell down in a swound.

395   How long in that same fit I lay,
I have not to declare;
But ere my living life returned,
I heard and in my soul discerned

Two voices in the air.

400 'Is it he?' quoth one, 'Is this the man?
By him who died on cross,
With his cruel bow he laid full low
The harmless Albatross.

The spirit who bideth by himself
405 In the land of mist and snow,
He loved the bird that loved the man
Who shot him with his bow.'

The other was a softer voice,
As soft as honey-dew:
410 Quoth he, 'The man hath penance done,
And penance more will do.'

PART VI
First Voice
'But tell me, tell me! speak again,
Thy soft response renewing—
What makes that ship drive on so fast?
415 What is the ocean doing?'

Second Voice
Still as a slave before his lord,
The ocean hath no blast;
His great bright eye most silently
Up to the Moon is cast—

420 If he may know which way to go;
For she guides him smooth or grim.
See, brother, see! how graciously
She looketh down on him.'

First Voice
'But why drives on that ship so fast,
425 Without or wave or wind?'

Second Voice
'The air is cut away before,
And closes from behind.

Fly, brother, fly! more high, more high!
Or we shall be belated:
430   For slow and slow that ship will go,
When the Mariner's trance is abated.'

I woke, and we were sailing on
As in a gentle weather:
'Twas night, calm night, the moon was high;
435   The dead men stood together.

All stood together on the deck,
For a charnel-dungeon fitter:
All fixed on me their stony eyes,
That in the Moon did glitter.

440   The pang, the curse, with which they died,
Had never passed away:
I could not draw my eyes from theirs,
Nor turn them up to pray.

And now this spell was snapt: once more
445   I viewed the ocean green,
And looked far forth, yet little saw
Of what had else been seen—

Like one, that on a lonesome road
Doth walk in fear and dread,
450   And having once turned round walks on,
And turns no more his head;
Because he knows, a frightful fiend
Doth close behind him tread.

But soon there breathed a wind on me,
455   Nor sound nor motion made:

Its path was not upon the sea,
In ripple or in shade.

It raised my hair, it fanned my cheek
Like a meadow-gale of spring—
460 It mingled strangely with my fears,
Yet it felt like a welcoming.

Swiftly, swiftly flew the ship,
Yet she sailed softly too:
Sweetly, sweetly blew the breeze—
465 On me alone it blew.

Oh! dream of joy! is this indeed
The light-house top I see?
Is this the hill? is this the kirk?
Is this mine own countree?

470 We drifted o'er the harbour-bar,
And I with sobs did pray—
O let me be awake, my God!
Or let me sleep alway.

The harbour-bay was clear as glass,
475 So smoothly it was strewn!
And on the bay the moonlight lay,
And the shadow of the Moon.

The rock shone bright, the kirk no less,
That stands above the rock:
480 The moonlight steeped in silentness
The steady weathercock.

And the bay was white with silent light,
Till rising from the same,
Full many shapes, that shadows were,
485 In crimson colours came.

A little distance from the prow

Those crimson shadows were:
I turned my eyes upon the deck—
Oh, Christ! what saw I there!

490   Each corse lay flat, lifeless and flat,
And, by the holy rood!
A man all light, a seraph-man,
On every corse there stood.

This seraph-band, each waved his hand:
495   It was a heavenly sight!
They stood as signals to the land,
Each one a lovely light;

This seraph-band, each waved his hand,
No voice did they impart—
500   No voice; but oh! the silence sank
Like music on my heart.

But soon I heard the dash of oars,
I heard the Pilot's cheer;
My head was turned perforce away
505   And I saw a boat appear.

The Pilot and the Pilot's boy,
I heard them coming fast:
Dear Lord in Heaven! it was a joy
The dead men could not blast.

510   I saw a third—I heard his voice:
It is the Hermit good!
He singeth loud his godly hymns
That he makes in the wood.
He'll shrieve my soul, he'll wash away
515   The Albatross's blood.

PART VII
This Hermit good lives in that wood
Which slopes down to the sea.

How loudly his sweet voice he rears!
He loves to talk with marineres
520   That come from a far countree.

He kneels at morn, and noon, and eve—
He hath a cushion plump:
It is the moss that wholly hides
The rotted old oak-stump.

525   The skiff-boat neared: I heard them talk,
'Why, this is strange, I trow!
Where are those lights so many and fair,
That signal made but now?'

'Strange, by my faith!' the Hermit said—
530   'And they answered not our cheer!
The planks looked warped! and see those sails,
How thin they are and sere!
I never saw aught like to them,
Unless perchance it were

535   Brown skeletons of leaves that lag
My forest-brook along;
When the ivy-tod is heavy with snow,
And the owlet whoops to the wolf below,
That eats the she-wolf's young.'

540   'Dear Lord! it hath a fiendish look—
(The Pilot made reply)
I am a-feared'—'Push on, push on!'
Said the Hermit cheerily.

The boat came closer to the ship,
545   But I nor spake nor stirred;
The boat came close beneath the ship,
And straight a sound was heard.

Under the water it rumbled on,
Still louder and more dread:
550   It reached the ship, it split the bay;

The ship went down like lead.

Stunned by that loud and dreadful sound,
Which sky and ocean smote,
Like one that hath been seven days drowned
555 My body lay afloat;
But swift as dreams, myself I found
Within the Pilot's boat.

Upon the whirl, where sank the ship,
The boat spun round and round;
560 And all was still, save that the hill
Was telling of the sound.

I moved my lips—the Pilot shrieked
And fell down in a fit;
The holy Hermit raised his eyes,
565 And prayed where he did sit.

I took the oars: the Pilot's boy,
Who now doth crazy go,
Laughed loud and long, and all the while
His eyes went to and fro.
570 'Ha! ha!' quoth he, 'full plain I see,
The Devil knows how to row.'

And now, all in my own countree,
I stood on the firm land!
The Hermit stepped forth from the boat,
575 And scarcely he could stand.

'O shrieve me, shrieve me, holy man!'
The Hermit crossed his brow.
'Say quick,' quoth he, 'I bid thee say—
What manner of man art thou?'

580 Forthwith this frame of mine was wrenched
With a woful agony,
Which forced me to begin my tale;

And then it left me free.

Since then, at an uncertain hour,
585 That agony returns:
And till my ghastly tale is told,
This heart within me burns.

I pass, like night, from land to land;
I have strange power of speech;
590 That moment that his face I see,
I know the man that must hear me:
To him my tale I teach.

What loud uproar bursts from that door!
The wedding-guests are there:
595 But in the garden-bower the bride
And bride-maids singing are:
And hark the little vesper bell,
Which biddeth me to prayer!

O Wedding-Guest! this soul hath been
600 Alone on a wide wide sea:
So lonely 'twas, that God himself
Scarce seemèd there to be.

O sweeter than the marriage-feast,
'Tis sweeter far to me,
605 To walk together to the kirk
With a goodly company!—

To walk together to the kirk,
And all together pray,
While each to his great Father bends,
610 Old men, and babes, and loving friends
And youths and maidens gay!

Farewell, farewell! but this I tell
To thee, thou Wedding-Guest!
He prayeth well, who loveth well

615   Both man and bird and beast.

He prayeth best, who loveth best
All things both great and small;
For the dear God who loveth us,
He made and loveth all.

620   The Mariner, whose eye is bright,
Whose beard with age is hoar,
Is gone: and now the Wedding-Guest
Turned from the bridegroom's door.

He went like one that hath been stunned,
625   And is of sense forlorn:
A sadder and a wiser man,
He rose the morrow morn.

KUBLA KHAN
Samuel Taylor Coleridge

Or, a vision in a dream. A Fragment.

1 In Xanadu did Kubla Khan
 A stately pleasure-dome decree:
 Where Alph, the sacred river, ran
 Through caverns measureless to man
5 Down to a sunless sea.
 So twice five miles of fertile ground
 With walls and towers were girdled round;
 And there were gardens bright with sinuous rills,
 Where blossomed many an incense-bearing tree;
10 And here were forests ancient as the hills,
 Enfolding sunny spots of greenery.

 But oh! that deep romantic chasm which slanted
 Down the green hill athwart a cedarn cover!
 A savage place! as holy and enchanted
15 As e'er beneath a waning moon was haunted
 By woman wailing for her demon-lover!
 And from this chasm, with ceaseless turmoil seething,
 As if this earth in fast thick pants were breathing,
 A mighty fountain momently was forced:
20 Amid whose swift half-intermitted burst
 Huge fragments vaulted like rebounding hail,
 Or chaffy grain beneath the thresher's flail:
 And 'mid these dancing rocks at once and ever
 It flung up momently the sacred river.
25 Five miles meandering with a mazy motion
 Through wood and dale the sacred river ran,
 Then reached the caverns measureless to man,
 And sank in tumult to a lifeless ocean;

And 'mid this tumult Kubla heard from far
30   Ancestral voices prophesying war!
    The shadow of the dome of pleasure
    Floated midway on the waves;
    Where was heard the mingled measure
    From the fountain and the caves.
35   It was a miracle of rare device,
    A sunny pleasure-dome with caves of ice!
    A damsel with a dulcimer
    In a vision once I saw:
    It was an Abyssinian maid
40   And on her dulcimer she played,
    Singing of Mount Abora.
    Could I revive within me
    Her symphony and song,
    To such a deep delight 'twould win me,
45   That with music loud and long,
    I would build that dome in air,
    That sunny dome! those caves of ice!
    And all who heard should see them there,
    And all should cry, Beware! Beware!
50   His flashing eyes, his floating hair!
    Weave a circle round him thrice,
    And close your eyes with holy dread
    For he on honey-dew hath fed,
    And drunk the milk of Paradise.

THE PAINS OF SLEEP

Samuel Taylor Coleridge

1   Ere on my bed my limbs I lay,
     It hath not been my use to pray
     With moving lips or bended knees;
     But silently, by slow degrees,
5   My spirit I to Love compose,
     In humble trust mine eye-lids close,
     With reverential resignation
     No wish conceived, no thought exprest,
     Only a sense of supplication;
10   A sense o'er all my soul imprest
     That I am weak, yet not unblest,
     Since in me, round me, every where
     Eternal strength and Wisdom are.

     But yester-night I prayed aloud
15   In anguish and in agony,
     Up-starting from the fiendish crowd
     Of shapes and thoughts that tortured me:
     A lurid light, a trampling throng,
     Sense of intolerable wrong,
20   And whom I scorned, those only strong!
     Thirst of revenge, the powerless will
     Still baffled, and yet burning still!
     Desire with loathing strangely mixed
     On wild or hateful objects fixed.
25   Fantastic passions! maddening brawl!
     And shame and terror over all!
     Deeds to be hid which were not hid,
     Which all confused I could not know
     Whether I suffered, or I did:
30   For all seemed guilt, remorse or woe,

My own or others still the same
Life-stifling fear, soul-stifling shame.

So two nights passed: the night's dismay
Saddened and stunned the coming day.
35 Sleep, the wide blessing, seemed to me
Distemper's worst calamity.
The third night, when my own loud scream
Had waked me from the fiendish dream,
O'ercome with sufferings strange and wild,
40 I wept as I had been a child;
And having thus by tears subdued
My anguish to a milder mood,
Such punishments, I said, were due
To natures deepliest stained with sin,—
45 For aye entempesting anew
The unfathomable hell within,
The horror of their deeds to view,
To know and loathe, yet wish and do!
Such griefs with such men well agree,
50 But wherefore, wherefore fall on me?
To be loved is all I need,
And whom I love, I love indeed.

FROST AT MIDNIGHT

Samuel Taylor Coleridge

1   The Frost performs its secret ministry,
    Unhelped by any wind. The owlet's cry
    Came loud—and hark, again! loud as before.
    The inmates of my cottage, all at rest,
5   Have left me to that solitude, which suits
    Abstruser musings: save that at my side
    My cradled infant slumbers peacefully.
    'Tis calm indeed! so calm, that it disturbs
    And vexes meditation with its strange
10   And extreme silentness. Sea, hill, and wood,
    This populous village! Sea, and hill, and wood,
    With all the numberless goings-on of life,
    Inaudible as dreams! the thin blue flame
    Lies on my low-burnt fire, and quivers not;
15   Only that film, which fluttered on the grate,
    Still flutters there, the sole unquiet thing.
    Methinks, its motion in this hush of nature
    Gives it dim sympathies with me who live,
    Making it a companionable form,
20   Whose puny flaps and freaks the idling Spirit
    By its own moods interprets, every where
    Echo or mirror seeking of itself,
    And makes a toy of Thought.

              But O! how oft,
    How oft, at school, with most believing mind,
25   Presageful, have I gazed upon the bars,
    To watch that fluttering *stranger* ! and as oft
    With unclosed lids, already had I dreamt
    Of my sweet birth-place, and the old church-tower,
    Whose bells, the poor man's only music, rang
30   From morn to evening, all the hot Fair-day,

So sweetly, that they stirred and haunted me
With a wild pleasure, falling on mine ear
Most like articulate sounds of things to come!
So gazed I, till the soothing things, I dreamt,
35   Lulled me to sleep, and sleep prolonged my dreams!
And so I brooded all the following morn,
Awed by the stern preceptor's face, mine eye
Fixed with mock study on my swimming book:
Save if the door half opened, and I snatched
40   A hasty glance, and still my heart leaped up,
For still I hoped to see the *stranger's* face,
Townsman, or aunt, or sister more beloved,
My play-mate when we both were clothed alike!

      Dear Babe, that sleepest cradled by my side,
45   Whose gentle breathings, heard in this deep calm,
Fill up the interspersèd vacancies
And momentary pauses of the thought!
My babe so beautiful! it thrills my heart
With tender gladness, thus to look at thee,
50   And think that thou shalt learn far other lore,
And in far other scenes! For I was reared
In the great city, pent 'mid cloisters dim,
And saw nought lovely but the sky and stars.
But *thou*, my babe! shalt wander like a breeze
55   By lakes and sandy shores, beneath the crags
Of ancient mountain, and beneath the clouds,
Which image in their bulk both lakes and shores
And mountain crags: so shalt thou see and hear
The lovely shapes and sounds intelligible
60   Of that eternal language, which thy God
Utters, who from eternity doth teach
Himself in all, and all things in himself.
Great universal Teacher! he shall mould
Thy spirit, and by giving make it ask.
65

Therefore all seasons shall be sweet to thee,
Whether the summer clothe the general earth
With greenness, or the redbreast sit and sing
Betwixt the tufts of snow on the bare branch
Of mossy apple-tree, while the night-thatch
70   Smokes in the sun-thaw; whether the eave-drops fall
Heard only in the trances of the blast,
Or if the secret ministry of frost
Shall hang them up in silent icicles,
Quietly shining to the quiet Moon.

GEORGE GORDON BYRON (1788–1824)

George Gordon Byron, often known by his nobleman's title, Lord Byron, was likely the most famous and most notorious of the Romantic poets. Byron's early life was traumatic. He was born with a deformed foot; abandoned by his father as a child; lived with a mother who may have been schizophrenic; and was sexually abused by his nurse. Byron attended Cambridge, developing several intense friendships, mostly with men. He was keenly aware of his personal magnetism and modeled the protagonists of his literary works (the famous brooding and passionate "Byronic heroes") after himself. Byron was inspired to travel the world, and visited many Mediterranean countries, including Portugal, Spain, Albania, Turkey, and Greece. After returning to England, Byron married Anne Isabella Milbanke, but divorced her when she accused him of incest and sodomy. Both charges seem to have been valid; Byron apparently had been intimate with his half sister Augusta and a number of young men. Friends warned him that he was at risk of being lynched, so he fled to Italy in 1816. Byron died suddenly at the age of thirty-six from a cold and fever. He had written a memoir, but it was burned by his friends who feared they would become part of the scandal that plagued Byron most of his life.

WHEN WE TWO PARTED

George Gordon Byron

1 When we two parted
  In silence and tears,
Half broken-hearted
  To sever for years,
5 Pale grew thy cheek and cold,
  Colder thy kiss;
Truly that hour foretold
  Sorrow to this.

The dew of the morning
  Sunk chill on my brow--
10 It felt like the warning
  Of what I feel now.
Thy vows are all broken,
  And light is thy fame;
I hear thy name spoken,
15 And share in its shame.

They name thee before me,
  A knell to mine ear;
A shudder comes o'er me--
  Why wert thou so dear?
They know not I knew thee,
20 Who knew thee too well--
Long, long shall I rue thee,
  Too deeply to tell.

In secret we met--
  In silence I grieve,
25 That thy heart could forget,
  Thy spirit deceive.
If I should meet thee
  After long years,
How should I greet thee?--
  With silence and tears.

GIRL OF CADIZ

George Gordon Byron

1   Like me, the lovely Girl of Cadiz.
Although her eyes be not of blue,
  Nor fair her locks, like English lassies,
How far its own expressive hue
5   The languid azure eye surpasses!

Prometheus-like, from heaven she stole
  The fire that through those silken lashes
In darkest glances seems to roll,
  From eyes that cannot hide their flashes;
10 And as along her bosom steal
  In lengthened flow her raven tresses,
You 'd swear each clustering lock could feel,
  And curled to give her neck caresses.

Our English maids are long to woo,
15   And frigid even in possession;
And if their charms be fair to view,
  Their lips are slow at love's confession;
But, born beneath a brighter sun,
  For love ordained the Spanish maid is,
20 And who, when fondly, fairly won,
  Enchants you like the Girl of Cadiz?

The Spanish maid is no coquette,
  Nor joys to see a lover tremble;
And if she love or if she hate,
25   Alike she knows not to dissemble.
Her heart can ne'er be bought or sold,—
  Howe'er it beats, it beats sincerely;
And, though it will not bend to gold,
  'T will love you long, and love you dearly.

30 The Spanish girl that meets your love
  Ne'er taunts you with a mock denial;
 For every thought is bent to prove
  Her passion in the hour of trial.
 When thronging foemen menace Spain
35 She dares the deed and shares the danger;
 And should her lover press the plain,
  She hurls the spear, her love's avenger.

 And when, beneath the evening star,
  She mingles in the gay Bolero,
40 Or sings to her attuned guitar
  Of Christian knight or Moorish hero,
 Or counts her beads with fairy hand
  Beneath the twinkling rays of Hesper,
 Or joins devotion's choral band
45 To chant the sweet and hallowed vesper,

 In each her charms the heart must move
  Of all who venture to behold her.
 Then let not maids less fair reprove,
  Because her bosom is not colder;
50 Through many a clime 't is mine to roam
  Where many a soft and melting maid is,
 But none abroad, and few at home,
  May match the dark-eyed Girl of Cadiz.

ADIEU, ADIEU! MY NATIVE SHORE

George Gordon Byron

1   Adieu, adieu! my native shore
Fades o'er the waters blue;
The night-winds sigh, the breakers roar,
And shrieks the wild sea-mew.
5   Yon sun that sets upon the sea
We follow in his flight;
Farewell awhile to him and thee,
My native Land-Good Night!

A few short hours, and he will rise
10   To give the morrow birth;
And I shall hail the main and skies,
But not my mother earth.
Deserted is my own good hall,
Its hearth is desolate;
15   Wild weeds are gathering on the wall;
My dog howls at the gate.

SHE WALKS IN BEAUTY

George Gordon Byron

1   She walks in beauty, like the night
     Of cloudless climes and starry skies;
     And all that's best of dark and bright
     Meet in her aspect and her eyes;
5   Thus mellowed to that tender light
     Which heaven to gaudy day denies.

     One shade the more, one ray the less,
     Had half impaired the nameless grace
     Which waves in every raven tress,
10   Or softly lightens o'er her face;
     Where thoughts serenely sweet express,
     How pure, how dear their dwelling-place.

     And on that cheek, and o'er that brow,
     So soft, so calm, yet eloquent,
15   The smiles that win, the tints that glow,
     But tell of days in goodness spent,
     A mind at peace with all below,
     A heart whose love is innocent!

PROMETHEUS

George Gordon Byron

1   Titan! to whose immortal eyes
        The sufferings of mortality,
        Seen in their sad reality,
    Were not as things that gods despise;
5   What was thy pity's recompense?
    A silent suffering, and intense;
    The rock, the vulture, and the chain,
    All that the proud can feel of pain,
    The agony they do not show,
10   The suffocating sense of woe,
        Which speaks but in its loneliness,
    And then is jealous lest the sky
    Should have a listener, nor will sigh
        Until its voice is echoless.

15   Titan! to thee the strife was given
        Between the suffering and the will,
        Which torture where they cannot kill;
    And the inexorable Heaven,
    And the deaf tyranny of Fate,
20   The ruling principle of Hate,
    Which for its pleasure doth create
    The things it may annihilate,
    Refus'd thee even the boon to die:
    The wretched gift Eternity
25   Was thine—and thou hast borne it well.
    All that the Thunderer wrung from thee
    Was but the menace which flung back
    On him the torments of thy rack;
    The fate thou didst so well foresee,
30   But would not to appease him tell;
    And in thy Silence was his Sentence,

And in his Soul a vain repentance,
And evil dread so ill dissembled,
That in his hand the lightnings trembled.

35 Thy Godlike crime was to be kind,
   To render with thy precepts less
   The sum of human wretchedness,
 And strengthen Man with his own mind;
 But baffled as thou wert from high,
40 Still in thy patient energy,
 In the endurance, and repulse
   Of thine impenetrable Spirit,
 Which Earth and Heaven could not convulse,
   A mighty lesson we inherit:
45 Thou art a symbol and a sign
   To Mortals of their fate and force;
 Like thee, Man is in part divine,
   A troubled stream from a pure source;
 And Man in portions can foresee
50 His own funereal destiny;
 His wretchedness, and his resistance,
 And his sad unallied existence:
 To which his Spirit may oppose
 Itself—and equal to all woes,
55   And a firm will, and a deep sense,
 Which even in torture can descry
   Its own concenter'd recompense,
 Triumphant where it dares defy,
 And making Death a Victory.

DARKNESS

George Gordon Byron

1   I had a dream, which was not all a dream.
The bright sun was extinguish'd, and the stars
Did wander darkling in the eternal space,
Rayless, and pathless, and the icy earth
5   Swung blind and blackening in the moonless air;
Morn came and went—and came, and brought no day,
And men forgot their passions in the dread
Of this their desolation; and all hearts
Were chill'd into a selfish prayer for light:
10   And they did live by watchfires—and the thrones,
The palaces of crowned kings—the huts,
The habitations of all things which dwell,
Were burnt for beacons; cities were consum'd,
And men were gather'd round their blazing homes
15   To look once more into each other's face;
Happy were those who dwelt within the eye
Of the volcanos, and their mountain-torch:
A fearful hope was all the world contain'd;
Forests were set on fire—but hour by hour
20   They fell and faded—and the crackling trunks
Extinguish'd with a crash—and all was black.
The brows of men by the despairing light
Wore an unearthly aspect, as by fits
The flashes fell upon them; some lay down
25   And hid their eyes and wept; and some did rest
Their chins upon their clenched hands, and smil'd;
And others hurried to and fro, and fed
Their funeral piles with fuel, and look'd up
With mad disquietude on the dull sky,
30   The pall of a past world; and then again
With curses cast them down upon the dust,
And gnash'd their teeth and howl'd: the wild birds shriek'd

And, terrified, did flutter on the ground,
And flap their useless wings; the wildest brutes
35   Came tame and tremulous; and vipers crawl'd
And twin'd themselves among the multitude,
Hissing, but stingless—they were slain for food.
And War, which for a moment was no more,
Did glut himself again: a meal was bought
40   With blood, and each sate sullenly apart
Gorging himself in gloom: no love was left;
All earth was but one thought—and that was death
Immediate and inglorious; and the pang
Of famine fed upon all entrails—men
45   Died, and their bones were tombless as their flesh;
The meagre by the meagre were devour'd,
Even dogs assail'd their masters, all save one,
And he was faithful to a corse, and kept
The birds and beasts and famish'd men at bay,
50   Till hunger clung them, or the dropping dead
Lur'd their lank jaws; himself sought out no food,
But with a piteous and perpetual moan,
And a quick desolate cry, licking the hand
Which answer'd not with a caress—he died.
55   The crowd was famish'd by degrees; but two
Of an enormous city did survive,
And they were enemies: they met beside
The dying embers of an altar-place
Where had been heap'd a mass of holy things
60   For an unholy usage; they rak'd up,
And shivering scrap'd with their cold skeleton hands
The feeble ashes, and their feeble breath
Blew for a little life, and made a flame
Which was a mockery; then they lifted up
65   Their eyes as it grew lighter, and beheld
Each other's aspects—saw, and shriek'd, and died—
Even of their mutual hideousness they died,
Unknowing who he was upon whose brow
Famine had written Fiend. The world was void,

70 The populous and the powerful was a lump,
Seasonless, herbless, treeless, manless, lifeless—
A lump of death—a chaos of hard clay.
The rivers, lakes and ocean all stood still,
And nothing stirr'd within their silent depths;
75 Ships sailorless lay rotting on the sea,
And their masts fell down piecemeal: as they dropp'd
They slept on the abyss without a surge—
The waves were dead; the tides were in their grave,
The moon, their mistress, had expir'd before;
80 The winds were wither'd in the stagnant air,
And the clouds perish'd; Darkness had no need
Of aid from them—She was the Universe.

SO WE'LL GO NO MORE A ROVING

George Gordon Byron

1 So, we'll go no more a roving
   So late into the night,
Though the heart be still as loving,
   And the moon be still as bright.

5 For the sword outwears its sheath,
   And the soul wears out the breast,
And the heart must pause to breathe,
   And love itself have rest.

Though the night was made for loving,
10   And the day returns too soon,
Yet we'll go no more a roving
   By the light of the moon.

THE ISLES OF GREECE

George Gordon Byron

1   The isles of Greece! the isles of Greece
        Where burning Sappho loved and sung,
    Where grew the arts of war and peace,
        Where Delos rose, and Phoebus sprung!
5   Eternal summer gilds them yet,
    But all, except their sun, is set.

    The Scian and the Teian muse,
        The hero's harp, the lover's lute,
    Have found the fame your shores refuse:
10   Their place of birth alone is mute
    To sounds which echo further west
    Than your sires' "Islands of the Blest".

    The mountains look on Marathon—
        And Marathon looks on the sea;
15   And musing there an hour alone,
        I dream'd that Greece might still be free;
    For standing on the Persians' grave,
    I could not deem myself a slave.

    A king sate on the rocky brow
20   Which looks o'er sea-born Salamis;
    And ships, by thousands, lay below,
        And men in nations;—all were his!
    He counted them at break of day—
    And when the sun set, where were they?

25   And where are they? and where art thou,
        My country? On thy voiceless shore
    The heroic lay is tuneless now—
        The heroic bosom beats no more!
    And must thy lyre, so long divine,

30   Degenerate into hands like mine?

         'Tis something in the dearth of fame,
               Though link'd among a fetter'd race,
         To feel at least a patriot's shame,
               Even as I sing, suffuse my face;
35   For what is left the poet here?
         For Greeks a blush--for Greece a tear.

         Must we but weep o'er days more blest?
               Must we but blush?—Our fathers bled.
         Earth! render back from out thy breast
40   A remnant of our Spartan dead!
         Of the three hundred grant but three,
         To make a new Thermopylae!

         What, silent still? and silent all?
               Ah! no;—the voices of the dead
45   Sound like a distant torrent's fall,
               And answer, 'Let one living head,
         But one, arise,—we come, we come!'
         'Tis but the living who are dumb.

         In vain--in vain: strike other chords;
50   Fill high the cup with Samian wine!
         Leave battles to the Turkish hordes,
               And shed the blood of Scio's vine:
         Hark! rising to the ignoble call—
         How answers each bold Bacchanal!

55   You have the Pyrrhic dance as yet;
               Where is the Pyrrhic phalanx gone?
         Of two such lessons, why forget
               The nobler and the manlier one?
         You have the letters Cadmus gave—
60   Think ye he meant them for a slave?

         Fill high the bowl with Samian wine!
               We will not think of themes like these!

It made Anacreon's song divine:
　　　He served—but served Polycrates—
65　A tyrant; but our masters then
Were still, at least, our countrymen.

The tyrant of the Chersonese
　　　Was freedom's best and bravest friend;
That tyrant was Miltiades!
70　　　O, that the present hour would lend
Another despot of the kind!
Such chains as his were sure to bind.

Fill high the bowl with Samian wine!
　　　On Suli's rock, and Parga's shore,
75　Exists the remnant of a line
　　　Such as the Doric mothers bore;
And there, perhaps, some seed is sown,
The Heracleidan blood might own.

Trust not for freedom to the Franks—
80　　　They have a king who buys and sells;
In native swords and native ranks
　　　The only hope of courage dwells:
But Turkish force and Latin fraud
Would break your shield, however broad.

85　Fill high the bowl with Samian wine!
　　　Our virgins dance beneath the shade—
I see their glorious black eyes shine;
　　　But gazing on each glowing maid,
My own the burning tear-drop laves,
90　To think such breasts must suckle slaves.

Place me on Sunium's marbled steep,
　　　Where nothing, save the waves and I,
May hear our mutual murmurs sweep;
　　　There, swan-like, let me sing and die:
95　A land of slaves shall ne'er be mine—
Dash down yon cup of Samian wine!

ON THIS DAY I COMPLETE MY THIRTY-SIXTH YEAR

George Gordon Byron

1 'Tis time this heart should be unmoved,
Since others it hath ceased to move:
Yet though I cannot be beloved,
Still let me love!

5 My days are in the yellow leaf;
The flowers and fruits of Love are gone;
The worm—the canker, and the grief
Are mine alone!

The fire that on my bosom preys
10 Is lone as some Volcanic Isle;
No torch is kindled at its blaze
A funeral pile.

The hope, the fear, the jealous care,
The exalted portion of the pain
15 And power of Love I cannot share,
But wear the chain.

But 'tis not *thus*—and 'tis not *here*
Such thoughts should shake my Soul, nor *now*,
Where Glory decks the hero's bier,
20 Or binds his brow.

The Sword, the Banner, and the Field,
Glory and Greece around us see!
The Spartan borne upon his shield
Was not more free.

25   Awake (not Greece—she *is* awake!)
          Awake, my Spirit! Think through *whom*
      Thy life-blood tracks its parent lake
                    And then strike home!

          Tread those reviving passions down
30   Unworthy Manhood—unto thee
      Indifferent should the smile or frown
                    Of beauty be.

          If thou regret'st thy Youth, *why live?*
            The land of honourable Death
35   Is here:—up to the Field, and give
                    Away thy breath!

          Seek out—less often sought than found—
            A Soldier's Grave, for thee the best;
      Then look around, and choose thy Ground,
40   And take thy rest.

                    MISSOLONGHI, *January 22*

STANZAS TO AUGUSTA

from Poems, 1816
George Gordon Byron

1   When all around grew drear and dark,
       And reason half withheld her ray—
       And hope but shed a dying spark
       Which more misled my lonely way;

5   In that deep midnight of the mind,
       And that internal strife of heart,
       When dreading to be deemed too kind,
       The weak despair—the cold depart;

       When fortune changed—and love fled far,
10   And hatred's shafts flew thick and fast,
       Thou wert the solitary star
       Which rose, and set not to the last.

       Oh, blest be thine unbroken light!
       That watched me as a seraph's eye,
15   And stood between me and the night,
       For ever shining sweetly nigh.

       And when the cloud upon us came,
       Which strove to blacken o'er thy ray—
       Then purer spread its gentle flame,
20   And dashed the darkness all away.

       Still may thy spirit dwell on mine,
       And teach it what to brave or brook—
       There's more in one soft word of thine
       Than in the world's defied rebuke.

25 Thou stood'st as stands a lovely tree
    That, still unbroke though gently bent,
    Still waves with fond fidelity
    Its boughs above a monument.

    The winds might rend, the skies might pour,
30 But there thou wert—and still wouldst be
    Devoted in the stormiest hour
    To shed thy weeping leaves o'er me.

    But thou and thine shall know no blight,
    Whatever fate on me may fall;
35 For heaven in sunshine will requite
    The kind—and thee the most of all.

    Then let the ties of baffled love
    Be broken—thine will never break;
    Thy heart can feel—but will not move;
40 Thy soul, though soft, will never shake.

    And these, when all was lost beside,
    Were found, and still are fixed in thee;—
    And bearing still a breast so tried,
    Earth is no desert—e'en to me.

PERCY BYSSHE SHELLEY (1792–1822)

Born into a wealthy family with exceptional social connections (his father was a Member of Parliament), Shelley was privileged. He did not, however, have an easy life. He attended Eton, the most famous British preparatory school, where he was bullied. During his freshman year at Oxford University, he was expelled for contributing to a pamphlet on atheism titled, "The Necessity of Atheism" (1811). Shelley's father was furious, but Shelley proved he was a man of his convictions; Shelley could have been readmitted if he had confessed he was a Christian, but he refused. He believed that Christianity was the worst form of tyranny. Shelley eloped with sixteen-year-old Harriet Westbrook, but their marriage was troubled from the start. Their daughter Elizabeth was born in 1813, but the next year, while Harriet was expecting their second child, Shelley abandoned her for another woman, Mary Wollstonecraft Godwin. Both Harriet and Mary gave birth to children fathered by Shelley the same year. Grief-stricken, Harriet committed suicide. Shelley married Mary only a few weeks later. The couple moved to Italy, where Shelley became close friends with Lord Byron. It was at this time he wrote his most memorable poems, including "Prometheus Unbound" and "Ode to the West Wind." In July of 1822, Shelley died in a shipwreck off the coast of Italy. He was only twenty-nine years old.

HYMN TO INTELLECTUAL BEAUTY

Percy Bysshe Shelley

1 The awful shadow of some unseen Power
  Floats though unseen among us; visiting
  This various world with as inconstant wing
 As summer winds that creep from flower to flower;
5 Like moonbeams that behind some piny mountain shower,
  It visits with inconstant glance
  Each human heart and countenance;
 Like hues and harmonies of evening,
  Like clouds in starlight widely spread,
10 Like memory of music fled,
  Like aught that for its grace may be
 Dear, and yet dearer for its mystery.

 Spirit of BEAUTY, that dost consecrate
  With thine own hues all thou dost shine upon
15 Of human thought or form, where art thou gone?
 Why dost thou pass away and leave our state,
 This dim vast vale of tears, vacant and desolate?
  Ask why the sunlight not for ever
  Weaves rainbows o'er yon mountain-river,
20 Why aught should fail and fade that once is shown,
  Why fear and dream and death and birth
  Cast on the daylight of this earth
  Such gloom, why man has such a scope
 For love and hate, despondency and hope?

25 No voice from some sublimer world hath ever
  To sage or poet these responses given:
  Therefore the names of Demon, Ghost, and Heaven,
 Remain the records of their vain endeavour:
 Frail spells whose utter'd charm might not avail to sever,
30 From all we hear and all we see,
  Doubt, chance and mutability.

Thy light alone—like mist o'er mountains driven,
        Or music by the night-wind sent
        Through strings of some still instrument,
35   Or moonlight on a midnight stream,
Gives grace and truth to life's unquiet dream.

Love, Hope, and Self-esteem, like clouds depart
        And come, for some uncertain moments lent.
        Man were immortal and omnipotent,
40   Didst thou, unknown and awful as thou art,
Keep with thy glorious train firm state within his heart.
        Thou messenger of sympathies,
        That wax and wane in lovers' eyes;
Thou, that to human thought art nourishment,
45   Like darkness to a dying flame!
        Depart not as thy shadow came,
        Depart not—lest the grave should be,
Like life and fear, a dark reality.

While yet a boy I sought for ghosts, and sped
50   Through many a listening chamber, cave and ruin,
        And starlight wood, with fearful steps pursuing
Hopes of high talk with the departed dead.
I call'd on poisonous names with which our youth is fed;
        I was not heard; I saw them not;
55   When musing deeply on the lot
Of life, at that sweet time when winds are wooing
        All vital things that wake to bring
        News of birds and blossoming,
        Sudden, thy shadow fell on me;
60   I shriek'd, and clasp'd my hands in ecstasy!

I vow'd that I would dedicate my powers
        To thee and thine: have I not kept the vow?
        With beating heart and streaming eyes, even now
I call the phantoms of a thousand hours
65   Each from his voiceless grave: they have in vision'd bowers
        Of studious zeal or love's delight
        Outwatch'd with me the envious night:

They know that never joy illum'd my brow
     Unlink'd with hope that thou wouldst free
70   This world from its dark slavery,
     That thou, O awful LOVELINESS,
Wouldst give whate'er these words cannot express.

The day becomes more solemn and serene
     When noon is past; there is a harmony
75   In autumn, and a lustre in its sky,
Which through the summer is not heard or seen,
As if it could not be, as if it had not been!
      Thus let thy power, which like the truth
      Of nature on my passive youth
80   Descended, to my onward life supply
      Its calm, to one who worships thee,
      And every form containing thee,
      Whom, SPIRIT fair, thy spells did bind
To fear himself, and love all human kind.

MUTABILITY

Percy Bysshe Shelley

1   We are as clouds that veil the midnight moon;
       How restlessly they speed and gleam and quiver,
    Streaking the darkness radiantly! yet soon
    Night closes round, and they are lost for ever:—

5   Or like forgotten lyres whose dissonant strings
       Give various response to each varying blast,
    To whose frail frame no second motion brings
       One mood or modulation like the last.

    We rest—a dream has power to poison sleep;
10   We rise—one wandering thought pollutes the day;
    We feel, conceive or reason, laugh or weep,
    Embrace fond woe, or cast our cares away:—

    It is the same!—For, be it joy or sorrow,
       The path of its departure still is free;
15   Man's yesterday may ne'er be like his morrow;
       Nought may endure but Mutability.

TO WORDSWORTH

Percy Bysshe Shelley

1   Poet of Nature, thou hast wept to know
       That things depart which never may return:
       Childhood and youth, friendship and love's first glow,
       Have fled like sweet dreams, leaving thee to mourn.
5   These common woes I feel. One loss is mine
       Which thou too feel'st, yet I alone deplore.
       Thou wert as a lone star, whose light did shine
       On some frail bark in winter's midnight roar:
       Thou hast like to a rock-built refuge stood
10   Above the blind and battling multitude:
       In honoured poverty thy voice did weave
       Songs consecrate to truth and liberty,—
       Deserting these, thou leavest me to grieve,
       Thus having been, that thou shouldst cease to be.

MONT BLANC

Percy Bysshe Shelley

I

1 The everlasting universe of things
Flows through the mind, and rolls its rapid waves,
Now dark—now glittering—now reflecting gloom—
Now lending splendour, where from secret springs
5 The source of human thought its tribute brings
Of waters—with a sound but half its own,
Such as a feeble brook will oft assume,
In the wild woods, among the mountains lone,
Where waterfalls around it leap for ever,
10 Where woods and winds contend, and a vast river
Over its rocks ceaselessly bursts and raves.

II

Thus thou, Ravine of Arve—dark, deep Ravine—
Thou many-colour'd, many-voiced vale,
Over whose pines, and crags, and caverns sail
15 Fast cloud-shadows and sunbeams: awful scene,
Where Power in likeness of the Arve comes down
From the ice-gulfs that gird his secret throne,
Bursting through these dark mountains like the flame
Of lightning through the tempest;—thou dost lie,
20 Thy giant brood of pines around thee clinging,
Children of elder time, in whose devotion
The chainless winds still come and ever came
To drink their odours, and their mighty swinging
To hear—an old and solemn harmony;
25 Thine earthly rainbows stretch'd across the sweep
Of the aethereal waterfall, whose veil
Robes some unsculptur'd image; the strange sleep
Which when the voices of the desert fail
Wraps all in its own deep eternity;

30   Thy caverns echoing to the Arve's commotion,
     A loud, lone sound no other sound can tame;
     Thou art pervaded with that ceaseless motion,
     Thou art the path of that unresting sound—
     Dizzy Ravine! and when I gaze on thee
35   I seem as in a trance sublime and strange
     To muse on my own separate fantasy,
     My own, my human mind, which passively
     Now renders and receives fast influencings,
     Holding an unremitting interchange
40   With the clear universe of things around;
     One legion of wild thoughts, whose wandering wings
     Now float above thy darkness, and now rest
     Where that or thou art no unbidden guest,
     In the still cave of the witch Poesy,
45   Seeking among the shadows that pass by
     Ghosts of all things that are, some shade of thee,
     Some phantom, some faint image; till the breast
     From which they fled recalls them, thou art there!

III

     Some say that gleams of a remoter world
50   Visit the soul in sleep, that death is slumber,
     And that its shapes the busy thoughts outnumber
     Of those who wake and live.—I look on high;
     Has some unknown omnipotence unfurl'd
     The veil of life and death? or do I lie
55   In dream, and does the mightier world of sleep
     Spread far around and inaccessibly
     Its circles? For the very spirit fails,
     Driven like a homeless cloud from steep to steep
     That vanishes among the viewless gales!
60   Far, far above, piercing the infinite sky,
     Mont Blanc appears—still, snowy, and serene;
     Its subject mountains their unearthly forms
     Pile around it, ice and rock; broad vales between
     Of frozen floods, unfathomable deeps,

65 Blue as the overhanging heaven, that spread
And wind among the accumulated steeps;
A desert peopled by the storms alone,
Save when the eagle brings some hunter's bone,
And the wolf tracks her there—how hideously
70 Its shapes are heap'd around! rude, bare, and high,
Ghastly, and scarr'd, and riven.—Is this the scene
Where the old Earthquake-daemon taught her young
Ruin? Were these their toys? or did a sea
Of fire envelop once this silent snow?
75 None can reply—all seems eternal now.
The wilderness has a mysterious tongue
Which teaches awful doubt, or faith so mild,
So solemn, so serene, that man may be,
But for such faith, with Nature reconcil'd;
80 Thou hast a voice, great Mountain, to repeal
Large codes of fraud and woe; not understood
By all, but which the wise, and great, and good
Interpret, or make felt, or deeply feel.

IV

The fields, the lakes, the forests, and the streams,
85 Ocean, and all the living things that dwell
Within the daedal earth; lightning, and rain,
Earthquake, and fiery flood, and hurricane,
The torpor of the year when feeble dreams
Visit the hidden buds, or dreamless sleep
90 Holds every future leaf and flower; the bound
With which from that detested trance they leap;
The works and ways of man, their death and birth,
And that of him and all that his may be;
All things that move and breathe with toil and sound
95 Are born and die; revolve, subside, and swell.
Power dwells apart in its tranquillity,
Remote, serene, and inaccessible:
And this, the naked countenance of earth,
On which I gaze, even these primeval mountains

100   Teach the adverting mind. The glaciers creep
      Like snakes that watch their prey, from their far fountains,
      Slow rolling on; there, many a precipice
      Frost and the Sun in scorn of mortal power
      Have pil'd: dome, pyramid, and pinnacle,
105   A city of death, distinct with many a tower
      And wall impregnable of beaming ice.
      Yet not a city, but a flood of ruin
      Is there, that from the boundaries of the sky
      Rolls its perpetual stream; vast pines are strewing
110   Its destin'd path, or in the mangled soil
      Branchless and shatter'd stand; the rocks, drawn down
      From yon remotest waste, have overthrown
      The limits of the dead and living world,
      Never to be reclaim'd. The dwelling-place
115   Of insects, beasts, and birds, becomes its spoil;
      Their food and their retreat for ever gone,
      So much of life and joy is lost. The race
      Of man flies far in dread; his work and dwelling
      Vanish, like smoke before the tempest's stream,
120   And their place is not known. Below, vast caves
      Shine in the rushing torrents' restless gleam,
      Which from those secret chasms in tumult welling
      Meet in the vale, and one majestic River,
      The breath and blood of distant lands, for ever
125   Rolls its loud waters to the ocean-waves,
      Breathes its swift vapours to the circling air.

V

      Mont Blanc yet gleams on high:—the power is there,
      The still and solemn power of many sights,
      And many sounds, and much of life and death.
130   In the calm darkness of the moonless nights,
      In the lone glare of day, the snows descend
      Upon that Mountain; none beholds them there,
      Nor when the flakes burn in the sinking sun,
      Or the star-beams dart through them. Winds contend

135   Silently there, and heap the snow with breath
       Rapid and strong, but silently! Its home
       The voiceless lightning in these solitudes
       Keeps innocently, and like vapour broods
       Over the snow. The secret Strength of things
140   Which governs thought, and to the infinite dome
       Of Heaven is as a law, inhabits thee!
       And what were thou, and earth, and stars, and sea,
       If to the human mind's imaginings
       Silence and solitude were vacancy?

OZYMANDIAS

Percy Bysshe Shelley

1   I met a traveller from an antique land,
Who said—"Two vast and trunkless legs of stone
Stand in the desert. . . . Near them, on the sand,
Half sunk a shattered visage lies, whose frown,
5   And wrinkled lip, and sneer of cold command,
Tell that its sculptor well those passions read
Which yet survive, stamped on these lifeless things,
The hand that mocked them, and the heart that fed;
And on the pedestal, these words appear:
10   'My name is Ozymandias, King of Kings;
Look on my Works, ye Mighty, and despair!'
Nothing beside remains. Round the decay
Of that colossal Wreck, boundless and bare
The lone and level sands stretch far away."

ENGLAND IN 1819

Percy Bysshe Shelley

1 An old, mad, blind, despised, and dying King;
Princes, the dregs of their dull race, who flow
Through public scorn,—mud from a muddy spring;
Rulers who neither see nor feel nor know,
5 But leechlike to their fainting country cling
Till they drop, blind in blood, without a blow.
A people starved and stabbed in th' untilled field;
An army, whom liberticide and prey
Makes as a two-edged sword to all who wield;
10 Golden and sanguine laws which tempt and slay;
Religion Christless, Godless—a book sealed;
A senate, Time's worst statute, unrepealed—
Are graves from which a glorious Phantom may
Burst, to illumine our tempestuous day.

ODE TO THE WEST WIND

Percy Bysshe Shelley

I

1 O wild West Wind, thou breath of Autumn's being,
Thou, from whose unseen presence the leaves dead
Are driven, like ghosts from an enchanter fleeing,

Yellow, and black, and pale, and hectic red,
5 Pestilence-stricken multitudes: O thou,
Who chariotest to their dark wintry bed

The winged seeds, where they lie cold and low,
Each like a corpse within its grave, until
Thine azure sister of the Spring shall blow

10 Her clarion o'er the dreaming earth, and fill
(Driving sweet buds like flocks to feed in air)
With living hues and odours plain and hill:

Wild Spirit, which art moving everywhere;
Destroyer and preserver; hear, oh hear!

II

15 Thou on whose stream, mid the steep sky's commotion,
Loose clouds like earth's decaying leaves are shed,
Shook from the tangled boughs of Heaven and Ocean,

Angels of rain and lightning: there are spread
On the blue surface of thine aëry surge,
20 Like the bright hair uplifted from the head

Of some fierce Maenad, even from the dim verge
Of the horizon to the zenith's height,
The locks of the approaching storm. Thou dirge

Of the dying year, to which this closing night
25   Will be the dome of a vast sepulchre,
Vaulted with all thy congregated might

Of vapours, from whose solid atmosphere
Black rain, and fire, and hail will burst: oh hear!

III
Thou who didst waken from his summer dreams
30   The blue Mediterranean, where he lay,
Lull'd by the coil of his crystalline streams,

Beside a pumice isle in Baiae's bay,
And saw in sleep old palaces and towers
Quivering within the wave's intenser day,

35   All overgrown with azure moss and flowers
So sweet, the sense faints picturing them! Thou
For whose path the Atlantic's level powers

Cleave themselves into chasms, while far below
The sea-blooms and the oozy woods which wear
The sapless foliage of the ocean, know

40   Thy voice, and suddenly grow gray with fear,
And tremble and despoil themselves: oh hear!

IV
If I were a dead leaf thou mightest bear;
If I were a swift cloud to fly with thee;
45   A wave to pant beneath thy power, and share

The impulse of thy strength, only less free
Than thou, O uncontrollable! If even
I were as in my boyhood, and could be

The comrade of thy wanderings over Heaven,
50   As then, when to outstrip thy skiey speed
Scarce seem'd a vision; I would ne'er have striven

As thus with thee in prayer in my sore need.
Oh, lift me as a wave, a leaf, a cloud!
I fall upon the thorns of life! I bleed!

55   A heavy weight of hours has chain'd and bow'd
One too like thee: tameless, and swift, and proud.

V

Make me thy lyre, even as the forest is:
What if my leaves are falling like its own!
The tumult of thy mighty harmonies

60   Will take from both a deep, autumnal tone,
Sweet though in sadness. Be thou, Spirit fierce,
My spirit! Be thou me, impetuous one!

Drive my dead thoughts over the universe
Like wither'd leaves to quicken a new birth!
65   And, by the incantation of this verse,

Scatter, as from an unextinguish'd hearth
Ashes and sparks, my words among mankind!
Be through my lips to unawaken'd earth

The trumpet of a prophecy! O Wind,
70   If Winter comes, can Spring be far behind?

LOVE'S PHILOSOPHY

Percy Bysshe Shelley

1   The fountains mingle with the river
      And the rivers with the ocean,
The winds of heaven mix for ever
      With a sweet emotion;
5   Nothing in the world is single;
      All things by a law divine
In one spirit meet and mingle.
      Why not I with thine?—

    See the mountains kiss high heaven
10   And the waves clasp one another;
No sister-flower would be forgiven
      If it disdained its brother;
And the sunlight clasps the earth
      And the moonbeams kiss the sea:
15   What is all this sweet work worth
      If thou kiss not me?

TO A SKYLARK

Percy Bysshe Shelley

1   Hail to thee, blithe Spirit!
Bird thou never wert,
That from Heaven, or near it,
Pourest thy full heart
5   In profuse strains of unpremeditated art.

Higher still and higher
From the earth thou springest
Like a cloud of fire;
The blue deep thou wingest,
10   And singing still dost soar, and soaring ever singest.

In the golden lightning
Of the sunken sun,
O'er which clouds are bright'ning,
Thou dost float and run;
15   Like an unbodied joy whose race is just begun.

The pale purple even
Melts around thy flight;
Like a star of Heaven,
In the broad day-light
20   Thou art unseen, but yet I hear thy shrill delight,

Keen as are the arrows
Of that silver sphere,
Whose intense lamp narrows
In the white dawn clear
25   Until we hardly see, we feel that it is there.

All the earth and air
With thy voice is loud,

As, when night is bare,
From one lonely cloud
30   The moon rains out her beams, and Heaven is overflow'd.

What thou art we know not;
What is most like thee?
From rainbow clouds there flow not
Drops so bright to see
35   As from thy presence showers a rain of melody.

Like a Poet hidden
In the light of thought,
Singing hymns unbidden,
Till the world is wrought
40   To sympathy with hopes and fears it heeded not:

Like a high-born maiden
In a palace-tower,
Soothing her love-laden
Soul in secret hour
45   With music sweet as love, which overflows her bower:

Like a glow-worm golden
In a dell of dew,
Scattering unbeholden
Its aërial hue
50   Among the flowers and grass, which screen it from the view:

Like a rose embower'd
In its own green leaves,
By warm winds deflower'd,
Till the scent it gives
55   Makes faint with too much sweet those heavy-winged thieves:

Sound of vernal showers
On the twinkling grass,
Rain-awaken'd flowers,

All that ever was
60 Joyous, and clear, and fresh, thy music doth surpass.

Teach us, Sprite or Bird,
What sweet thoughts are thine:
I have never heard
Praise of love or wine
65 That panted forth a flood of rapture so divine.

Chorus Hymeneal,
Or triumphal chant,
Match'd with thine would be all
But an empty vaunt,
70 A thing wherein we feel there is some hidden want.

What objects are the fountains
Of thy happy strain?
What fields, or waves, or mountains?
What shapes of sky or plain?
75 What love of thine own kind? what ignorance of pain?

With thy clear keen joyance
Languor cannot be:
Shadow of annoyance
Never came near thee:
80 Thou lovest: but ne'er knew love's sad satiety.

Waking or asleep,
Thou of death must deem
Things more true and deep
Than we mortals dream,
85 Or how could thy notes flow in such a crystal stream?

We look before and after,
And pine for what is not:
Our sincerest laughter
With some pain is fraught;

90 Our sweetest songs are those that tell of saddest thought.

Yet if we could scorn
Hate, and pride, and fear;
If we were things born
Not to shed a tear,
95 I know not how thy joy we ever should come near.

Better than all measures
Of delightful sound,
Better than all treasures
That in books are found,
100 Thy skill to poet were, thou scorner of the ground!

Teach me half the gladness
That thy brain must know,
Such harmonious madness
From my lips would flow
105 The world should listen then, as I am listening now.

TO NIGHT

Percy Bysshe Shelley

1   Swiftly walk o'er the western wave,
        Spirit of Night!
Out of the misty eastern cave,
Where, all the long and lone daylight,
5   Thou wovest dreams of joy and fear,
Which make thee terrible and dear,—
        Swift be thy flight!

Wrap thy form in a mantle gray,
        Star-inwrought!
10   Blind with thine hair the eyes of Day;
Kiss her until she be wearied out,
Then wander o'er city, and sea, and land,
Touching all with thine opiate wand—
        Come, long-sought!

15   When I arose and saw the dawn,
        I sighed for thee;
When light rode high, and the dew was gone,
And noon lay heavy on flower and tree,
And the weary Day turned to his rest,
20   Lingering like an unloved guest.
        I sighed for thee.

Thy brother Death came, and cried,
        Wouldst thou me?
Thy sweet child Sleep, the filmy-eyed,
25   Murmured like a noontide bee,
Shall I nestle near thy side?
Wouldst thou me?—And I replied,
        No, not thee!

Death will come when thou art dead,
30   Soon, too soon—
Sleep will come when thou art fled;
Of neither would I ask the boon
I ask of thee, belovèd Night—
Swift be thine approaching flight,
35   Come soon, soon!

MUSIC WHEN SOFT VOICES DIE (TO —)

Percy Bysshe Shelley

1   Music, when soft voices die,
         Vibrates in the memory—
         Odours, when sweet violets sicken,
         Live within the sense they quicken.

5   Rose leaves, when the rose is dead,
         Are heaped for the belovèd's bed;
         And so thy thoughts, when thou art gone,
         Love itself shall slumber on.

TO THE MOON

Percy Bysshe Shelley

I

1   Art thou pale for weariness
Of climbing heaven and gazing on the earth,
Wandering companionless
Among the stars that have a different birth, —
5   And ever changing, like a joyless eye
That finds no object worth its constancy?

II

Thou chosen sister of the Spirit,
That gazes on thee till in thee it pities ...

THE WANING MOON

Percy Bysshe Shelley

1   And like a dying lady, lean and pale,
Who totters forth, wrapp'd in a gauzy veil,
Out of her chamber, led by the insane
And feeble wanderings of her fading brain,
5   The moon arose up in the murky East,
A white and shapeless mass.

STANZAS WRITTEN IN DEJECTION, NEAR NAPLES

Percy Bysshe Shelley

1 The sun is warm, the sky is clear,
  The waves are dancing fast and bright,
  Blue isles and snowy mountains wear
  The purple noon's transparent might,
5 The breath of the moist earth is light,
  Around its unexpanded buds;
  Like many a voice of one delight,
  The winds, the birds, the ocean floods,
The City's voice itself, is soft like Solitude's.

10 I see the Deep's untrampled floor
  With green and purple seaweeds strown;
  I see the waves upon the shore,
  Like light dissolved in star-showers, thrown:
  I sit upon the sands alone,—
15 The lightning of the noontide ocean
  Is flashing round me, and a tone
  Arises from its measured motion,
How sweet! did any heart now share in my emotion.

  Alas! I have nor hope nor health,
20 Nor peace within nor calm around,
  Nor that content surpassing wealth
  The sage in meditation found,
  And walked with inward glory crowned—
  Nor fame, nor power, nor love, nor leisure.
25 Others I see whom these surround—
  Smiling they live, and call life pleasure;
To me that cup has been dealt in another measure.

Yet now despair itself is mild,
Even as the winds and waters are;
30   I could lie down like a tired child,
And weep away the life of care
    Which I have borne and yet must bear,
Till death like sleep might steal on me,
    And I might feel in the warm air
35   My cheek grow cold, and hear the sea
Breathe o'er my dying brain its last monotony.

Some might lament that I were cold,
    As I, when this sweet day is gone,
Which my lost heart, too soon grown old,
40   Insults with this untimely moan;
    They might lament—for I am one
Whom men love not,—and yet regret,
    Unlike this day, which, when the sun
Shall on its stainless glory set,
45   Will linger, though enjoyed, like joy in memory yet.

LIFT NOT THE PAINTED VEIL

Percy Bysshe Shelley

1 Lift not the painted veil which those who live
 Call Life: though unreal shapes be pictured there,
 And it but mimic all we would believe
 With colours idly spread,—behind, lurk Fear
5 And Hope, twin Destinies; who ever weave
 Their shadows, o'er the chasm, sightless and drear.
 I knew one who had lifted it—he sought,
 For his lost heart was tender, things to love,
 But found them not, alas! nor was there aught
10 The world contains, the which he could approve.
 Through the unheeding many he did move,
 A splendour among shadows, a bright blot
 Upon this gloomy scene, a Spirit that strove
 For truth, and like the Preacher found it not.

JOHN KEATS (1795-1821)

John Keats was the oldest of four children born to working class parents, Thomas and Frances (Jennings) Keats. He was trained as a surgeon's apprentice, but his true vocation was poetry writing. He published his first volume of poems in 1817. Leigh Hunt, a well-respected poet in his own right and editor of the *Examiner*, introduced Keats to the literary circle that included Percy Bysshe Shelley and George Gordon Byron. In 1818, at the age of twenty-three, Keats fell in love with eighteen-year-old Fanny Brawne, and much of his best poetry was written to or about Fanny. Some of Keats's best known poems include "La Belle Dame Sans Merci," "Ode to a Nightingale," and "To Autumn." About a year later, he developed tuberculosis--the disease that had already killed his older brother and his mother. Though he was dying, Keats nevertheless continued to write poetry and letters to Fanny throughout his illness. He moved from England to Italy to try to save his health, but succumbed to tuberculosis in Rome at only twenty-five years old.

ODE TO A NIGHTINGALE

John Keats

1 My heart aches, and a drowsy numbness pains
  My sense, as though of hemlock I had drunk,
Or emptied some dull opiate to the drains
  One minute past, and Lethe-wards had sunk:
5 'Tis not through envy of thy happy lot,
  But being too happy in thine happiness,—
   That thou, light-winged Dryad of the trees
    In some melodious plot
  Of beechen green, and shadows numberless,
10   Singest of summer in full-throated ease.

O, for a draught of vintage! that hath been
  Cool'd a long age in the deep-delved earth,
Tasting of Flora and the country green,
  Dance, and Provençal song, and sunburnt mirth!
15 O for a beaker full of the warm South,
  Full of the true, the blushful Hippocrene,
   With beaded bubbles winking at the brim,
    And purple-stained mouth;
  That I might drink, and leave the world unseen,
20   And with thee fade away into the forest dim:

Fade far away, dissolve, and quite forget
  What thou among the leaves hast never known,
The weariness, the fever, and the fret
  Here, where men sit and hear each other groan;
25 Where palsy shakes a few, sad, last gray hairs,
  Where youth grows pale, and spectre-thin, and dies;
   Where but to think is to be full of sorrow
    And leaden-eyed despairs,
  Where Beauty cannot keep her lustrous eyes,
30   Or new Love pine at them beyond to-morrow.

Away! away! for I will fly to thee,
    Not charioted by Bacchus and his pards,
But on the viewless wings of Poesy,
    Though the dull brain perplexes and retards:
35 Already with thee! tender is the night,
      And haply the Queen-Moon is on her throne,
        Cluster'd around by all her starry Fays;
          But here there is no light,
    Save what from heaven is with the breezes blown
40   Through verdurous glooms and winding mossy ways.

I cannot see what flowers are at my feet,
    Nor what soft incense hangs upon the boughs,
But, in embalmed darkness, guess each sweet
    Wherewith the seasonable month endows
45 The grass, the thicket, and the fruit-tree wild;
      White hawthorn, and the pastoral eglantine;
        Fast fading violets cover'd up in leaves;
          And mid-May's eldest child,
    The coming musk-rose, full of dewy wine,
50   The murmurous haunt of flies on summer eves.

Darkling I listen; and, for many a time
    I have been half in love with easeful Death,
Call'd him soft names in many a mused rhyme,
    To take into the air my quiet breath;
55   Now more than ever seems it rich to die,
    To cease upon the midnight with no pain,
      While thou art pouring forth thy soul abroad
        In such an ecstasy!
    Still wouldst thou sing, and I have ears in vain—
60   To thy high requiem become a sod.

Thou wast not born for death, immortal Bird!
    No hungry generations tread thee down;
The voice I hear this passing night was heard

In ancient days by emperor and clown:
65 Perhaps the self-same song that found a path
Through the sad heart of Ruth, when, sick for home,
She stood in tears amid the alien corn;
The same that oft-times hath
Charm'd magic casements, opening on the foam
70 Of perilous seas, in faery lands forlorn.

Forlorn! the very word is like a bell
To toll me back from thee to my sole self!
Adieu! the fancy cannot cheat so well
As she is fam'd to do, deceiving elf.
75 Adieu! adieu! thy plaintive anthem fades
Past the near meadows, over the still stream,
Up the hill-side; and now 'tis buried deep
In the next valley-glades:
Was it a vision, or a waking dream?
80 Fled is that music:—Do I wake or sleep?

ODE TO PSYCHE

John Keats

1 O Goddess! hear these tuneless numbers, wrung
   By sweet enforcement and remembrance dear,
 And pardon that thy secrets should be sung
   Even into thine own soft-conched ear:
5 Surely I dreamt to-day, or did I see
   The winged Psyche with awaken'd eyes?
 I wander'd in a forest thoughtlessly,
   And, on the sudden, fainting with surprise,
 Saw two fair creatures, couched side by side
10   In deepest grass, beneath the whisp'ring roof
   Of leaves and trembled blossoms, where there ran
    A brooklet, scarce espied:

 'Mid hush'd, cool-rooted flowers, fragrant-eyed,
   Blue, silver-white, and budded Tyrian,
15 They lay calm-breathing, on the bedded grass;
   Their arms embraced, and their pinions too;
   Their lips touch'd not, but had not bade adieu,
 As if disjoined by soft-handed slumber,
 And ready still past kisses to outnumber
20   At tender eye-dawn of aurorean love:
   The winged boy I knew;
 But who wast thou, O happy, happy dove?
   His Psyche true!

 O latest born and loveliest vision far
25   Of all Olympus' faded hierarchy!
 Fairer than Phoebe's sapphire-region'd star,
   Or Vesper, amorous glow-worm of the sky;
 Fairer than these, though temple thou hast none,
   Nor altar heap'd with flowers;
30 Nor virgin-choir to make delicious moan
   Upon the midnight hours;
 No voice, no lute, no pipe, no incense sweet

From chain-swung censer teeming;
No shrine, no grove, no oracle, no heat
35 Of pale-mouth'd prophet dreaming.

O brightest! though too late for antique vows,
Too, too late for the fond believing lyre,
When holy were the haunted forest boughs,
Holy the air, the water, and the fire;
40 Yet even in these days so far retir'd
From happy pieties, thy lucent fans,
Fluttering among the faint Olympians,
I see, and sing, by my own eyes inspir'd.
So let me be thy choir, and make a moan
45 Upon the midnight hours;
Thy voice, thy lute, thy pipe, thy incense sweet
From swinged censer teeming;
Thy shrine, thy grove, thy oracle, thy heat
Of pale-mouth'd prophet dreaming.

50 Yes, I will be thy priest, and build a fane
In some untrodden region of my mind,
Where branched thoughts, new grown with pleasant pain,
Instead of pines shall murmur in the wind:
Far, far around shall those dark-cluster'd trees
55 Fledge the wild-ridged mountains steep by steep;
And there by zephyrs, streams, and birds, and bees,
The moss-lain Dryads shall be lull'd to sleep;
And in the midst of this wide quietness
A rosy sanctuary will I dress
60 With the wreath'd trellis of a working brain,
With buds, and bells, and stars without a name,
With all the gardener Fancy e'er could feign,
Who breeding flowers, will never breed the same:
And there shall be for thee all soft delight
65 That shadowy thought can win,
A bright torch, and a casement ope at night,
To let the warm Love in!

ODE TO A GRECIAN URN

John Keats

1   Thou still unravish'd bride of quietness,
          Thou foster-child of silence and slow time,
      Sylvan historian, who canst thus express
          A flowery tale more sweetly than our rhyme:
5   What leaf-fring'd legend haunts about thy shape
          Of deities or mortals, or of both,
                In Tempe or the dales of Arcady?
          What men or gods are these? What maidens loth?
      What mad pursuit? What struggle to escape?
10   What pipes and timbrels? What wild ecstasy?

      Heard melodies are sweet, but those unheard
          Are sweeter; therefore, ye soft pipes, play on;
      Not to the sensual ear, but, more endear'd,
          Pipe to the spirit ditties of no tone:
15   Fair youth, beneath the trees, thou canst not leave
          Thy song, nor ever can those trees be bare;
                Bold Lover, never, never canst thou kiss,
      Though winning near the goal yet, do not grieve;
          She cannot fade, though thou hast not thy bliss,
20   For ever wilt thou love, and she be fair!

      Ah, happy, happy boughs! that cannot shed
          Your leaves, nor ever bid the Spring adieu;
      And, happy melodist, unwearied,
          For ever piping songs for ever new;
25   More happy love! more happy, happy love!
          For ever warm and still to be enjoy'd,
                For ever panting, and for ever young;
      All breathing human passion far above,
          That leaves a heart high-sorrowful and cloy'd,
30   A burning forehead, and a parching tongue.

Who are these coming to the sacrifice?
    To what green altar, O mysterious priest,
Lead'st thou that heifer lowing at the skies,
    And all her silken flanks with garlands drest?
35   What little town by river or sea shore,
    Or mountain-built with peaceful citadel,
        Is emptied of this folk, this pious morn?
And, little town, thy streets for evermore
    Will silent be; and not a soul to tell
40   Why thou art desolate, can e'er return.

O Attic shape! Fair attitude! with brede
    Of marble men and maidens overwrought,
With forest branches and the trodden weed;
    Thou, silent form, dost tease us out of thought
45   As doth eternity: Cold Pastoral!
    When old age shall this generation waste,
        Thou shalt remain, in midst of other woe
Than ours, a friend to man, to whom thou say'st,
    "Beauty is truth, truth beauty,—that is all
50   Ye know on earth, and all ye need to know."

ODE TO INDOLENCE

John Keats

'They toil not, neither do they spin.'

1   One morn before me were three figures seen,
      With bowèd necks, and joinèd hands, side-faced;
And one behind the other stepp'd serene,
      In placid sandals, and in white robes graced;
5   They pass'd, like figures on a marble urn,
      When shifted round to see the other side;
They came again; as when the urn once more
      Is shifted round, the first seen shades return;
      And they were strange to me, as may betide
10   With vases, to one deep in Phidian lore.

How is it, Shadows! that I knew ye not?
      How came ye muffled in so hush a mask?
Was it a silent deep-disguisèd plot
      To steal away, and leave without a task
15   My idle days? Ripe was the drowsy hour;
      The blissful cloud of summer-indolence
Benumb'd my eyes; my pulse grew less and less;
      Pain had no sting, and pleasure's wreath no flower:
      O, why did ye not melt, and leave my sense
20   Unhaunted quite of all but—nothingness?
A third time pass'd they by, and, passing, turn'd

So, ye three Ghosts, adieu! Ye cannot raise
      My head cool-bedded in the flowery grass;
25   For I would not be dieted with praise,
      A pet-lamb in a sentimental farce!
      Fade softly from my eyes, and be once more
      In masque-like figures on the dreamy urn;
Farewell! I yet have visions for the night,

30   And for the day faint visions there is store;
        Vanish, ye Phantoms! from my idle spright,
            Into the clouds, and never more return!

        Each one the face a moment whiles to me;
        Then faded, and to follow them I burn'd
35   And ached for wings, because I knew the three;
            The first was a fair Maid, and Love her name;
            The second was Ambition, pale of cheek,
        And ever watchful with fatiguèd eye;
            The last, whom I love more, the more of blame
40   Is heap'd upon her, maiden most unmeek,—
        I knew to be my demon Poesy.

        They faded, and, forsooth! I wanted wings:
            O folly! What is Love? and where is it?
        And for that poor Ambition! it springs
45   From a man's little heart's short fever-fit;
            For Poesy!—no,—she has not a joy,—
            At least for me,—so sweet as drowsy noons,
        And evenings steep'd in honey'd indolence;
            O, for an age so shelter'd from annoy,
50   That I may never know how change the moons,
        Or hear the voice of busy common-sense!

        And once more came they by:—alas! wherefore?
            My sleep had been embroider'd with dim dreams;
        My soul had been a lawn besprinkled o'er
55   With flowers, and stirring shades, and baffled beams:
            The morn was clouded, but no shower fell,
            Tho' in her lids hung the sweet tears of May;
        The open casement press'd a new-leaved vine,
            Let in the budding warmth and throstle's lay;
60   O Shadows! 'twas a time to bid farewell!
        Upon your skirts had fallen no tears of mine.

LA BELLE DAME SANS MERCI: A BALLAD

John Keats

1   O what can ail thee, knight-at-arms,
       Alone and palely loitering?
The sedge has withered from the lake,
       And no birds sing.

5   O what can ail thee, knight-at-arms,
       So haggard and so woe-begone?
The squirrel's granary is full,
       And the harvest's done.

I see a lily on thy brow,
10   With anguish moist and fever-dew,
And on thy cheeks a fading rose
       Fast withereth too.

I met a lady in the meads,
       Full beautiful—a faery's child,
15   Her hair was long, her foot was light,
       And her eyes were wild.

I made a garland for her head,
       And bracelets too, and fragrant zone;
She looked at me as she did love,
20   And made sweet moan

I set her on my pacing steed,
       And nothing else saw all day long,
For sidelong would she bend, and sing
       A faery's song.

25   She found me roots of relish sweet,
       And honey wild, and manna-dew,

And sure in language strange she said—
    'I love thee true'.

She took me to her Elfin grot,
30   And there she wept and sighed full sore,
And there I shut her wild wild eyes
    With kisses four.

And there she lullèd me asleep,
    And there I dreamed—Ah! woe betide!—
35 The latest dream I ever dreamt
    On the cold hill side.

I saw pale kings and princes too,
    Pale warriors, death-pale were they all;
They cried—'La Belle Dame sans Merci
40   Hath thee in thrall!'

I saw their starved lips in the gloam,
    With horrid warning gapèd wide,
And I awoke and found me here,
    On the cold hill's side.

45 And this is why I sojourn here,
    Alone and palely loitering,
Though the sedge is withered from the lake,
    And no birds sing.

TO AUTUMN

John Keats

1   Season of mists and mellow fruitfulness,
        Close bosom-friend of the maturing sun;
     Conspiring with him how to load and bless
        With fruit the vines that round the thatch-eves run;
5   To bend with apples the moss'd cottage-trees,
        And fill all fruit with ripeness to the core;
            To swell the gourd, and plump the hazel shells
        With a sweet kernel; to set budding more,
     And still more, later flowers for the bees,
10   Until they think warm days will never cease,
        For summer has o'er-brimm'd their clammy cells.

     Who hath not seen thee oft amid thy store?
        Sometimes whoever seeks abroad may find
     Thee sitting careless on a granary floor,
15   Thy hair soft-lifted by the winnowing wind;
     Or on a half-reap'd furrow sounad asleep,
        Drows'd with the fume of poppies, while thy hook
            Spares the next swath and all its twined flowers:
     And sometimes like a gleaner thou dost keep
20   Steady thy laden head across a brook;
        Or by a cyder-press, with patient look,
            Thou watchest the last oozings hours by hours.

     Where are the songs of spring? Ay, Where are they?
        Think not of them, thou hast thy music too,—
25   While barred clouds bloom the soft-dying day,
        And touch the stubble-plains with rosy hue;
     Then in a wailful choir the small gnats mourn
        Among the river sallows, borne aloft
            Or sinking as the light wind lives or dies;
30   And full-grown lambs loud bleat from hilly bourn;
        Hedge-crickets sing; and now with treble soft
        The red-breast whistles from a garden-croft;
            And gathering swallows twitter in the skies.

TO HOMER

John Keats

1   Standing aloof in giant ignorance,
    Of thee I hear and of the Cyclades,
As one who sits ashore and longs perchance
    To visit dolphin-coral in deep seas.
5   So thou wast blind;—but then the veil was rent,
    For Jove uncurtain'd Heaven to let thee live,
And Neptune made for thee a spumy tent,
    And Pan made sing for thee his forest-hive;
Aye on the shores of darkness there is light,
10   And precipices show untrodden green,
There is a budding morrow in midnight,
    There is a triple sight in blindness keen;
Such seeing hadst thou, as it once befel
To Dian, Queen of Earth, and Heaven, and Hell.

TO SLEEP

John Keats

1   O soft embalmer of the still midnight,
       Shutting, with careful fingers and benign,
Our gloom-pleas'd eyes, embower'd from the light,
       Enshaded in forgetfulness divine:
5   O soothest Sleep! if so it please thee, close
       In midst of this thine hymn my willing eyes,
Or wait the "Amen," ere thy poppy throws
       Around my bed its lulling charities.
Then save me, or the passed day will shine
10   Upon my pillow, breeding many woes,—
       Save me from curious Conscience, that still lords
Its strength for darkness, burrowing like a mole;
       Turn the key deftly in the oiled wards,
And seal the hushed Casket of my Soul.

WHEN I HAVE FEARS THAT I MAY CEASE TO BE

John Keats

1   When I have fears that I may cease to be
   Before my pen has gleaned my teeming brain,
Before high-pilèd books, in charactery,
   Hold like rich garners the full ripened grain;
5   When I behold, upon the night's starred face,
   Huge cloudy symbols of a high romance,
And think that I may never live to trace
   Their shadows with the magic hand of chance;
And when I feel, fair creature of an hour,
10   That I shall never look upon thee more,
Never have relish in the faery power
   Of unreflecting love—then on the shore
Of the wide world I stand alone, and think
Till love and fame to nothingness do sink.

BRIGHT STAR

John Keats

1   Bright star, would I were stedfast as thou art—
          Not in lone splendour hung aloft the night
      And watching, with eternal lids apart,
          Like nature's patient, sleepless Eremite,
5   The moving waters at their priestlike task
          Of pure ablution round earth's human shores,
      Or gazing on the new soft-fallen mask
          Of snow upon the mountains and the moors—
      No—yet still stedfast, still unchangeable,
10   Pillow'd upon my fair love's ripening breast,
      To feel for ever its soft fall and swell,
          Awake for ever in a sweet unrest,
      Still, still to hear her tender-taken breath,
      And so live ever—or else swoon to death.

ON SEEING THE ELGIN MARBLES

John Keats

1   My spirit is too weak—mortality
    Weighs heavily on me like unwilling sleep,
    And each imagined pinnacle and steep
Of godlike hardship tells me I must die
5   Like a sick eagle looking at the sky.
    Yet 'tis a gentle luxury to weep
    That I have not the cloudy winds to keep
Fresh for the opening of the morning's eye.
Such dim-conceived glories of the brain
10   Bring round the heart an undescribable feud;
So do these wonders a most dizzy pain,
    That mingles Grecian grandeur with the rude
Wasting of old time—with a billowy main—
    A sun—a shadow of a magnitude.

ELIZABETH BARRETT BROWNING (1806-1861)

Elizabeth Barrett Browning was the oldest of twelve children, born to parents who had immigrated to England from Jamaica. Barrett Browning experienced frail health for most of her life; she developed a lung ailment at the age of fourteen that never went away and suffered a spinal injury, the result of a horseback riding accident. A smart and deeply religious young woman, Barrett Browning taught herself Hebrew so that she could study the Old Testament in its original language. She also learned Greek and translated Aeschylus's *Prometheus Bound* into English. Barrett Browning wrote her first book of poetry at the age of twelve; two years later, in 1820, her father was able to sell the rights to a book of her poems. By the time her collection *Poems* was published in 1844, she was famous. Her success led to a relationship with her future husband and fellow poet, Robert Browning, who wrote to her as an admirer of her work. Her father bitterly disapproved of the match, but the couple continued to exchange hundreds of love poems and letters; twenty months later, they eloped and moved to Florence, Italy. *Sonnets from the Portuguese* (1850), widely considered her best work, was written during the period leading up to her marriage. The couple produced a son, Robert Barrett Browning, in 1849.

GRIEF

Elizabeth Barrett Browning

1   I tell you, hopeless grief is passionless;
    That only men incredulous of despair,
    Half-taught in anguish, through the midnight air
    Beat upward to God's throne in loud access
5   Of shrieking and reproach. Full desertness,
    In souls as countries, lieth silent-bare
    Under the blanching, vertical eye-glare
    Of the absolute heavens. Deep-hearted man, express
    Grief for thy dead in silence like to death—
10   Most like a monumental statue set
    In everlasting watch and moveless woe
    Till itself crumble to the dust beneath.
    Touch it; the marble eyelids are not wet:
    If it could weep, it could arise and go.

TO GEORGE SAND: A DESIRE

Elizabeth Barrett Browning

1   Thou large-brained woman and large-hearted man,
Self-called George Sand ! whose soul, amid the lions
Of thy tumultuous senses, moans defiance
And answers roar for roar, as spirits can:
5   I would some mild miraculous thunder ran
Above the applauded circus, in appliance
Of thine own nobler nature's strength and science,
Drawing two pinions, white as wings of swan,
From thy strong shoulders, to amaze the place
10   With holier light ! that thou to woman's claim
And man's, mightst join beside the angel's grace
Of a pure genius sanctified from blame
Till child and maiden pressed to thine embrace
To kiss upon thy lips a stainless fame.

TO GEORGE SAND: A RECOGNITION

Elizabeth Barrett Browning

1   True genius, but true woman! dost deny
    Thy woman's nature with a manly scorn
    And break away the gauds and armlets worn
    By weaker women in captivity?
5   Ah, vain denial! that revolted cry
    Is sobbed in by a woman's voice forlorn—
    Thy woman's hair, my sister, all unshorn
    Floats back dishevelled strength in agony
    Disproving thy man's name: and while before
10   The world thou burnest in a poet-fire,
    We see thy woman-heart beat evermore
    Through the large flame. Beat purer, heart, and higher,
    Till God unsex thee on the heavenly shore,
    Where unincarnate spirits purely aspire!

1: I THOUGHT ONCE HOW THEOCRITUS HAD SUNG

from Sonnets from the Portuguese
Elizabeth Barrett Browning

1   I thought once how Theocritus had sung
     Of the sweet years, the dear and wished for years,
     Who each one in a gracious hand appears
     To bear a gift for mortals, old or young:
5   And, as I mused it in his antique tongue,
     I saw, in gradual vision through my tears,
     The sweet, sad years, the melancholy years,
     Those of my own life, who by turns had flung
     A shadow across me. Straightway I was 'ware,
10   So weeping, how a mystic Shape did move
     Behind me, and drew me backward by the hair,
     And a voice said in mastery, while I strove, ...
     "Guess now who holds thee?"—"Death," I said. But there,
     The silver answer rang—"Not Death, but Love."

5: I LIFT MY HEAVY HEART UP SOLEMNLY

from Sonnets from the Portuguese
Elizabeth Barrett Browning

1   I lift my heavy heart up solemnly,
As once Electra her sepulchral urn,
And, looking in thine eyes, I overturn
The ashes at thy feet. Behold and see
5   What a great heap of grief lay hid in me,
And how the red wild sparkles dimly burn
Through the ashen greyness. If thy foot in scorn
Could tread them out to darkness utterly,
It might be well perhaps. But if instead
10   Thou wait beside me for the wind to blow
The grey dust up,... those laurels on thine head,
O My beloved, will not shield thee so,
That none of all the fires shall scorch and shred
The hair beneath. Stand further off then! Go.

14: IF THOU MUST LOVE ME, LET IT BE FOR NOUGHT

from Sonnets from the Portuguese
Elizabeth Barrett Browning

1   If thou must love me, let it be for nought
    Except for love's sake only. Do not say
    "I love her for her smile—her look—her way
    Of speaking gently,—for a trick of thought
5   That falls in well with mine, and certes brought
    A sense of pleasant ease on such a day"—
    For these things in themselves, Belovèd, may
    Be changed, or change for thee,—and love, so wrought,
    May be unwrought so. Neither love me for
10   Thine own dear pity's wiping my cheeks dry,—
    A creature might forget to weep, who bore
    Thy comfort long, and lose thy love thereby!
    But love me for love's sake, that evermore
    Thou may'st love on, through love's eternity.

20: BELOVED, MY BELOVED, WHEN I THINK

from Sonnets from the Portuguese
Elizabeth Barrett Browning

1   Beloved, my Beloved, when I think
    That thou wast in the world a year ago,
    What time I sate alone here in the snow
    And saw no footprint, heard the silence sink
5   No moment at thy voice ... but, link by link,
    Went counting all my chains, as if that so
    They never could fall off at any blow
    Struck by thy possible hand ... why, thus I drink
    Of life's great cup of wonder! Wonderful,
10   Never to feel thee thrill the day or night
    With personal act or speech,—nor ever cull
    Some prescience of thee with the blossoms white
    Thou sawest growing! Atheists are as dull,
    Who cannot guess God's presence out of sight.

22: WHEN OUR TWO SOULS STAND UP ERECT AND STRONG

from Sonnets from the Portuguese
Elizabeth Barrett Browning

1   When our two souls stand up erect and strong,
    Face to face, silent, drawing nigh and nigher,
    Until the lengthening wings break into fire
    At either curvéd point, — what bitter wrong
5   Can the earth do to us, that we should not long
    Be here contented ? Think. In mounting higher,
    The angels would press on us, and aspire
    To drop some golden orb of perfect song
    Into our deep, dear silence. Let us stay
10   Rather on earth, Belovèd, — where the unfit
    Contrarious moods of men recoil away
    And isolate pure spirits, and permit
    A place to stand and love in for a day,
    With darkness and the death-hour rounding it.

35: IF I LEAVE ALL FOR THEE, WILT THOU EXCHANGE

from Sonnets from the Portuguese
Elizabeth Barrett Browning

1   If I leave all for thee, wilt thou exchange
And be all to me? Shall I never miss
Home-talk and blessing and the common kiss
That comes to each in turn, nor count it strange,
5   When I look up, to drop on a new range
Of walls and floors ... another home than this?
Nay, wilt thou fill that place by me which is
Filled by dead eyes too tender to know change?
That's hardest. If to conquer love, has tried,
10   To conquer grief, tries more ... as all things prove;
For grief indeed is love and grief beside.
Alas, I have grieved so I am hard to love.
Yet love me—wilt thou? Open thine heart wide,
And fold within, the wet wings of thy dove.

43: HOW DO I LOVE THEE? LET ME COUNT THE WAYS

from Sonnets from the Portuguese
Elizabeth Barrett Browning

1   How do I love thee? Let me count the ways.
I love thee to the depth and breadth and height
My soul can reach, when feeling out of sight
For the ends of being and ideal grace.
5   I love thee to the level of every day's
Most quiet need, by sun and candle-light.
I love thee freely, as men strive for right;
I love thee purely, as they turn from praise.
I love thee with the passion put to use
10   In my old griefs, and with my childhood's faith.
I love thee with a love I seemed to lose
With my lost saints. I love thee with the breath,
Smiles, tears, of all my life; and, if God choose,
I shall but love thee better after death.

44: BELOVED, THOU HAST BROUGHT ME MANY FLOWERS

from Sonnets from the Portuguese
Elizabeth Barrett Browning

1   Beloved, thou hast brought me many flowers
Plucked in the garden, all the summer through
And winter, and it seemed as if they grew
In this close room, nor missed the sun and showers,
5   So, in the like name of that love of ours,
Take back these thoughts which here unfolded too,
And which on warm and cold days I withdrew
From my heart's ground. Indeed, those beds and bowers
Be overgrown with bitter weeds and rue,
10 And wait thy weeding; yet here's eglantine,
Here's ivy!— take them, as I used to do
Thy flowers, and keep them where they shall not pine.
Instruct thine eyes to keep their colours true,
And tell thy soul, their roots are left in mine.

from *AURORA LEIGH: BOOK ONE*

Elizabeth Barrett Browning

1   I am like,
They tell me, my dear father. Broader brows
Howbeit, upon a slenderer undergrowth
Of delicate features,–paler, near as grave;
5   But then my mother's smile breaks up the whole,
And makes it better sometaimes than itself.

So, nine full years, our days were hid with God
Among his mountains. I was just thirteen,
Still growing like the plants from unseen roots
10   In tongue-tied Springs,–and suddenly awoke
To full life and its needs and agonies,
With an intense, strong, struggling heart beside
A stone-dead father. Life, struck sharp on death,
Makes awful lightning. His last word was, 'Love–'
15   'Love, my child, love, love!'–(then he had done with grief)
'Love, my child.' Ere I answered he was gone,
And none was left to love in all the world.

There, ended childhood: what succeeded next
I recollect as, after fevers, men
20   Thread back the passage of delirium,
Missing the turn still, baffled by the door;
Smooth endless days, notched here and there with knives;
A weary, wormy darkness, spurred i' the flank
With flame, that it should eat and end itself
25   Like some tormented scorpion. Then, at last,
I do remember clearly, how there came
A stranger with authority, not right,
(I thought not) who commanded, caught me up
From old Assunta's neck; how, with a shriek,
30   She let me go,–while I, with ears too full
Of my father's silence, to shriek back a word,

In all a child's astonishment at grief
Stared at the wharfage where she stood and moaned,
My poor Assunta, where she stood and moaned!
35   The white walls, the blue hills, my Italy,
Drawn backward from the shuddering steamer-deck,
Like one in anger drawing back her skirts
Which suppliants catch at. Then the bitter sea
Inexorably pushed between us both,
40   And sweeping up the ship with my despair
Threw us out as a pasture to the stars.
Ten nights and days we voyaged on the deep;
Ten nights and days, without the common face
Of any day or night; the moon and sun
45   Cut off from the green reconciling earth,
To starve into a blind ferocity
And glare unnatural; the very sky
(Dropping its bell-net down upon the sea
As if no human heart should 'scape alive,)
50   Bedraggled with the desolating salt,
Until it seemed no more than holy heaven
To which my father went. All new, and strange—
The universe turned stranger, for a child.

Then, land!—then, England! oh, the frosty cliffs
55   Looked cold upon me. Could I find a home
Among those mean red houses through the fog?
And when I heard my father's language first
From alien lips which had no kiss for mine,
I wept aloud, then laughed, then wept, then wept,—
60   And some one near me said the child was mad
Through much sea-sickness. The train swept us on.
Was this my father's England? the great isle?
The ground seemed cut up from the fellowship
Or verdure, field from field, as man from man;
65   The skies themselves looked low and positive,
As almost you could touch them with a hand,
And dared to do it, they were so far off
From God's celestial crystals; all things, blurred
And dull and vague. Did Shakspeare and his mates

70   Absorb the light here?–not a hill or stone
      With heart to strike a radiant colour up
      Or active outline on the indifferent air!

      I think I see my father's sister stand
      Upon the hall-step of her country-house
75   To give me welcome. She stood straight and calm,
      Her somewhat narrow forehead braided tight
      As if for taming accidental thoughts
      From possible pulses; brown hair pricked with grey
      By frigid use of life, (she was not old,
80   Although my father's elder by a year)
      A nose drawn sharply, yet in delicate lines;
      A close mild mouth, a little soured about
      The ends, through speaking unrequited loves,
      Or peradventure niggardly half-truths;
85   Eyes of no colour,–once they might have smiled,
      But never, never have forgot themselves
      In smiling; cheeks in which was yet a rose
      Of perished summers, like a rose in a book,
      Kept more for ruth than pleasure,–if past bloom,
90   Past fading also.
                  She had lived we'll say,
      A harmless life, she called a virtuous life,
      A quiet life, which was not life at all,
      (But that, she had not lived enough to know)
      Between the vicar and the county squires,
95   The lord-lieutenant looking down sometimes
      From the empyreal, to assure their souls
      Against chance vulgarisms, and, in the abyss,
      The apothecary looked on once a year,
      To prove their soundness of humility.
100   The poor-club exercised her Christian gifts
      Of knitting stockings, stitching petticoats,
      Because we are of one flesh after all
      And need one flannel, (with a proper sense
      Of difference in the quality)–and still
105   The book-club guarded from your modern trick
      Of shaking dangerous questions from the crease,

Preserved her intellectual. She had lived
A sort of cage-bird life, born in a cage,
Accounting that to leap from perch to perch
110   Was act and joy enough for any bird.
Dear heaven, how silly are the things that live
In thickets and eat berries!
                    I, alas,
A wild bird scarcely fledged, was brought to her cage,
And she was there to meet me. Very kind.
115   Bring the clean water; give out the fresh seed.
She stood upon the steps to welcome me,
Calm, in black garb. I clung about her neck,–
Young babes, who catch at every shred of wool
To draw the new light closer, catch and cling
120   Less blindly. In my ears, my father's word
Hummed ignorantly, as the sea in shells,
'Love, love, my child,' She, black there with my grief,
Might feel my love–she was his sister once–
I clung to her. A moment, she seemed moved.
125   Kissed me with cold lips, suffered me to cling,
And drew me feebly through the hall, into
The room she sate in.
                    There, with some strange spasm
Of pain and passion, she wrung loose my hands
Imperiously, and held me at arm's length,
130   And with two grey-steel naked-bladed eyes
Searched through my face,–ay, stabbed it through and through,
Through brows and cheeks and chin, as if to find
A wicked murderer in my innocent face,
If not here, there perhaps. Then, drawing breath,
135   She struggled for her ordinary calm,
And missed it rather,–told me not to shrink,
As if she had told me not to lie or swear,–
'She loved my father, and would love me too
As long as I deserved it.' Very kind.

from *AURORA LEIGH: BOOK FIVE*

Elizabeth Barrett Browning

1   Aurora Leigh, be humble. Shall I hope
    To speak my poems in mysterious tune
    With man and nature,–with the lava-lymph
    That trickles from successive galaxies
5   Still drop by drop adown the finger of God,
    In still new worlds?–with summer-days in this,
    That scarce dare breathe, they are so beautiful?–
    With spring's delicious trouble in the ground
    Tormented by the quickened blood of roots.
10   And softly pricked by golden crocus-sheaves
    In token of the harvest-time of flowers?–
    With winters and with autumns,–and beyond,
    With the human heart's large seasons,–when it hopes
    And fears, joys, grieves, and loves?–with all that strain
15   Of sexual passion, which devours the flesh
    In a sacrament of souls? with mother's breasts,
    Which, round the new made creatures hanging there,
    Throb luminous and harmonious like pure spheres?–
    With multitudinous life, and finally
20   With the great out-goings of ecstatic souls,
    Who, in a rush of too long prisoned flame,
    Their radiant faces upward, burn away
    This dark of the body, issuing on a world
    Beyond our mortal?–can I speak my verse
25   So plainly in tune to these things and the rest,
    That men shall feel it catch them on the quick,
    As having the same warrant over them
    To hold and move them, if they will or no,
    Alike imperious as the primal rhythm
30   Of that theurgic nature? I must fail,
    Who fail at the beginning to hold and move
    One man,–and he my cousin, and he my friend,

And he born tender, made intelligent,
Inclined to ponder the precipitous sides
35   Of difficult questions; yet, obtuse to me,–
Of me, incurious! likes me very well,
And wishes me a paradise of good,
Good looks, good means, and good digestion!–ay,
But otherwise evades me, puts me off
40   With kindness, with a tolerant gentleness,–
Too light a book for a grave man's reading! Go,
Aurora Leigh: be humble.
                There it is;
We women are too apt to look to one,
Which proves a certain impotence in art.
45   We strain our natures at doing something great,
Far less because it's something great to do,
Than, haply, that we, so, commend ourselves
As being not small, and more appreciable
To some one friend. We must have mediators
50   Betwixt our highest conscience and the judge;
Some sweet saint's blood must quicken in our palms.
Or all the life in heaven seems slow and cold:
Good only, being perceived as the end of good,
And God alone pleased,–that's too poor, we think,
55   And not enough for us, by any means.
Ay–Romney, I remember, told me once
We miss the abstract, when we comprehend!
We miss it most when we aspire, . . and fail.

Yet, so, I will not.–This vile woman's way
60   Of trailing garments, shall not trip me up.
I'll have no traffic with the personal thought
In art's pure temple. Must I work in vain,
Without the approbation of a man?
It cannot be; it shall not. Fame itself,
65   That approbation of the general race,
Presents a poor end, (though the arrow speed,
Shot straight with vigorous finger to the white,)

And the highest fame was never reached except
By what was aimed above it. Art for art,
70   And good for God Himself, the essential Good!
We'll keep our aims sublime, our eyes erect,
Although our woman-hands should shake and fail;
And if we fail . . But must we?–
                    Shall I fail?
The Greeks said grandly in their tragic phrase,
75   'Let no one be called happy till his death.'
To which I add,–Let no one till his death
Be called unhappy. Measure not the work
Until the day's out and the labour done;
Then bring your gauges. If the day's work's scant,
80   Why, call it scant; affect no compromise;
And, in that we have nobly striven at least,
Deal with us nobly, women though we be,
And honour us with truth, if not with praise.

A MUSICAL INSTRUMENT

Elizabeth Barrett Browning

1   What was he doing, the great god Pan,
        Down in the reeds by the river ?
    Spreading ruin and scattering ban,
    Splashing and paddling with hoofs of a goat,
5   And breaking the golden lilies afloat
        With the dragon-fly on the river.

    He tore out a reed, the great god Pan,
        From the deep cool bed of the river :
    The limpid water turbidly ran,
10 And the broken lilies a-dying lay,
    And the dragon-fly had fled away,
        Ere he brought it out of the river.

    High on the shore sate the great god Pan,
        While turbidly flowed the river ;
15 And hacked and hewed as a great god can,
    With his hard bleak steel at the patient reed,
    Till there was not a sign of a leaf indeed
        To prove it fresh from the river.

    He cut it short, did the great god Pan,
20   (How tall it stood in the river !)
    Then drew the pith, like the heart of a man,
    Steadily from the outside ring,
    And notched the poor dry empty thing
        In holes, as he sate by the river.

25 This is the way,' laughed the great god Pan,
        Laughed while he sate by the river,)
    The only way, since gods began
    To make sweet music, they could succeed.'

Then, dropping his mouth to a hole in the reed,
30   He blew in power by the river.

Sweet, sweet, sweet, O Pan !
    Piercing sweet by the river !
Blinding sweet, O great god Pan !
The sun on the hill forgot to die,
35   And the lilies revived, and the dragon-fly
        Came back to dream on the river.

Yet half a beast is the great god Pan,
    To laugh as he sits by the river,
Making a poet out of a man :
40   The true gods sigh for the cost and pain, —
For the reed which grows nevermore again
        As a reed with the reeds in the river.

ALFRED TENNYSON (1809-1892)

Alfred Tennyson, also known as Alfred, Lord Tennyson, after being awarded the title of Baron in 1884, was the most famous Victorian poet. In 1850, Tennyson was appointed Poet Laureate of Great Britain and Ireland, a position he held throughout most of Victoria's reign, up to his death in 1892. No other Poet Laureate before or since has served as long a tenure. Tennyson had a difficult childhood. His brilliant father, who tutored his son in classical and modern languages, was prone to drunkenness, mental breakdowns, and financial disasters. Tennyson also had a brother who became an opium addict and another who was committed to an insane asylum. Tennyson began writing poetry very young; by the age of twelve he had completed a 6,000-line epic poem. He attended Trinity College, Cambridge, and became a member of a student literary group known as "the Apostles." By 1831, however, his family's financial problems forced him to leave Cambridge. Tennyson experienced grave financial insecurity throughout the next decade. After he became engaged to Emily Sellwood, he lost his inheritance to a bad investment which resulted in her parents calling off the engagement. Fortunately, Tennyson's *Poems*, published in 1842, became instantly popular and propelled him to wealth and fame, enabling him to marry Sellwood. The couple had two sons. Tennyson also developed a significant relationship with a younger student and poet, Arthur Hallam. Hallam died unexpectedly of a stroke at the age of twenty-two, prompting Tennyson's most famous poem, "In Memoriam, A.H.H."

THE KRAKEN

Lord Alfred Tennyson

1   Below the thunders of the upper deep,
     Far, far beneath in the abysmal sea,
     His ancient, dreamless, uninvaded sleep
     The Kraken sleepeth: faintest sunlights flee
5   About his shadowy sides; above him swell
     Huge sponges of millennial growth and height;
     And far away into the sickly light,
     From many a wondrous grot and secret cell
     Unnumbered and enormous polypi
10   Winnow with giant arms the slumbering green.
     There hath he lain for ages, and will lie
     Battening upon huge sea worms in his sleep,
     Until the latter fire shall heat the deep;
     Then once by man and angels to be seen,
15   In roaring he shall rise and on the surface die.

MARIANA

Lord Alfred Tennyson

"Mariana in the moated grange"
(Shakespeare, *Measure for Measure*)

1 With blackest moss the flower-plots
 Were thickly crusted, one and all:
 The rusted nails fell from the knots
 That held the pear to the gable-wall.
5 The broken sheds look'd sad and strange:
 Unlifted was the clinking latch;
 Weeded and worn the ancient thatch
 Upon the lonely moated grange.
 She only said, "My life is dreary,
10 He cometh not," she said;
 She said, "I am aweary, aweary,
 I would that I were dead!"

 Her tears fell with the dews at even;
 Her tears fell ere the dews were dried;
15 She could not look on the sweet heaven,
 Either at morn or eventide.
 After the flitting of the bats,
 When thickest dark did trance the sky,
 She drew her casement-curtain by,
20 And glanced athwart the glooming flats.
 She only said, "The night is dreary,
 He cometh not," she said;
 She said, "I am aweary, aweary,
 I would that I were dead!"

25 Upon the middle of the night,
 Waking she heard the night-fowl crow:
 The cock sung out an hour ere light:

From the dark fen the oxen's low
Came to her: without hope of change,
30   In sleep she seem'd to walk forlorn,
Till cold winds woke the gray-eyed morn
About the lonely moated grange.
She only said, "The day is dreary,
He cometh not," she said;
35   She said, "I am aweary, aweary,
I would that I were dead!"

About a stone-cast from the wall
A sluice with blacken'd waters slept,
And o'er it many, round and small,
40   The cluster'd marish-mosses crept.
Hard by a poplar shook alway,
All silver-green with gnarled bark:
For leagues no other tree did mark
The level waste, the rounding gray.
45   She only said, "My life is dreary,
He cometh not," she said;
She said "I am aweary, aweary
I would that I were dead!"

And ever when the moon was low,
50   And the shrill winds were up and away,
In the white curtain, to and fro,
She saw the gusty shadow sway.
But when the moon was very low
And wild winds bound within their cell,
55   The shadow of the poplar fell
Upon her bed, across her brow.
She only said, "The night is dreary,
He cometh not," she said;
She said "I am aweary, aweary,
60   I would that I were dead!"

All day within the dreamy house,
The doors upon their hinges creak'd;
The blue fly sung in the pane; the mouse
Behind the mouldering wainscot shriek'd,
65 Or from the crevice peer'd about.
Old faces glimmer'd thro' the doors
Old footsteps trod the upper floors,
Old voices called her from without.
She only said, "My life is dreary,
70 He cometh not," she said;
She said, "I am aweary, aweary,
I would that I were dead!"

The sparrow's chirrup on the roof,
The slow clock ticking, and the sound
75 Which to the wooing wind aloof
The poplar made, did all confound
Her sense; but most she loathed the hour
When the thick-moted sunbeam lay
Athwart the chambers, and the day
80 Was sloping toward his western bower.
Then said she, "I am very dreary,
He will not come," she said;
She wept, "I am aweary, aweary,
Oh God, that I were dead!"

THE LADY OF SHALOTT (1832)

Lord Alfred Tennyson

Part I

1 On either side the river lie
Long fields of barley and of rye,
That clothe the wold and meet the sky;
And thro' the field the road runs by
5   To many-tower'd Camelot;
The yellow-leaved waterlily
The green-sheathed daffodilly
Tremble in the water chilly
   Round about Shalott.

10 Willows whiten, aspens shiver.
The sunbeam showers break and quiver
In the stream that runneth ever
By the island in the river
   Flowing down to Camelot.
15 Four gray walls, and four gray towers
Overlook a space of flowers,
And the silent isle imbowers
   The Lady of Shalott.

Underneath the bearded barley,
20 The reaper, reaping late and early,
Hears her ever chanting cheerly,
Like an angel, singing clearly,
   O'er the stream of Camelot.
Piling the sheaves in furrows airy,
25 Beneath the moon, the reaper weary
Listening whispers, ' 'Tis the fairy,
   Lady of Shalott.'

The little isle is all inrail'd

With a rose-fence, and overtrail'd
30 With roses: by the marge unhail'd
The shallop flitteth silken sail'd,
    Skimming down to Camelot.
A pearl garland winds her head:
She leaneth on a velvet bed,
35 Full royally apparelled,
    The Lady of Shalott.

Part II
No time hath she to sport and play:
A charmed web she weaves alway.
A curse is on her, if she stay
40 Her weaving, either night or day,
    To look down to Camelot.
She knows not what the curse may be;
Therefore she weaveth steadily,
Therefore no other care hath she,
45   The Lady of Shalott.

She lives with little joy or fear.
Over the water, running near,
The sheepbell tinkles in her ear.
Before her hangs a mirror clear,
50   Reflecting tower'd Camelot.
And as the mazy web she whirls,
She sees the surly village churls,
And the red cloaks of market girls
    Pass onward from Shalott.

55 Sometimes a troop of damsels glad,
An abbot on an ambling pad,
Sometimes a curly shepherd lad,
Or long-hair'd page in crimson clad,
    Goes by to tower'd Camelot:
60 And sometimes thro' the mirror blue
The knights come riding two and two:
She hath no loyal knight and true,

The Lady of Shalott.

But in her web she still delights
65   To weave the mirror's magic sights,
For often thro' the silent nights
A funeral, with plumes and lights
    And music, came from Camelot:
Or when the moon was overhead
70   Came two young lovers lately wed;
'I am half sick of shadows,' said
    The Lady of Shalott.

Part III
A bow-shot from her bower-eaves,
He rode between the barley-sheaves,
75   The sun came dazzling thro' the leaves,
And flam'd upon the brazen greaves
    Of bold Sir Lancelot.
A red-cross knight for ever kneel'd
To a lady in his shield,
80   That sparkled on the yellow field,
    Beside remote Shalott.

The gemmy bridle glitter'd free,
Like to some branch of stars we see
Hung in the golden Galaxy.
85   The bridle bells rang merrily
    As he rode down from Camelot:
And from his blazon'd baldric slung
A mighty silver bugle hung,
And as he rode his armour rung,
90   Beside remote Shalott.

All in the blue unclouded weather
Thick-jewell'd shone the saddle-leather,
The helmet and the helmet-feather

Burn'd like one burning flame together,
95   As he rode down from Camelot.
As often thro' the purple night,
Below the starry clusters bright,
Some bearded meteor, trailing light,
        Moves over green Shalott.

100   His broad clear brow in sunlight glow'd;
On burnish'd hooves his war-horse trode;
From underneath his helmet flow'd
His coal-black curls as on he rode,
        As he rode down from Camelot.
105   From the bank and from the river
He flash'd into the crystal mirror,
'Tirra lirra, tirra lirra:'
        Sang Sir Lancelot.

She left the web, she left the loom
110   She made three paces thro' the room
She saw the water-flower bloom,
She saw the helmet and the plume,
        She look'd down to Camelot.
Out flew the web and floated wide;
115   The mirror crack'd from side to side;
'The curse is come upon me,' cried
        The Lady of Shalott.

Part IV
In the stormy east-wind straining,
The pale yellow woods were waning,
120   The broad stream in his banks complaining,
Heavily the low sky raining
        Over tower'd Camelot;
Outside the isle a shallow boat
Beneath a willow lay afloat,
125   Below the carven stern she wrote,
        The Lady of Shalott.

A cloudwhite crown of pearl she dight,
All raimented in snowy white
That loosely flew (her zone in sight
130   Clasp'd with one blinding diamond bright)
      Her wide eyes fix'd on Camelot,
Though the squally east-wind keenly
Blew, with folded arms serenely
By the water stood the queenly
135   Lady of Shalott.

With a steady stony glance—
Like some bold seer in a trance,
Beholding all his own mischance,
Mute, with a glassy countenance—
140   She look'd down to Camelot.
It was the closing of the day:
She loos'd the chain, and down she lay;
The broad stream bore her far away,
      The Lady of Shalott.

145   As when to sailors while they roam,
By creeks and outfalls far from home,
Rising and dropping with the foam,
From dying swans wild warblings come,
      Blown shoreward; so to Camelot
150   Still as the boathead wound along
The willowy hills and fields among,
They heard her chanting her deathsong,
      The Lady of Shalott.

A longdrawn carol, mournful, holy,
155   She chanted loudly, chanted lowly,
Till her eyes were darken'd wholly,
And her smooth face sharpen'd slowly,
      Turn'd to tower'd Camelot:
For ere she reach'd upon the tide

160 The first house by the water-side,
Singing in her song she died,
    The Lady of Shalott.

Under tower and balcony,
By garden wall and gallery,
165 A pale, pale corpse she floated by,
Deadcold, between the houses high,
    Dead into tower'd Camelot.
Knight and burgher, lord and dame,
To the planked wharfage came:
170 Below the stern they read her name,
    The Lady of Shalott.

They cross'd themselves, their stars they blest,
Knight, minstrel, abbot, squire, and guest.
There lay a parchment on her breast,
175 That puzzled more than all the rest,
    The wellfed wits at Camelot.
'The web was woven curiously,
The charm is broken utterly,
Draw near and fear not,—this is I,
180   The Lady of Shalott.'

ULYSSES

Lord Alfred Tennyson

1   It little profits that an idle king,
By this still hearth, among these barren crags,
Match'd with an aged wife, I mete and dole
Unequal laws unto a savage race,
5   That hoard, and sleep, and feed, and know not me.
I cannot rest from travel: I will drink
Life to the lees: All times I have enjoy'd
Greatly, have suffer'd greatly, both with those
That loved me, and alone, on shore, and when
10   Thro' scudding drifts the rainy Hyades
Vext the dim sea: I am become a name;
For always roaming with a hungry heart
Much have I seen and known; cities of men
And manners, climates, councils, governments,
15   Myself not least, but honour'd of them all;
And drunk delight of battle with my peers,
Far on the ringing plains of windy Troy.
I am a part of all that I have met;
Yet all experience is an arch wherethro'
20   Gleams that untravell'd world whose margin fades
For ever and forever when I move.
How dull it is to pause, to make an end,
To rust unburnish'd, not to shine in use!
As tho' to breathe were life! Life piled on life
25   Were all too little, and of one to me
Little remains: but every hour is saved
From that eternal silence, something more,
A bringer of new things; and vile it were
For some three suns to store and hoard myself,
30   And this gray spirit yearning in desire
To follow knowledge like a sinking star,
Beyond the utmost bound of human thought.

This is my son, mine own Telemachus,
To whom I leave the sceptre and the isle,—
35 Well-loved of me, discerning to fulfil
This labour, by slow prudence to make mild
A rugged people, and thro' soft degrees
Subdue them to the useful and the good.
Most blameless is he, centred in the sphere
40 Of common duties, decent not to fail
In offices of tenderness, and pay
Meet adoration to my household gods,
When I am gone. He works his work, I mine.

There lies the port; the vessel puffs her sail:
45 There gloom the dark, broad seas. My mariners,
Souls that have toil'd, and wrought, and thought with me—
That ever with a frolic welcome took
The thunder and the sunshine, and opposed
Free hearts, free foreheads—you and I are old;
50 Old age hath yet his honour and his toil;
Death closes all: but something ere the end,
Some work of noble note, may yet be done,
Not unbecoming men that strove with Gods.
The lights begin to twinkle from the rocks:
55 The long day wanes: the slow moon climbs: the deep
Moans round with many voices. Come, my friends,
'Tis not too late to seek a newer world.
Push off, and sitting well in order smite
The sounding furrows; for my purpose holds
60 To sail beyond the sunset, and the baths
Of all the western stars, until I die.
It may be that the gulfs will wash us down:
It may be we shall touch the Happy Isles,
And see the great Achilles, whom we knew.
65 Tho' much is taken, much abides; and tho'
We are not now that strength which in old days
Moved earth and heaven, that which we are, we are;
One equal temper of heroic hearts,
Made weak by time and fate, but strong in will
70 To strive, to seek, to find, and not to yield.

BREAK, BREAK, BREAK

Lord Alfred Tennyson

1   Break, break, break,
    On thy cold gray stones, O Sea!
And I would that my tongue could utter
    The thoughts that arise in me.

5   O, well for the fisherman's boy,
    That he shouts with his sister at play!
O, well for the sailor lad,
    That he sings in his boat on the bay!

And the stately ships go on
10   To their haven under the hill;
But O for the touch of a vanish'd hand,
    And the sound of a voice that is still!

Break, break, break
    At the foot of thy crags, O Sea!
15 But the tender grace of a day that is dead
    Will never come back to me.

LOCKSLEY HALL

Lord Alfred Tennyson

1 Comrades, leave me here a little, while as yet 't is early morn:
Leave me here, and when you want me, sound upon the bugle-horn.

'T is the place, and all around it, as of old, the curlews call,
Dreary gleams about the moorland flying over Locksley Hall;

5 Locksley Hall, that in the distance overlooks the sandy tracts,
And the hollow ocean-ridges roaring into cataracts.

Many a night from yonder ivied casement, ere I went to rest,
Did I look on great Orion sloping slowly to the West.

Many a night I saw the Pleiads, rising thro' the mellow shade,
10 Glitter like a swarm of fire-flies tangled in a silver braid.

Here about the beach I wander'd, nourishing a youth sublime
With the fairy tales of science, and the long result of Time;

When the centuries behind me like a fruitful land reposed;
When I clung to all the present for the promise that it closed:

15 When I dipt into the future far as human eye could see;
Saw the Vision of the world and all the wonder that would be.—

In the Spring a fuller crimson comes upon the robin's breast;
In the Spring the wanton lapwing gets himself another crest;

In the Spring a livelier iris changes on the burnish'd dove;
20 In the Spring a young man's fancy lightly turns to thoughts of love.

Then her cheek was pale and thinner than should be for one so young,
And her eyes on all my motions with a mute observance hung.

And I said, "My cousin Amy, speak, and speak the truth to me,

Trust me, cousin, all the current of my being sets to thee."

25   On her pallid cheek and forehead came a colour and a light,
As I have seen the rosy red flushing in the northern night.

And she turn'd—her bosom shaken with a sudden storm of sighs—
All the spirit deeply dawning in the dark of hazel eyes—

Saying, "I have hid my feelings, fearing they should do me wrong";
30   Saying, "Dost thou love me, cousin?" weeping, "I have loved thee long."

Love took up the glass of Time, and turn'd it in his glowing hands;
Every moment, lightly shaken, ran itself in golden sands.

Love took up the harp of Life, and smote on all the chords with might;
Smote the chord of Self, that, trembling, pass'd in music out of sight.

35   Many a morning on the moorland did we hear the copses ring,
And her whisper throng'd my pulses with the fulness of the Spring.

Many an evening by the waters did we watch the stately ships,
And our spirits rush'd together at the touching of the lips.

O my cousin, shallow-hearted! O my Amy, mine no more!
40   O the dreary, dreary moorland! O the barren, barren shore!

Falser than all fancy fathoms, falser than all songs have sung,
Puppet to a father's threat, and servile to a shrewish tongue!

Is it well to wish thee happy?—having known me—to decline
On a range of lower feelings and a narrower heart than mine!

45   Yet it shall be; thou shalt lower to his level day by day,
What is fine within thee growing coarse to sympathize with clay.

As the husband is, the wife is: thou art mated with a clown,
And the grossness of his nature will have weight to drag thee down.

He will hold thee, when his passion shall have spent its novel force,
50   Something better than his dog, a little dearer than his horse.

What is this? his eyes are heavy; think not they are glazed with wine.
Go to him, it is thy duty, kiss him, take his hand in thine.

It may be my lord is weary, that his brain is overwrought:
Soothe him with thy finer fancies, touch him with thy lighter thought.

55 He will answer to the purpose, easy things to understand—
Better thou wert dead before me, tho' I slew thee with my hand!

Better thou and I were lying, hidden from the heart's disgrace,
Roll'd in one another's arms, and silent in a last embrace.

Cursed be the social wants that sin against the strength of youth!
60 Cursed be the social lies that warp us from the living truth!

Cursed be the sickly forms that err from honest Nature's rule!
Cursed be the gold that gilds the straiten'd forehead of the fool!

Well—'t is well that I should bluster!—Hadst thou less unworthy proved—
Would to God—for I had loved thee more than ever wife was loved.

65 Am I mad, that I should cherish that which bears but bitter fruit?
I will pluck it from my bosom, tho' my heart be at the root.

Never, tho' my mortal summers to such length of years should come
As the many-winter'd crow that leads the clanging rookery home.

Where is comfort? in division of the records of the mind?
70 Can I part her from herself, and love her, as I knew her, kind?

I remember one that perish'd; sweetly did she speak and move;
Such a one do I remember, whom to look at was to love.

Can I think of her as dead, and love her for the love she bore?
No—she never loved me truly; love is love for evermore.

75 Comfort? comfort scorn'd of devils! this is truth the poet sings,
That a sorrow's crown of sorrow is remembering happier things.

Drug thy memories, lest thou learn it, lest thy heart be put to proof,
In the dead unhappy night, and when the rain is on the roof.

Like a dog, he hunts in dreams, and thou art staring at the wall,
80   Where the dying night-lamp flickers, and the shadows rise and fall.

Then a hand shall pass before thee, pointing to his drunken sleep,
To thy widow'd marriage-pillows, to the tears that thou wilt weep.

Thou shalt hear the "Never, never," whisper'd by the phantom years,
And a song from out the distance in the ringing of thine ears;

85   And an eye shall vex thee, looking ancient kindness on thy pain.
Turn thee, turn thee on thy pillow; get thee to thy rest again.

Nay, but Nature brings thee solace; for a tender voice will cry.
'T is a purer life than thine, a lip to drain thy trouble dry.

Baby lips will laugh me down; my latest rival brings thee rest.
90   Baby fingers, waxen touches, press me from the mother's breast.

O, the child too clothes the father with a dearness not his due.
Half is thine and half is his: it will be worthy of the two.

O, I see thee old and formal, fitted to thy petty part,
With a little hoard of maxims preaching down a daughter's heart.

95   "They were dangerous guides the feelings—she herself was not exempt—
Truly, she herself had suffer'd"—Perish in thy self-contempt!

Overlive it—lower yet—be happy! wherefore should I care?
I myself must mix with action, lest I wither by despair.

What is that which I should turn to, lighting upon days like these?
100   Every door is barr'd with gold, and opens but to golden keys.

Every gate is throng'd with suitors, all the markets overflow.
I have but an angry fancy; what is that which I should do?

I had been content to perish, falling on the foeman's ground,
When the ranks are roll'd in vapour, and the winds are laid with sound.

105   But the jingling of the guinea helps the hurt that Honour feels,

And the nations do but murmur, snarling at each other's heels.

Can I but relive in sadness? I will turn that earlier page.
Hide me from my deep emotion, O thou wondrous Mother-Age!

Make me feel the wild pulsation that I felt before the strife,
When I heard my days before me, and the tumult of my life;

Yearning for the large excitement that the coming years would yield,
Eager-hearted as a boy when first he leaves his father's field,

And at night along the dusky highway near and nearer drawn,
Sees in heaven the light of London flaring like a dreary dawn;

And his spirit leaps within him to be gone before him then,
Underneath the light he looks at, in among the throngs of men:

Men, my brothers, men the workers, ever reaping something new:
That which they have done but earnest of the things that they shall do:

For I dipt into the future, far as human eye could see,
Saw the Vision of the world, and all the wonder that would be;

Saw the heavens fill with commerce, argosies of magic sails,
Pilots of the purple twilight dropping down with costly bales;

Heard the heavens fill with shouting, and there rain'd a ghastly dew
From the nations' airy navies grappling in the central blue;

Far along the world-wide whisper of the south-wind rushing warm,
With the standards of the peoples plunging thro' the thunder-storm;

Till the war-drum throbb'd no longer, and the battle-flags were furl'd
In the Parliament of man, the Federation of the world.

There the common sense of most shall hold a fretful realm in awe,
And the kindly earth shall slumber, lapt in universal law.

So I triumph'd ere my passion sweeping thro' me left me dry,
Left me with the palsied heart, and left me with the jaundiced eye;

Eye, to which all order festers, all things here are out of joint:
Science moves, but slowly, slowly, creeping on from point to point:

135 Slowly comes a hungry people, as a lion, creeping nigher,
Glares at one that nods and winks behind a slowly-dying fire.

Yet I doubt not thro' the ages one increasing purpose runs,
And the thoughts of men are widen'd with the process of the suns.

What is that to him that reaps not harvest of his youthful joys,
140 Tho' the deep heart of existence beat for ever like a boy's?

Knowledge comes, but wisdom lingers, and I linger on the shore,
And the individual withers, and the world is more and more.

Knowledge comes, but wisdom lingers, and he bears a laden breast,
Full of sad experience, moving toward the stillness of his rest.

145 Hark, my merry comrades call me, sounding on the bugle-horn,
They to whom my foolish passion were a target for their scorn:

Shall it not be scorn to me to harp on such a moulder'd string?
I am shamed thro' all my nature to have loved so slight a thing.

Weakness to be wroth with weakness! woman's pleasure, woman's pain—
150 Nature made them blinder motions bounded in a shallower brain:

Woman is the lesser man, and all thy passions, match'd with mine,
Are as moonlight unto sunlight, and as water unto wine—

Here at least, where nature sickens, nothing. Ah, for some retreat
Deep in yonder shining Orient, where my life began to beat;

155 Where in wild Mahratta-battle fell my father evil-starr'd,—
I was left a trampled orphan, and a selfish uncle's ward.

Or to burst all links of habit—there to wander far away,
On from island unto island at the gateways of the day.

Larger constellations burning, mellow moons and happy skies,
160 Breadths of tropic shade and palms in cluster, knots of Paradise.

Never comes the trader, never floats an European flag,
Slides the bird o'er lustrous woodland, swings the trailer from the crag;

Droops the heavy-blossom'd bower, hangs the heavy-fruited tree—
Summer isles of Eden lying in dark-purple spheres of sea.

165 There methinks would be enjoyment more than in this march of mind,
In the steamship, in the railway, in the thoughts that shake mankind.

There the passions cramp'd no longer shall have scope and breathing space;
I will take some savage woman, she shall rear my dusky race.

Iron-jointed, supple-sinew'd, they shall dive, and they shall run,
170 Catch the wild goat by the hair, and hurl their lances in the sun;

Whistle back the parrot's call, and leap the rainbows of the brooks,
Not with blinded eyesight poring over miserable books—

Fool, again the dream, the fancy! but I know my words are wild,
But I count the gray barbarian lower than the Christian child.

175 I, to herd with narrow foreheads, vacant of our glorious gains,
Like a beast with lower pleasures, like a beast with lower pains!

Mated with a squalid savage—what to me were sun or clime?
I the heir of all the ages, in the foremost files of time—

I that rather held it better men should perish one by one,
180 Than that earth should stand at gaze like Joshua's moon in Ajalon!

Not in vain the distance beacons. Forward, forward let us range,
Let the great world spin for ever down the ringing grooves of change.

Thro' the shadow of the globe we sweep into the younger day;
Better fifty years of Europe than a cycle of Cathay.

185 Mother-Age (for mine I knew not) help me as when life begun:
Rift the hills, and roll the waters, flash the lightnings, weigh the Sun.

O, I see the crescent promise of my spirit hath not set.
Ancient founts of inspiration well thro' all my fancy yet.

Howsoever these things be, a long farewell to Locksley Hall!
190   Now for me the woods may wither, now for me the roof-tree fall.

Comes a vapour from the margin, blackening over heath and holt,
Cramming all the blast before it, in its breast a thunderbolt.

Let it fall on Locksley Hall, with rain or hail, or fire or snow;
For the mighty wind arises, roaring seaward, and I go.

TEARS, IDLE TEARS

Lord Alfred Tennyson

1   Tears, idle tears, I know not what they mean,
        Tears from the depth of some divine despair
        Rise in the heart, and gather to the eyes,
        In looking on the happy Autumn-fields,
5   And thinking of the days that are no more.

        Fresh as the first beam glittering on a sail,
        That brings our friends up from the underworld,
        Sad as the last which reddens over one
        That sinks with all we love below the verge;
10   So sad, so fresh, the days that are no more.

        Ah, sad and strange as in dark summer dawns
        The earliest pipe of half-awaken'd birds
        To dying ears, when unto dying eyes
        The casement slowly grows a glimmering square;
15   So sad, so strange, the days that are no more.

        Dear as remember'd kisses after death,
        And sweet as those by hopeless fancy feign'd
        On lips that are for others; deep as love,
        Deep as first love, and wild with all regret;
20   O Death in Life, the days that are no more!

from *IN MEMORIAM A.H.H.*

Lord Alfred Tennyson

1   Ring out, wild bells, to the wild sky,
　　　The flying cloud, the frosty light:
　　　The year is dying in the night;
　　Ring out, wild bells, and let him die.

5   Ring out the old, ring in the new,
　　　Ring, happy bells, across the snow:
　　　The year is going, let him go;
　　Ring out the false, ring in the true.

　　Ring out the grief that saps the mind
10　　　For those that here we see no more;
　　　Ring out the feud of rich and poor,
　　Ring in redress to all mankind.

　　Ring out a slowly dying cause,
　　　And ancient forms of party strife;
15　　　Ring in the nobler modes of life,
　　With sweeter manners, purer laws.

　　Ring out the want, the care, the sin,
　　　The faithless coldness of the times;
　　　Ring out, ring out my mournful rhymes
20　But ring the fuller minstrel in.

　　Ring out false pride in place and blood,
　　　The civic slander and the spite;
　　　Ring in the love of truth and right,
　　Ring in the common love of good.

25　Ring out old shapes of foul disease;

Ring out the narrowing lust of gold;
Ring out the thousand wars of old,
Ring in the thousand years of peace.

Ring in the valiant man and free,
30   The larger heart, the kindlier hand;
Ring out the darkness of the land,
Ring in the Christ that is to be.

CHARGE OF THE LIGHT BRIGADE

Lord Alfred Tennyson

I

1   Half a league, half a league,
Half a league onward,
All in the valley of Death
   Rode the six hundred.
5   "Forward, the Light Brigade!
Charge for the guns!" he said.
Into the valley of Death
   Rode the six hundred.

II
"Forward, the Light Brigade!"
10   Was there a man dismayed?
Not though the soldier knew
   Someone had blundered.
   Theirs not to make reply,
   Theirs not to reason why,
15   Theirs but to do and die.
Into the valley of Death
   Rode the six hundred.

III

Cannon to right of them,
Cannon to left of them,
20   Cannon in front of them
      Volleyed and thundered;
Stormed at with shot and shell,
Boldly they rode and well,
Into the jaws of Death,
25   Into the mouth of hell
      Rode the six hundred.

IV

Flashed all their sabres bare,
Flashed as they turned in air
Sabring the gunners there,
30   Charging an army, while
      All the world wondered.
Plunged in the battery-smoke
Right through the line they broke;
Cossack and Russian
35   Reeled from the sabre stroke
      Shattered and sundered.
Then they rode back, but not
      Not the six hundred.

V

Cannon to right of them,
40   Cannon to left of them,
Cannon behind them
      Volleyed and thundered;
Stormed at with shot and shell,
While horse and hero fell.
45   They that had fought so well
Came through the jaws of Death,
Back from the mouth of hell,
All that was left of them,
      Left of six hundred.

VI

50 When can their glory fade?
O the wild charge they made!
All the world wondered.
Honour the charge they made!
Honour the Light Brigade,
55   Noble six hundred!

CROSSING THE BAR

Lord Alfred Tennyson

1   Sunset and evening star,
And one clear call for me!
And may there be no moaning of the bar,
When I put out to sea,

5   But such a tide as moving seems asleep,
Too full for sound and foam,
When that which drew from out the boundless deep
Turns again home.

Twilight and evening bell,
10   And after that the dark!
And may there be no sadness of farewell,
When I embark;

For tho' from out our bourne of Time and Place
The flood may bear me far,
15 I hope to see my Pilot face to face
When I have crost the bar.

ROBERT BROWNING (1812-1889)

Browning was the son of artistic parents; his father was a bank clerk who collected over 6,000 books and painted in his free time, and his mother played the piano. By the age of fourteen, he knew four languages. Browning was an aspiring but unrecognized poet and playwright when, in 1844, he sought out and fell in love with the already-famous Elizabeth Barrett. The couple eloped in 1846 and moved to Italy. They had a son, Robert Barrett Browning, and both parents doted on him. Browning cared for his invalid wife and their son, and though both were working on their poetry, Robert Browning published little during the marriage. After his wife's early death in 1861, Browning returned to England with their son, and in his later years, he became a famous poet in his own right. He was known best for his philosophical poems, such as his long narrative poem, *The Ring and the Book* (1868-69), and psychologically realistic dramatic monologues, such as "My Last Duchess" and "Porphyria's Lover." Browning lived to witness the founding of the Browning Society in 1881, a literary club dedicated to the study of his work.

THE REAL AND SURE AND TRUE

Robert Browning

1 Marriage on earth seems such a counterfeit,
  Mere imitation of the inimitable:
  In heaven we have the real and true and sure.
  'Tis there they neither marry nor are given
5 In marriage but are as the angels: right,
  Oh how right that is, how like Jesus Christ
  To say that! Marriage-making for the earth,
  With gold so much,— birth, power, repute so much,
  Or beauty, youth so much, in lack of these!
10 Be as the angels rather, who, apart,
  Know themselves into one, are found at length
  Married, but marry never, no, nor give
  In marriage; they are man and wife at once
  When the true time is: here we have to wait
15 Not so long neither! Could we by a wish
  Have what we will and get the future now,
  Would we wish aught done undone in the past?
  So, let him wait God's instant men call years;
  Meantime hold hard by truth and his great soul,
20 Do out the duty! Through such souls alone
  God stooping shows sufficient of His light
  For us i' the dark to rise by. And I rise.

PORPHYRIA'S LOVER

Robert Browning

1   The rain set early in to-night,
      The sullen wind was soon awake,
It tore the elm-tops down for spite,
      And did its worst to vex the lake:
5   I listened with heart fit to break.
When glided in Porphyria; straight
      She shut the cold out and the storm,
And kneeled and made the cheerless grate
      Blaze up, and all the cottage warm;
10   Which done, she rose, and from her form
Withdrew the dripping cloak and shawl,
      And laid her soiled gloves by, untied
Her hat and let the damp hair fall,
      And, last, she sat down by my side
15   And called me. When no voice replied,
She put my arm about her waist,
      And made her smooth white shoulder bare,
And all her yellow hair displaced,
      And, stooping, made my cheek lie there,
20   And spread, o'er all, her yellow hair,
Murmuring how she loved me — she
      Too weak, for all her heart's endeavour,
To set its struggling passion free
      From pride, and vainer ties dissever,
25   And give herself to me for ever.
But passion sometimes would prevail,
      Nor could to-night's gay feast restrain
A sudden thought of one so pale
      For love of her, and all in vain:
30   So, she was come through wind and rain.
Be sure I looked up at her eyes
      Happy and proud; at last I knew

Porphyria worshipped me; surprise
  Made my heart swell, and still it grew
35   While I debated what to do.
That moment she was mine, mine, fair,
  Perfectly pure and good: I found
A thing to do, and all her hair
  In one long yellow string I wound
40   Three times her little throat around,
And strangled her. No pain felt she;
  I am quite sure she felt no pain.
As a shut bud that holds a bee,
  I warily oped her lids: again
45   Laughed the blue eyes without a stain.
And I untightened next the tress
  About her neck; her cheek once more
Blushed bright beneath my burning kiss:
  I propped her head up as before,
50   Only, this time my shoulder bore
Her head, which droops upon it still:
  The smiling rosy little head,
So glad it has its utmost will,
  That all it scorned at once is fled,
55   And I, its love, am gained instead!
Porphyria's love: she guessed not how
  Her darling one wish would be heard.
And thus we sit together now,
  And all night long we have not stirred,
60   And yet God has not said a word!

MY LAST DUCHESS

Robert Browning

FERRARA

1   That's my last Duchess painted on the wall,
Looking as if she were alive. I call
That piece a wonder, now; Fra Pandolf's hands
Worked busily a day, and there she stands.
5   Will't please you sit and look at her? I said
"Fra Pandolf" by design, for never read
Strangers like you that pictured countenance,
The depth and passion of its earnest glance,
But to myself they turned (since none puts by
10   The curtain I have drawn for you, but I)
And seemed as they would ask me, if they durst,
How such a glance came there; so, not the first
Are you to turn and ask thus. Sir, 'twas not
Her husband's presence only, called that spot
15   Of joy into the Duchess' cheek; perhaps
Fra Pandolf chanced to say, "Her mantle laps
Over my lady's wrist too much," or "Paint
Must never hope to reproduce the faint
Half-flush that dies along her throat." Such stuff
20   Was courtesy, she thought, and cause enough
For calling up that spot of joy. She had
A heart—how shall I say?— too soon made glad,
Too easily impressed; she liked whate'er
She looked on, and her looks went everywhere.
25   Sir, 'twas all one! My favour at her breast,
The dropping of the daylight in the West,
The bough of cherries some officious fool
Broke in the orchard for her, the white mule
She rode with round the terrace—all and each
30   Would draw from her alike the approving speech,

Or blush, at least. She thanked men—good! but thanked
Somehow—I know not how—as if she ranked
My gift of a nine-hundred-years-old name
With anybody's gift. Who'd stoop to blame
35 This sort of trifling? Even had you skill
In speech—which I have not—to make your will
Quite clear to such an one, and say, "Just this
Or that in you disgusts me; here you miss,
Or there exceed the mark"—and if she let
40 Herself be lessoned so, nor plainly set
Her wits to yours, forsooth, and made excuse—
E'en then would be some stooping; and I choose
Never to stoop. Oh, sir, she smiled, no doubt,
Whene'er I passed her; but who passed without
45 Much the same smile? This grew; I gave commands;
Then all smiles stopped together. There she stands
As if alive. Will't please you rise? We'll meet
The company below, then. I repeat,
The Count your master's known munificence
50 Is ample warrant that no just pretense
Of mine for dowry will be disallowed;
Though his fair daughter's self, as I avowed
At starting, is my object. Nay, we'll go
Together down, sir. Notice Neptune, though,
55 Taming a sea-horse, thought a rarity,
Which Claus of Innsbruck cast in bronze for me!

SOLILOQUY OF THE SPANISH CLOISTER

Robert Browning

1 Gr-r-r—there go, my heart's abhorrence!
  Water your damned flower-pots, do!
If hate killed men, Brother Lawrence,
  God's blood, would not mine kill you!
5 What? your myrtle-bush wants trimming?
  Oh, that rose has prior claims—
Needs its leaden vase filled brimming?
  Hell dry you up with its flames!

At the meal we sit together;
10 Salve tibi! I must hear
Wise talk of the kind of weather,
  Sort of season, time of year:
Not a plenteous cork crop: scarcely
  Dare we hope oak-galls, I doubt;
15 What's the Latin name for "parsley"?
  What's the Greek name for "swine's snout"?

Whew! We'll have our platter burnished,
  Laid with care on our own shelf!
With a fire-new spoon we're furnished,
20 And a goblet for ourself,
Rinsed like something sacrificial
  Ere 'tis fit to touch our chaps—
Marked with L. for our initial!
  (He-he! There his lily snaps!)

25 Saint, forsooth! While Brown Dolores
  Squats outside the Convent bank
With Sanchicha, telling stories,
  Steeping tresses in the tank,
Blue-black, lustrous, thick like horsehairs,

30   —Can't I see his dead eye glow,
        Bright as 'twere a Barbary corsair's?
          (That is, if he'd let it show!)

        When he finishes refection,
          Knife and fork he never lays
35   Cross-wise, to my recollection,
          As do I, in Jesu's praise.
        I the Trinity illustrate,
          Drinking watered orange pulp—
        In three sips the Arian frustrate;
40   While he drains his at one gulp!

        Oh, those melons! if he's able
          We're to have a feast; so nice!
        One goes to the Abbot's table,
          All of us get each a slice.
45   How go on your flowers? None double?
          Not one fruit-sort can you spy?
        Strange!—And I, too, at such trouble,
          Keep them close-nipped on the sly!

        There's a great text in Galatians,
50   Once you trip on it, entails
        Twenty-nine district damnations,
          One sure, if another fails;
        If I trip him just a-dying,
          Sure of heaven as sure can be,
55   Spin him round and send him flying
          Off to hell, a Manichee?

        Or, my scrofulous French novel
          On grey paper with blunt type!
        Simply glance at it, you grovel
60   Hand and foot in Belial's gripe;
        If I double down its pages
          At the woeful sixteenth print,

When he gathers his greengages,
　Ope a sieve and slip it in't?

65　Or, there's Satan!—one might venture
　　Pledge one's soul to him, yet leave
Such a flaw in the indenture
　　As he'd miss till, past retrieve,
Blasted lay that rose-acacia
70　　We're so proud of! Hy, Zy, Hine...
'St, there's Vespers! Plena gratia
　Ave, Virgo! Gr-r-r—you swine!

THE LOST LEADER

Robert Browning

1   Just for a handful of silver he left us,
    Just for a riband to stick in his coat—
    Found the one gift of which fortune bereft us,
    Lost all the others she lets us devote;
5   They, with the gold to give, doled him out silver,
    So much was theirs who so little allowed:
    How all our copper had gone for his service!
    Rags—were they purple, his heart had been proud!
    We that had loved him so, followed him, honoured him,
10   Lived in his mild and magnificent eye,
    Learned his great language, caught his clear accents,
    Made him our pattern to live and to die!
    Shakespeare was of us, Milton was for us,
    Burns, Shelley, were with us,—they watch from their graves!
15   He alone breaks from the van and the freemen,
    —He alone sinks to the rear and the slaves!

    We shall march prospering,—not thro' his presence;
    Songs may inspirit us,—not from his lyre;
    Deeds will be done,—while he boasts his quiescence,
20   Still bidding crouch whom the rest bade aspire:
    Blot out his name, then, record one lost soul more,
    One task more declined, one more footpath untrod,
    One more devils'-triumph and sorrow for angels,
    One wrong more to man, one more insult to God!
25   Life's night begins: let him never come back to us!
    There would be doubt, hesitation and pain,
    Forced praise on our part—the glimmer of twilight,
    Never glad confident morning again!
    Best fight on well, for we taught him—strike gallantly,
30   Menace our heart ere we master his own;
    Then let him receive the new knowledge and wait us,
    Pardoned in heaven, the first by the throne!

THE BISHOP ORDERS HIS TOMB AT SAINT PRAXED'S CHURCH

Robert Browning

Rome, 15—

1   Vanity, saith the preacher, vanity!
Draw round my bed: is Anselm keeping back?
Nephews—sons mine . . . ah God, I know not! Well—
She, men would have to be your mother once,

5   Old Gandolf envied me, so fair she was!
What's done is done, and she is dead beside,
Dead long ago, and I am Bishop since,
And as she died so must we die ourselves,
And thence ye may perceive the world's a dream.

10   Life, how and what is it? As here I lie
In this state-chamber, dying by degrees,
Hours and long hours in the dead night, I ask
"Do I live, am I dead?" Peace, peace seems all.
Saint Praxed's ever was the church for peace;

15   And so, about this tomb of mine. I fought
With tooth and nail to save my niche, ye know:
—Old Gandolf cozened me, despite my care;
Shrewd was that snatch from out the corner South
He graced his carrion with, God curse the same!

20   Yet still my niche is not so cramped but thence
One sees the pulpit o' the epistle-side,
And somewhat of the choir, those silent seats,
And up into the aery dome where live
The angels, and a sunbeam's sure to lurk:

25   And I shall fill my slab of basalt there,
And 'neath my tabernacle take my rest,
With those nine columns round me, two and two,
The odd one at my feet where Anselm stands:
Peach-blossom marble all, the rare, the ripe

30   As fresh-poured red wine of a mighty pulse.
      —Old Gandolf with his paltry onion-stone,
      Put me where I may look at him! True peach,
      Rosy and flawless: how I earned the prize!
      Draw close: that conflagration of my church
35   —What then? So much was saved if aught were missed!
      My sons, ye would not be my death? Go dig
      The white-grape vineyard where the oil-press stood,
      Drop water gently till the surface sink,
      And if ye find . . . Ah God, I know not, I! ...
40   Bedded in store of rotten fig-leaves soft,
      And corded up in a tight olive-frail,
      Some lump, ah God, of lapis lazuli,
      Big as a Jew's head cut off at the nape,
      Blue as a vein o'er the Madonna's breast ...
45   Sons, all have I bequeathed you, villas, all,
      That brave Frascati villa with its bath,
      So, let the blue lump poise between my knees,
      Like God the Father's globe on both His hands
      Ye worship in the Jesu Church so gay,
50   For Gandolf shall not choose but see and burst!
      Swift as a weaver's shuttle fleet our years:
      Man goeth to the grave, and where is he?
      Did I say basalt for my slab, sons? Black—
      'Twas ever antique-black I meant! How else
55   Shall ye contrast my frieze to come beneath?
      The bas-relief in bronze ye promised me,
      Those Pans and Nymphs ye wot of, and perchance
      Some tripod, thyrsus, with a vase or so,
      The Saviour at his sermon on the mount,
60   Saint Praxed in a glory, and one Pan
      Ready to twitch the Nymph's last garment off,
      And Moses with the tables . . . but I know
      Ye mark me not! What do they whisper thee,
      Child of my bowels, Anselm? Ah, ye hope
65   To revel down my villas while I gasp
      Bricked o'er with beggar's mouldy travertine

Which Gandolf from his tomb-top chuckles at!
Nay, boys, ye love me—all of jasper, then!
'Tis jasper ye stand pledged to, lest I grieve.
70 My bath must needs be left behind, alas!
One block, pure green as a pistachio-nut,
There's plenty jasper somewhere in the world—
And have I not Saint Praxed's ear to pray
Horses for ye, and brown Greek manuscripts,
75 And mistresses with great smooth marbly limbs?
—That's if ye carve my epitaph aright,
Choice Latin, picked phrase, Tully's every word,
No gaudy ware like Gandolf's second line—
Tully, my masters? Ulpian serves his need!
80 And then how I shall lie through centuries,
And hear the blessed mutter of the mass,
And see God made and eaten all day long,
And feel the steady candle-flame, and taste
Good strong thick stupefying incense-smoke!
85 For as I lie here, hours of the dead night,
Dying in state and by such slow degrees,
I fold my arms as if they clasped a crook,
And stretch my feet forth straight as stone can point,
And let the bedclothes, for a mortcloth, drop
90 Into great laps and folds of sculptor's-work:
And as yon tapers dwindle, and strange thoughts
Grow, with a certain humming in my ears,
About the life before I lived this life,
And this life too, popes, cardinals and priests,
95 Saint Praxed at his sermon on the mount,
Your tall pale mother with her talking eyes,
And new-found agate urns as fresh as day,
And marble's language, Latin pure, discreet,
—Aha, ELUCESCEBAT quoth our friend?
100 No Tully, said I, Ulpian at the best!
Evil and brief hath been my pilgrimage.
All lapis, all, sons! Else I give the Pope
My villas! Will ye ever eat my heart?

Ever your eyes were as a lizard's quick,
105 They glitter like your mother's for my soul,
  Or ye would heighten my impoverished frieze,
  Piece out its starved design, and fill my vase
  With grapes, and add a vizor and a Term,
  And to the tripod ye would tie a lynx
110 That in his struggle throws the thyrsus down,
  To comfort me on my entablature
  Whereon I am to lie till I must ask
  "Do I live, am I dead?" There, leave me, there!
  For ye have stabbed me with ingratitude
115 To death—ye wish it—God, ye wish it! Stone—
  Gritstone, a-crumble! Clammy squares which sweat
  As if the corpse they keep were oozing through—
  And no more lapis to delight the world!
  Well, go! I bless ye. Fewer tapers there,
120 But in a row: and, going, turn your backs
  —Ay, like departing altar-ministrants,
  And leave me in my church, the church for peace,
  That I may watch at leisure if he leers—
  Old Gandolf, at me, from his onion-stone,
125 As still he envied me, so fair she was!

FRA LIPPO LIPPI

Robert Browning

[Florentine painter, 1412-69]

1   I am poor brother Lippo, by your leave!
You need not clap your torches to my face.
Zooks, what's to blame? you think you see a monk!
What, 'tis past midnight, and you go the rounds,
5   And here you catch me at an alley's end
Where sportive ladies leave their doors ajar?
The Carmine's my cloister: hunt it up,
Do,—harry out, if you must show your zeal,
Whatever rat, there, haps on his wrong hole,
10   And nip each softling of a wee white mouse,
Weke, weke, that's crept to keep him company!
Aha, you know your betters! Then, you'll take
Your hand away that's fiddling on my throat,
And please to know me likewise. Who am I?
15   Why, one, sir, who is lodging with a friend
Three streets off—he's a certain . . . how d'ye call?
Master—a . . . Cosimo of the Medici,
I' the house that caps the corner. Boh! you were best!
Remember and tell me, the day you're hanged,
20   How you affected such a gullet's-gripe!
But you, sir, it concerns you that your knaves
Pick up a manner nor discredit you:
Zooks, are we pilchards, that they sweep the streets
And count fair price what comes into their net?
25   He's Judas to a tittle, that man is!
Just such a face! Why, sir, you make amends.
Lord, I'm not angry! Bid your hang-dogs go
Drink out this quarter-florin to the health
Of the munificent House that harbours me
30   (And many more beside, lads! more beside!)

And all's come square again. I'd like his face—
His, elbowing on his comrade in the door
With the pike and lantern,—for the slave that holds
John Baptist's head a-dangle by the hair
35 With one hand ("Look you, now," as who should say)
And his weapon in the other, yet unwiped!
It's not your chance to have a bit of chalk,
A wood-coal or the like? or you should see!
Yes, I'm the painter, since you style me so.
40 What, brother Lippo's doings, up and down,
You know them and they take you? like enough!
I saw the proper twinkle in your eye—
'Tell you, I liked your looks at very first.
Let's sit and set things straight now, hip to haunch.
45 Here's spring come, and the nights one makes up bands
To roam the town and sing out carnival,
And I've been three weeks shut within my mew,
A-painting for the great man, saints and saints
And saints again. I could not paint all night—
50 Ouf! I leaned out of window for fresh air.
There came a hurry of feet and little feet,
A sweep of lute strings, laughs, and whifts of song, —
Flower o' the broom,
Take away love, and our earth is a tomb!
55 Flower o' the quince,
I let Lisa go, and what good in life since?
Flower o' the thyme—and so on. Round they went.
Scarce had they turned the corner when a titter
Like the skipping of rabbits by moonlight,—three slim shapes,
60 And a face that looked up . . . zooks, sir, flesh and blood,
That's all I'm made of! Into shreds it went,
Curtain and counterpane and coverlet,
All the bed-furniture—a dozen knots,
There was a ladder! Down I let myself,
65 Hands and feet, scrambling somehow, and so dropped,
And after them. I came up with the fun
Hard by Saint Laurence, hail fellow, well met,—

Flower o' the rose,
If I've been merry, what matter who knows?
70 And so as I was stealing back again
To get to bed and have a bit of sleep
Ere I rise up to-morrow and go work
On Jerome knocking at his poor old breast
With his great round stone to subdue the flesh,
75 You snap me of the sudden. Ah, I see!
Though your eye twinkles still, you shake your head—
Mine's shaved—a monk, you say—the sting 's in that!
If Master Cosimo announced himself,
Mum's the word naturally; but a monk!
80 Come, what am I a beast for? tell us, now!
I was a baby when my mother died
And father died and left me in the street.
I starved there, God knows how, a year or two
On fig-skins, melon-parings, rinds and shucks,
85 Refuse and rubbish. One fine frosty day,
My stomach being empty as your hat,
The wind doubled me up and down I went.
Old Aunt Lapaccia trussed me with one hand,
(Its fellow was a stinger as I knew)
90 And so along the wall, over the bridge,
By the straight cut to the convent. Six words there,
While I stood munching my first bread that month:
"So, boy, you're minded," quoth the good fat father
Wiping his own mouth, 'twas refection-time,—
95 "To quit this very miserable world?
Will you renounce" . . . "the mouthful of bread?" thought I;
By no means! Brief, they made a monk of me;
I did renounce the world, its pride and greed,
Palace, farm, villa, shop, and banking-house,
100 Trash, such as these poor devils of Medici
Have given their hearts to—all at eight years old.
Well, sir, I found in time, you may be sure,
'Twas not for nothing—the good bellyful,
The warm serge and the rope that goes all round,

105 And day-long blessed idleness beside!
   "Let's see what the urchin's fit for"—that came next.
   Not overmuch their way, I must confess.
   Such a to-do! They tried me with their books:
   Lord, they'd have taught me Latin in pure waste!
110 Flower o' the clove.
   All the Latin I construe is, "amo" I love!
   But, mind you, when a boy starves in the streets
   Eight years together, as my fortune was,
   Watching folk's faces to know who will fling
115 The bit of half-stripped grape-bunch he desires,
   And who will curse or kick him for his pains,—
   Which gentleman processional and fine,
   Holding a candle to the Sacrament,
   Will wink and let him lift a plate and catch
120 The droppings of the wax to sell again,
   Or holla for the Eight and have him whipped,—
   How say I?—nay, which dog bites, which lets drop
   His bone from the heap of offal in the street,—
   Why, soul and sense of him grow sharp alike,
125 He learns the look of things, and none the less
   For admonition from the hunger-pinch.
   I had a store of such remarks, be sure,
   Which, after I found leisure, turned to use.
   I drew men's faces on my copy-books,
130 Scrawled them within the antiphonary's marge,
   Joined legs and arms to the long music-notes,
   Found eyes and nose and chin for A's and B's,
   And made a string of pictures of the world
   Betwixt the ins and outs of verb and noun,
135 On the wall, the bench, the door. The monks looked black.
   "Nay," quoth the Prior, "turn him out, d'ye say?
   In no wise. Lose a crow and catch a lark.
   What if at last we get our man of parts,
   We Carmelites, like those Camaldolese
140 And Preaching Friars, to do our church up fine
   And put the front on it that ought to be!"

And hereupon he bade me daub away.
Thank you! my head being crammed, the walls a blank,
Never was such prompt disemburdening.
145   First, every sort of monk, the black and white,
I drew them, fat and lean: then, folk at church,
From good old gossips waiting to confess
Their cribs of barrel-droppings, candle-ends,—
To the breathless fellow at the altar-foot,
150   Fresh from his murder, safe and sitting there
With the little children round him in a row
Of admiration, half for his beard and half
For that white anger of his victim's son
Shaking a fist at him with one fierce arm,
155   Signing himself with the other because of Christ
(Whose sad face on the cross sees only this
After the passion of a thousand years)
Till some poor girl, her apron o'er her head,
(Which the intense eyes looked through) came at eve
160   On tiptoe, said a word, dropped in a loaf,
Her pair of earrings and a bunch of flowers
(The brute took growling), prayed, and so was gone.
I painted all, then cried "'Tis ask and have;
Choose, for more's ready!"—laid the ladder flat,
165   And showed my covered bit of cloister-wall.
The monks closed in a circle and praised loud
Till checked, taught what to see and not to see,
Being simple bodies,—"That's the very man!
Look at the boy who stoops to pat the dog!
170   That woman's like the Prior's niece who comes
To care about his asthma: it's the life!"
But there my triumph's straw-fire flared and funked;
Their betters took their turn to see and say:
The Prior and the learned pulled a face
175   And stopped all that in no time. "How? what's here?
Quite from the mark of painting, bless us all!
Faces, arms, legs, and bodies like the true
As much as pea and pea! it's devil's-game!

Your business is not to catch men with show,
180 With homage to the perishable clay,
But lift them over it, ignore it all,
Make them forget there's such a thing as flesh.
Your business is to paint the souls of men—
Man's soul, and it's a fire, smoke . . . no, it's not . . .
185 It's vapour done up like a new-born babe—
(In that shape when you die it leaves your mouth)
It's . . . well, what matters talking, it's the soul!
Give us no more of body than shows soul!
Here's Giotto, with his Saint a-praising God,
190 That sets us praising—why not stop with him?
Why put all thoughts of praise out of our head
With wonder at lines, colours, and what not?
Paint the soul, never mind the legs and arms!
Rub all out, try at it a second time.
195 Oh, that white smallish female with the breasts,
She's just my niece . . . Herodias, I would say,—
Who went and danced and got men's heads cut off!
Have it all out!" Now, is this sense, I ask?
A fine way to paint soul, by painting body
200 So ill, the eye can't stop there, must go further
And can't fare worse! Thus, yellow does for white
When what you put for yellow's simply black,
And any sort of meaning looks intense
When all beside itself means and looks nought.
205 Why can't a painter lift each foot in turn,
Left foot and right foot, go a double step,
Make his flesh liker and his soul more like,
Both in their order? Take the prettiest face,
The Prior's niece . . . patron-saint—is it so pretty
210 You can't discover if it means hope, fear,
Sorrow or joy? won't beauty go with these?
Suppose I've made her eyes all right and blue,
Can't I take breath and try to add life's flash,
And then add soul and heighten them three-fold?
215 Or say there's beauty with no soul at all—

(I never saw it—put the case the same—)
If you get simple beauty and nought else,
You get about the best thing God invents:
That's somewhat: and you'll find the soul you have missed,
220   Within yourself, when you return him thanks.
"Rub all out!" Well, well, there's my life, in short,
And so the thing has gone on ever since.
I'm grown a man no doubt, I've broken bounds:
You should not take a fellow eight years old
225   And make him swear to never kiss the girls.
I'm my own master, paint now as I please—
Having a friend, you see, in the Corner-house!
Lord, it's fast holding by the rings in front—
Those great rings serve more purposes than just
230   To plant a flag in, or tie up a horse!
And yet the old schooling sticks, the old grave eyes
Are peeping o'er my shoulder as I work,
The heads shake still—"It's art's decline, my son!
You're not of the true painters, great and old;
235   Brother Angelico's the man, you'll find;
Brother Lorenzo stands his single peer:
Fag on at flesh, you'll never make the third!"
Flower o' the pine,
You keep your mistr . . . manners, and I'll stick to mine!
240   I'm not the third, then: bless us, they must know!
Don't you think they're the likeliest to know,
They with their Latin? So, I swallow my rage,
Clench my teeth, suck my lips in tight, and paint
To please them—sometimes do and sometimes don't;
245   For, doing most, there's pretty sure to come
A turn, some warm eve finds me at my saints—
A laugh, a cry, the business of the world—
(Flower o' the peach
Death for us all, and his own life for each!)
250   And my whole soul revolves, the cup runs over,
The world and life's too big to pass for a dream,
And I do these wild things in sheer despite,

And play the fooleries you catch me at,
In pure rage! The old mill-horse, out at grass
255   After hard years, throws up his stiff heels so,
Although the miller does not preach to him
The only good of grass is to make chaff.
What would men have? Do they like grass or no—
May they or mayn't they? all I want's the thing
260   Settled for ever one way. As it is,
You tell too many lies and hurt yourself:
You don't like what you only like too much,
You do like what, if given you at your word,
You find abundantly detestable.
265   For me, I think I speak as I was taught;
I always see the garden and God there
A-making man's wife: and, my lesson learned,
The value and significance of flesh,
I can't unlearn ten minutes afterwards.

270   You understand me: I'm a beast, I know.
But see, now—why, I see as certainly
As that the morning-star's about to shine,
What will hap some day. We've a youngster here
Comes to our convent, studies what I do,
275   Slouches and stares and lets no atom drop:
His name is Guidi—he'll not mind the monks—
They call him Hulking Tom, he lets them talk—
He picks my practice up—he'll paint apace.
I hope so—though I never live so long,
280   I know what's sure to follow. You be judge!
You speak no Latin more than I, belike;
However, you're my man, you've seen the world
—The beauty and the wonder and the power,
The shapes of things, their colours, lights and shades,
285   Changes, surprises,—and God made it all!
—For what? Do you feel thankful, ay or no,
For this fair town's face, yonder river's line,
The mountain round it and the sky above,

Much more the figures of man, woman, child,
290 These are the frame to? What's it all about?
To be passed over, despised? or dwelt upon,
Wondered at? oh, this last of course!—you say.
But why not do as well as say,—paint these
Just as they are, careless what comes of it?
295 God's works—paint any one, and count it crime
To let a truth slip. Don't object, "His works
Are here already; nature is complete:
Suppose you reproduce her—(which you can't)
There's no advantage! you must beat her, then."
300 For, don't you mark? we're made so that we love
First when we see them painted, things we have passed
Perhaps a hundred times nor cared to see;
And so they are better, painted—better to us,
Which is the same thing. Art was given for that;
305 God uses us to help each other so,
Lending our minds out. Have you noticed, now,
Your cullion's hanging face? A bit of chalk,
And trust me but you should, though! How much more,
If I drew higher things with the same truth!
310 That were to take the Prior's pulpit-place,
Interpret God to all of you! Oh, oh,
It makes me mad to see what men shall do
And we in our graves! This world's no blot for us,
Nor blank; it means intensely, and means good:
315 To find its meaning is my meat and drink.
"Ay, but you don't so instigate to prayer!"
Strikes in the Prior: "when your meaning's plain
It does not say to folk—remember matins,
Or, mind you fast next Friday!" Why, for this
320 What need of art at all? A skull and bones,
Two bits of stick nailed crosswise, or, what's best,
A bell to chime the hour with, does as well.
I painted a Saint Laurence six months since
At Prato, splashed the fresco in fine style:
325 "How looks my painting, now the scaffold's down?"

I ask a brother: "Hugely," he returns—
"Already not one phiz of your three slaves
Who turn the Deacon off his toasted side,
But's scratched and prodded to our heart's content,
330 The pious people have so eased their own
With coming to say prayers there in a rage:
We get on fast to see the bricks beneath.
Expect another job this time next year,
For pity and religion grow i' the crowd—
335 Your painting serves its purpose!" Hang the fools!

—That is—you'll not mistake an idle word
Spoke in a huff by a poor monk, God wot,
Tasting the air this spicy night which turns
The unaccustomed head like Chianti wine!
340 Oh, the church knows! don't misreport me, now!
It's natural a poor monk out of bounds
Should have his apt word to excuse himself:
And hearken how I plot to make amends.
I have bethought me: I shall paint a piece
345 . . . There's for you! Give me six months, then go, see
Something in Sant' Ambrogio's! Bless the nuns!
They want a cast o' my office. I shall paint
God in the midst, Madonna and her babe,
Ringed by a bowery, flowery angel-brood,
350 Lilies and vestments and white faces, sweet
As puff on puff of grated orris-root
When ladies crowd to Church at midsummer.
And then i' the front, of course a saint or two—
Saint John' because he saves the Florentines,
355 Saint Ambrose, who puts down in black and white
The convent's friends and gives them a long day,
And Job, I must have him there past mistake,
The man of Uz (and Us without the z,
Painters who need his patience). Well, all these
360 Secured at their devotion, up shall come
Out of a corner when you least expect,

As one by a dark stair into a great light,
Music and talking, who but Lippo! I!—
Mazed, motionless, and moonstruck—I'm the man!
365 Back I shrink—what is this I see and hear?
I, caught up with my monk's-things by mistake,
My old serge gown and rope that goes all round,
I, in this presence, this pure company!
Where's a hole, where's a corner for escape?
370 Then steps a sweet angelic slip of a thing
Forward, puts out a soft palm—"Not so fast!"
—Addresses the celestial presence, "nay—
He made you and devised you, after all,
Though he's none of you! Could Saint John there draw—
375 His camel-hair make up a painting brush?
We come to brother Lippo for all that,
Iste perfecit opus! So, all smile—
I shuffle sideways with my blushing face
Under the cover of a hundred wings
380 Thrown like a spread of kirtles when you're gay
And play hot cockles, all the doors being shut,
Till, wholly unexpected, in there pops
The hothead husband! Thus I scuttle off
To some safe bench behind, not letting go
385 The palm of her, the little lily thing
That spoke the good word for me in the nick,
Like the Prior's niece . . . Saint Lucy, I would say.
And so all's saved for me, and for the church
A pretty picture gained. Go, six months hence!
390 Your hand, sir, and good-bye: no lights, no lights!
The street's hushed, and I know my own way back,
Don't fear me! There's the grey beginning. Zooks!
Painters who need his patience). Well, all these
Secured at their devotion, up shall come
395 Out of a corner when you least expect,
As one by a dark stair into a great light,
Music and talking, who but Lippo! I!—
Mazed, motionless, and moonstruck—I'm the man!

Back I shrink—what is this I see and hear?
400 I, caught up with my monk's-things by mistake,
My old serge gown and rope that goes all round,
I, in this presence, this pure company!
Where's a hole, where's a corner for escape?
Then steps a sweet angelic slip of a thing
405 Forward, puts out a soft palm—"Not so fast!"
—Addresses the celestial presence, "nay—
He made you and devised you, after all,
Though he's none of you! Could Saint John there draw—
His camel-hair make up a painting brush?
410 We come to brother Lippo for all that,
Iste perfecit opus! So, all smile—
I shuffle sideways with my blushing face
Under the cover of a hundred wings
Thrown like a spread of kirtles when you're gay
415 And play hot cockles, all the doors being shut,
Till, wholly unexpected, in there pops
The hothead husband! Thus I scuttle off
To some safe bench behind, not letting go
The palm of her, the little lily thing
420 That spoke the good word for me in the nick,
Like the Prior's niece . . . Saint Lucy, I would say.
And so all's saved for me, and for the church
A pretty picture gained. Go, six months hence!
Your hand, sir, and good-bye: no lights, no lights!
425 The street's hushed, and I know my own way back,
Don't fear me! There's the grey beginning. Zooks!

EMILY BRONTË (1818–1848)

Emily Brontë, best known for her novel *Wuthering Heights* (1847), was one of a trio of sisters who became famous Victorian authors. (Charlotte wrote the enduringly famous *Jane Eyre*, and several other novels, while Anne is best remembered for *The Tenant of Wildfell Hall*.) But before they were novelists, Charlotte, Anne, and Emily were poets, who published their work in a single volume in 1846, using the masculine-sounding pseudonyms of Currer, Acton, and Ellis Bell. Ellis's (Emily's) poems were the best reviewed, and continue to be the ones recognized for their unsentimental emotional intensity.

Brontë's life was full of family illnesses and death. When she was only three, her mother died. Her older sisters, Maria and Elizabeth, developed typhoid fever (or tuberculosis) while away at boarding school and died soon after, in 1825. In 1842, the aunt who had become a second mother to the children also passed away. Brother Branwell, a talented painter and writer but also an alcoholic and opium addict, died in 1848. Emily herself became ill with tuberculosis and followed her brother the same year. Anne's death followed a few months after Emily's, in 1849; Charlotte continued to write but also died young, in 1855, at the age of thirty-eight.

REMEMBRANCE

Emily Brontë

1   Cold in the earth—and the deep snow piled above thee,
Far, far removed, cold in the dreary grave!
Have I forgot, my only Love, to love thee,
Severed at last by Time's all-severing wave?

5   Now, when alone, do my thoughts no longer hover
Over the mountains, on that northern shore,
Resting their wings where heath and fern-leaves cover
Thy noble heart forever, ever more?

Cold in the earth—and fifteen wild Decembers,
10   From those brown hills, have melted into spring:
Faithful, indeed, is the spirit that remembers
After such years of change and suffering!

Sweet Love of youth, forgive, if I forget thee,
While the world's tide is bearing me along;
15   Other desires and other hopes beset me,
Hopes which obscure, but cannot do thee wrong!

No later light has lightened up my heaven,
No second morn has ever shone for me;
All my life's bliss from thy dear life was given,
20   All my life's bliss is in the grave with thee.

But, when the days of golden dreams had perished,
And even Despair was powerless to destroy,
Then did I learn how existence could be cherished,
Strengthened, and fed without the aid of joy.

25   Then did I check the tears of useless passion—
Weaned my young soul from yearning after thine;

Sternly denied its burning wish to hasten
Down to that tomb already more than mine.

And, even yet, I dare not let it languish,
30   Dare not indulge in memory's rapturous pain;
Once drinking deep of that divinest anguish,
How could I seek the empty world again?

SONG

Emily Brontë

1   The linnet in the rocky dells,
The moor-lark in the air,
The bee among the heather bells
That hide my lady fair:

5   The wild deer browse above her breast;
The wild birds raise their brood;
And they, her smiles of love caressed,
Have left her solitude!

I ween, that when the grave's dark wall
10   Did first her form retain,
They thought their hearts could ne'er recall
The light of joy again.

They thought the tide of grief would flow
Unchecked through future years;
15   But where is all their anguish now,
And where are all their tears?

Well, let them fight for honour's breath,
Or pleasure's shade pursue—
The dweller in the land of death
20   Is changed and careless too.

And, if their eyes should watch and weep
Till sorrow's source were dry,
She would not, in her tranquil sleep,
Return a single sigh!

25   Blow, west-wind, by the lonely mound,
And murmur, summer-streams—
There is no need of other sound
To soothe my lady's dreams.

THE PRISONER

Emily Brontë

1   In the dungeon-crypts idly did I stray,
Reckless of the lives wasting there away;
"Draw the ponderous bars! open, Warder stern!"
He dared not say me nay--the hinges harshly turn.

5   "Our guests are darkly lodged," I whisper'd, gazing through
The vault, whose grated eye showed heaven more gray than blue;
(This was when glad Spring laughed in awaking pride;)
"Ay, darkly lodged enough!" returned my sullen guide.

Then, God forgive my youth; forgive my careless tongue;
10   I scoffed, as the chill chains on the damp flagstones rung:
"Confined in triple walls, art thou so much to fear,
That we must bind thee down and clench thy fetters here?"

The captive raised her face; it was as soft and mild
As sculptured marble saint, or slumbering unwean'd child;
15   It was so soft and mild, it was so sweet and fair,
Pain could not trace a line, nor grief a shadow there!

The captive raised her hand and pressed it to her brow;
"I have been struck," she said, "and I am suffering now;
Yet these are little worth, your bolts and irons strong;
20   And, were they forged in steel, they could not hold me long."

Hoarse laughed the jailor grim: "Shall I be won to hear;
Dost think, fond, dreaming wretch, that I shall grant thy prayer?
Or, better still, wilt melt my master's heart with groans?
Ah! sooner might the sun thaw down these granite stones.

25   "My master's voice is low, his aspect bland and kind,
But hard as hardest flint the soul that lurks behind;
And I am rough and rude, yet not more rough to see
Than is the hidden ghost that has its home in me."

About her lips there played a smile of almost scorn,
30   "My friend," she gently said, "you have not heard me mourn;
When you my kindred's lives, MY lost life, can restore,
Then may I weep and sue,--but never, friend, before!

"Still, let my tyrants know, I am not doomed to wear
Year after year in gloom, and desolate despair;
35   A messenger of Hope comes every night to me,
And offers for short life, eternal liberty.

"He comes with western winds, with evening's wandering airs,
With that clear dusk of heaven that brings the thickest stars.
Winds take a pensive tone, and stars a tender fire,
40   And visions rise, and change, that kill me with desire.

"Desire for nothing known in my maturer years,
When Joy grew mad with awe, at counting future tears.
When, if my spirit's sky was full of flashes warm,
I knew not whence they came, from sun or thunder-storm.

45   "But, first, a hush of peace--a soundless calm descends;
The struggle of distress, and fierce impatience ends;
Mute music soothes my breast--unuttered harmony,
That I could never dream, till Earth was lost to me.

"Then dawns the Invisible; the Unseen its truth reveals;
50   My outward sense is gone, my inward essence feels:
Its wings are almost free--its home, its harbour found,
Measuring the gulph, it stoops and dares the final bound,

"Oh I dreadful is the check--intense the agony--
When the ear begins to hear, and the eye begins to see;
55   When the pulse begins to throb, the brain to think again;
The soul to feel the flesh, and the flesh to feel the chain.

"Yet I would lose no sting, would wish no torture less;
The more that anguish racks, the earlier it will bless;
And robed in fires of hell, or bright with heavenly shine,
60   If it but herald death, the vision is divine!"

She ceased to speak, and we, unanswering, turned to go--
We had no further power to work the captive woe:
Her cheek, her gleaming eye, declared that man had given
A sentence, unapproved, and overruled by Heaven.

THE OLD STOIC

Emily Brontë

1   Riches I hold in light esteem,
      And Love I laugh to scorn;
And lust of fame was but a dream,
      That vanished with the morn:

5   And if I pray, the only prayer
      That moves my lips for me
Is, "Leave the heart that now I bear,
      And give me liberty!"

    Yes, as my swift days near their goal:
10   'Tis all that I implore;
In life and death a chainless soul,
      With courage to endure.

HOPE

Emily Brontë

1   Hope was but a timid friend;
    She sat without the grated den,
    Watching how my fate would tend,
    Even as selfish-hearted men.

5   She was cruel in her fear;
    Through the bars one dreary day,
    I looked out to see her there,
    And she turned her face away!

    Like a false guard, false watch keeping,
10   Still, in strife, she whispered peace;
    She would sing while I was weeping;
    If I listened, she would cease.

    False she was, and unrelenting;
    When my last joys strewed the ground,
15   Even Sorrow saw, repenting,
    Those sad relics scattered round;

    Hope, whose whisper would have given
    Balm to all my frenzied pain,
    Stretched her wings, and soared to heaven,
20   Went, and ne'er returned again!

HOW CLEAR SHE SHINES

Emily Brontë

1   How clear she shines ! How quietly
     I lie beneath her guardian light;
    While heaven and earth are whispering me,
     " To morrow, wake, but, dream to-night."
5   Yes, Fancy, come, my Fairy love !
     These throbbing temples softly kiss;
    And bend my lonely couch above
     And bring me rest, and bring me bliss.

    The world is going; dark world, adieu !
10   Grim world, conceal thee till the day;
    The heart, thou canst not all subdue,
     Must still resist, if thou delay !

    Thy love I will not, will not share;
     Thy hatred only wakes a smile;
15   Thy griefs may wound–thy wrongs may tear,
     But, oh, thy lies shall ne'er beguile !
    While gazing on the stars that glow
     Above me, in that stormless sea,
    I long to hope that all the woe
20   Creation knows, is held in thee !

    And, this shall be my dream to-night;
     I'll think the heaven of glorious spheres
    Is rolling on its course of light
     In endless bliss, through endless years;
25   I'll think, there's not one world above,
     Far as these straining eyes can see,
    Where Wisdom ever laughed at Love,
     Or Virtue crouched to Infamy;

Where, writhing 'neath the strokes of Fate,
30   The mangled wretch was forced to smile;
To match his patience 'gainst her hate,
    His heart rebellious all the while.
Where Pleasure still will lead to wrong,
    And helpless Reason warn in vain;
35   And Truth is weak, and Treachery strong;
    And Joy the surest path to Pain;
And Peace, the lethargy of Grief;
    And Hope, a phantom of the soul;
And Life, a labour, void and brief;
40   And Death, the despot of the whole !

THE NIGHT-WIND

Emily Brontë

1   In summer's mellow midnight,
       A cloudless moon shone through
       Our open parlour window,
       And rose-trees wet with dew.

5   I sat in silent musing;
       The soft wind waved my hair;
       It told me heaven was glorious,
       And sleeping earth was fair.

       I needed not its breathing
10   To bring such thoughts to me;
       But still it whispered lowly,
       How dark the woods will be!

       "The thick leaves in my murmur
       Are rustling like a dream,
15   And all their myriad voices
       Instinct with spirit seem."

       I said, "Go, gentle singer,
       Thy wooing voice is kind:
       But do not think its music
20   Has power to reach my mind.

       "Play with the scented flower,
       The young tree's supple bough,
       And leave my human feelings
       In their own course to flow."

25   The wanderer would not heed me;
       Its kiss grew warmer still.
       "O come!" it sighed so sweetly;
       "I'll win thee 'gainst thy will.

"Were we not friends from childhood?
30   Have I not loved thee long?
As long as thou, the solemn night,
Whose silence wakes my song.

"And when thy heart is resting
Beneath the church-aisle stone,
35   I shall have time for mourning,
And THOU for being alone."

NO COWARD SOUL IS MINE

Emily Brontë

1   No coward soul is mine
No trembler in the world's storm-troubled sphere
I see Heaven's glories shine
And Faith shines equal arming me from Fear

5   O God within my breast
Almighty ever-present Deity
Life, that in me hast rest,
As I Undying Life, have power in Thee

Vain are the thousand creeds
10   That move men's hearts, unutterably vain,
Worthless as withered weeds
Or idlest froth amid the boundless main

To waken doubt in one
Holding so fast by thy infinity,
15   So surely anchored on
The steadfast rock of Immortality.

With wide-embracing love
Thy spirit animates eternal years
Pervades and broods above,
20   Changes, sustains, dissolves, creates and rears

Though earth and moon were gone
And suns and universes ceased to be
And Thou wert left alone
Every Existence would exist in thee

25   There is not room for Death
Nor atom that his might could render void
Since thou art Being and Breath
And what thou art may never be destroyed.

AH! WHY, BECAUSE THE DAZZLING SUN

Emily Brontë

1   Ah! why, because the dazzling sun
Restored my earth to joy
Have you departed, every one,
And left a desert sky?

5   All through the night, your glorious eyes
Were gazing down in mine,
And with a full heart's thankful sighs
I blessed that watch divine!

I was at peace, and drank your beams
10   As they were life to me
And revelled in my changeful dreams
Like petrel on the sea.

Thought followed thought—star followed star
Through boundless regions on,
15   While one sweet influence, near and far,
Thrilled through and proved us one.

Why did the morning rise to break
So great, so pure a spell,
And scorch with fire the tranquil cheek
20   Where your cool radiance fell?

Blood-red he rose, and arrow-straight,
His fierce beams struck my brow;
The soul of Nature sprang elate,
But mine sank sad and low!

25   My lids closed down—yet through their veil
I saw him blazing still;
And bathe in gold the misty dale,
And flash upon the hill.

I turned me to the pillow then
30   To call back Night, and see
Your worlds of solemn light, again
Throb with my heart and me!

It would not do—the pillow glowed
And glowed both roof and floor,
35   And birds sang loudly in the wood,
And fresh winds shook the door.

The curtains waved, the wakened flies
Were murmuring round my room,
Imprisoned there, till I should rise
And give them leave to roam.
40

O Stars and Dreams and Gentle Night;
O Night and Stars return!
And hide me from the hostile light
That does not warm, but burn—

45

That drains the blood of suffering men;
Drinks tears, instead of dew:
Let me sleep through his blinding reign,
And only wake with you!

FALL, LEAVES, FALL

Emily Brontë

1   Fall, leaves, fall; die, flowers, away;
Lengthen night and shorten day;
Every leaf speaks bliss to me
Fluttering from the autumn tree.
5   I shall smile when wreaths of snow
Blossom where the rose should grow;
I shall sing when night's decay
Ushers in a drearier day.

I AM THE ONLY BEING WHOSE DOOM

Emily Brontë

1   I am the only being whose doom
No tongue would ask, no eye would mourn;
I never caused a thought of gloom,
A smile of joy, since I was born.

5   In secret pleasure, secret tears,
This changeful life has slipped away,
As friendless after eighteen years,
As lone as on my natal day.

There have been times I cannot hide,
10   There have been times when this was drear,
When my sad soul forgot its pride
And longed for one to love me here.

But those were in the early glow
Of feelings since subdued by care;
15   And they have died so long ago,
I hardly now believe they were.

First melted off the hope of youth,
Then fancy's rainbow fast withdrew;
And then experience told me truth
20   In mortal bosoms never grew.

'Twas grief enough to think mankind
All hollow, servile, insincere;
But worse to trust to my own mind
And find the same corruption there

LONG NEGLECT HAS WORN AWAY

Emily Brontë

1   Long neglect has worn away
     Half the sweet enchanting smile;
     Time has turned the bloom to gray;
     Mold and damp the face defile.

5   But that lock of silky hair,
     Still beneath the picture twined,
     Tells what once those features were,
     Paints their image on the mind.

     Fair the hand that traced that line,
10   "Dearest, ever deem me true";
     Swiftly flew the fingers fine
     When the pen that motto drew.

LOVE AND FRIENDSHIP

Emily Brontë

1   Love is like the wild rose-briar,
Friendship like the holly-tree—
The holly is dark when the rose-briar blooms
But which will bloom most constantly?

5   The wild rose-briar is sweet in spring,
Its summer blossoms scent the air;
Yet wait till winter comes again
And who will call the wild-briar fair?

Then scorn the silly rose-wreath now
10   And deck thee with the holly's sheen,
That when December blights thy brow
He still may leave thy garland green.

THE NIGHT IS DARKENING ROUND ME

Emily Brontë

1 The night is darkening round me,
The wild winds coldly blow;
But a tyrant spell has bound me,
And I cannot, cannot go.

5 The giant trees are bending
Their bare boughs weighed with snow;
The storm is fast descending,
And yet I cannot go.

Clouds beyond clouds above me,
10 Wastes beyond wastes below;
But nothing drear can move me;
I will not, cannot go.

OFTEN REBUKED, YET ALWAYS BACK RETURNING

Emily Brontë

1 Often rebuked, yet always back returning
  To those first feelings that were born with me,
 And leaving busy chase of wealth and learning
  For idle dreams of things which cannot be:

5 To-day, I will seek not the shadowy region;
  Its unsustaining vastness waxes drear;
 And visions rising, legion after legion,
  Bring the unreal world too strangely near.

 I'll walk, but not in old heroic traces,
10 And not in paths of high morality,
 And not among the half-distinguished faces,
  The clouded forms of long-past history.

 I'll walk where my own nature would be leading:
  It vexes me to choose another guide:
15 Where the gray flocks in ferny glens are feeding;
  Where the wild wind blows on the mountain side.

 What have those lonely mountains worth revealing?
  More glory and more grief than I can tell:
 The earth that wakes one human heart to feeling
20 Can centre both the worlds of Heaven and Hell.

PLEAD FOR ME

Emily Brontë

1   O thy bright eyes must answer now,
When Reason, with a scornful brow,
Is mocking at my overthrow;
O thy sweet tongue must plead for me
5   And tell why I have chosen thee!

Stern Reason is to judgment come
Arrayed in all her forms of gloom:
Wilt thou my advocate be dumb?
No, radiant angel, speak and say
10   Why I did cast the world away;

Why I have persevered to shun
The common paths that others run;
And on a strange road journeyed on
Heedless alike of Wealth and Power—
15   Of Glory's wreath and Pleasure's flower.

These once indeed seemed Beings divine,
And they perchance heard vows of mine
And saw my offerings on their shrine—
But, careless gifts are seldom prized,
20   And mine were worthily despised;

So with a ready heart I swore
To seek their altar-stone no more,
And gave my spirit to adore
Thee, ever present, phantom thing—
25   My slave, my comrade, and my King!

A slave because I rule thee still;
Incline thee to my changeful will

And make thy influence good or ill—
A comrade, for by day and night
30 Thou art my intimate delight—

My Darling Pain that wounds and sears
And wrings a blessing out from tears
By deadening me to real cares;
And yet, a king—though prudence well
35 Have taught thy subject to rebel.

And am I wrong to worship where
Faith cannot doubt nor Hope despair,
Since my own soul can grant my prayer?
Speak, God of Visions, plead for me
40 And tell why I have chosen thee!

SHALL EARTH NO MORE INSPIRE THEE

Emily Brontë

1 Shall earth no more inspire thee,
  Thou lonely dreamer now?
  Since passion may not fire thee
  Shall Nature cease to bow?

5 Thy mind is ever moving
  In regions dark to thee;
  Recall its useless roving—
  Come back and dwell with me.

  I know my mountain breezes
10 Enchant and soothe thee still—
  I know my sunshine pleases
  Despite thy wayward will.

  When day with evening blending
  Sinks from the summer sky,
15 I've seen thy spirit bending
  In fond idolatry.

  I've watched thee every hour;
  I know my mighty sway,
  I know my magic power
20 To drive thy griefs away.

  Few hearts to mortals given
  On earth so wildly pine;
  Yet none would ask a heaven
  More like this earth than thine.

25 Then let my winds caress thee;
  Thy comrade let me be—
  Since nought beside can bless thee,
  Return and dwell with me.

STANZAS

Emily Brontë

1   I'll not weep that thou art going to leave me,
There's nothing lovely here;
And doubly will the dark world grieve me,
While thy heart suffers there.

5   I'll not weep, because the summer's glory
Must always end in gloom;
And, follow out the happiest story—
It closes with a tomb!

And I am weary of the anguish
10   Increasing winters bear;
Weary to watch the spirit languish
Through years of dead despair.

So, if a tear, when thou art dying,
Should haply fall from me,
15   It is but that my soul is sighing,
To go and rest with thee.

THE TWO CHILDREN

Emily Brontë

1   Heavy hangs the raindrop
    From the burdened spray;
    Heavy broods the damp mist
    On uplands far away;

5   Heavy looms the dull sky,
    Heavy rolls the sea—
    And heavy beats the young heart
    Beneath that lonely tree.

    Never has a blue streak
10   Cleft the clouds since morn—
    Never has his grim Fate
    Smiled since he was born.

    Frowning on the infant,
    Shadowing childhood's joy,
15   Guardian angel knows not
    That melancholy boy.

    Day is passing swiftly
    Its sad and sombre prime;
    Youth is fast invading
20   Sterner manhood's time.

    All the flowers are praying
    For sun before they close,
    And he prays too, unknowing,
    That sunless human rose!

25   Blossoms, that the west wind
    Has never wooed to blow,
    Scentless are your petals,
    Your dew as cold as snow.

Soul, where kindred kindness
30   No early promise woke,
Barren is your beauty
As weed upon the rock.

Wither, Brothers, wither,
You were vainly given—
35   Earth reserves no blessing
For the unblessed of Heaven!

Child of Delight! with sunbright hair,
And seablue, seadeep eyes;
Spirit of Bliss, what brings thee here,
40   Beneath these sullen skies?

Thou shouldst live in eternal spring,
Where endless day is never dim;
Why, seraph, has thy erring wing
Borne thee down to weep with him?

45   "Ah, not from heaven am I descended,
And I do not come to mingle tears;
But sweet is day, though with shadows blended;
And, though clouded, sweet are youthful years.

"I, the image of light and gladness,
50   Saw and pitied that mournful boy,
And I swore to take his gloomy sadness,
And give to him my beamy joy.

"Heavy and dark the night is closing;
Heavy and dark may its biding be:
Better for all from grief reposing,
55   And better for all who watch like me.

"Guardian angel, he lacks no longer;
Evil fortune he need not fear:
Fate is strong, but Love is stronger;
And more unsleeping than angel's care."

GEORGE ELIOT (1819-1880)

George Eliot was the pseudonym of Mary Ann Evans—the name under which all her fiction and poetry was published and the name by which she continues to be known. Although she was far more famous for her novels, especially *Adam Bede, The Mill on the Floss, Silas Marner, and Middlemarch,* Eliot also considered herself a serious poet. For example, a less-known drama Eliot wrote, The *Spanish Gypsy*, shows her mastery of Shakespearean iambic pentameter. George Eliot's poetry has attracted increasing critical attention in the twenty-first century. Eliot's poetry and novels present a moral message; they consistently advocate thoughtful self-discipline and sympathy towards fellow human beings, especially the less fortunate and the social outcasts. Because George Eliot chose to live with her already-married lover, George Henry Lewes, she suffered the loss of family ties, many old friends, and— before her novels made her famous—her social respectability. Considered a second Shakespeare by contemporary admirers, Eliot became the most popular, critically acclaimed, and highest-paid Victorian female author.

I GRANT YOU AMPLE LEAVE

George Eliot

1   "I grant you ample leave
To use the hoary formula 'I am'
Naming the emptiness where thought is not;
But fill the void with definition, 'I'
5   Will be no more a datum than the words
You link false inference with, the 'Since' & 'so'
That, true or not, make up the atom-whirl.
Resolve your 'Ego', it is all one web
With vibrant ether clotted into worlds:
10   Your subject, self, or self-assertive 'I'
Turns nought but object, melts to molecules,
Is stripped from naked Being with the rest
Of those rag-garments named the Universe.
Or if, in strife to keep your 'Ego' strong
15   You make it weaver of the etherial light,
Space, motion, solids & the dream of Time —
Why, still 'tis Being looking from the dark,
The core, the centre of your consciousness,
That notes your bubble-world: sense, pleasure, pain,
20   What are they but a shifting otherness,
Phantasmal flux of moments? —"

IN A LONDON DRAWINGROOM

George Eliot

1   The sky is cloudy, yellowed by the smoke.
For view there are the houses opposite
Cutting the sky with one long line of wall
Like solid fog: far as the eye can stretch
5   Monotony of surface & of form
Without a break to hang a guess upon.
No bird can make a shadow as it flies,
For all is shadow, as in ways o'erhung
By thickest canvass, where the golden rays
10   Are clothed in hemp. No figure lingering
Pauses to feed the hunger of the eye
Or rest a little on the lap of life.
All hurry on & look upon the ground,
Or glance unmarking at the passers by
15   The wheels are hurrying too, cabs, carriages
All closed, in multiplied identity.
The world seems one huge prison-house & court
Where men are punished at the slightest cost,
With lowest rate of colour, warmth & joy.

COUNT THAT DAY LOST

George Eliot

1 If you sit down at set of sun
  And count the acts that you have done,
  And, counting, find
  One self-denying deed, one word
5 That eased the heart of him who heard,
  One glance most kind
  That fell like sunshine where it went—
  Then you may count that day well spent.

  But if, through all the livelong day,
10 You've cheered no heart, by yea or nay—
  If, through it all
  You've nothing done that you can trace
  That brought the sunshine to one face—
  No act most small
15 That helped some soul and nothing cost—
  Then count that day as worse than lost.

BROTHER AND SISTER

George Eliot

I.

1   I cannot choose but think upon the time
When our two lives grew like two buds that kiss
At lightest thrill from the bee's swinging chime,
Because the one so near the other is.

5   He was the elder and a little man
Of forty inches, bound to show no dread,
And I the girl that puppy-like now ran,
Now lagged behind my brother's larger tread.

I held him wise, and when he talked to me
10   Of snakes and birds, and which God loved the best,
I thought his knowledge marked the boundary
Where men grew blind, though angels knew the rest.

If he said "Hush!" I tried to hold my breath;
Wherever he said "Come!" I stepped in faith.

II.

15   Long years have left their writing on my brow,
But yet the freshness and the dew-fed beam
Of those young mornings are about me now,
When we two wandered toward the far-off stream

With rod and line. Our basket held a store
20   Baked for us only, and I thought with joy
That I should have my share, though he had more,
Because he was the elder and a boy.

The firmaments of daisies since to me
Have had those mornings in their opening eyes,

25 The bunchèd cowslip's pale transparency
    Carries that sunshine of sweet memories,

    And wild-rose branches take their finest scent
    From those blest hours of infantine content.

III.
    Our mother bade us keep the trodden ways,
30 Stroked down my tippet, set my brother's frill,
    Then with the benediction of her gaze
    Clung to us lessening, and pursued us still

    Across the homestead to the rookery elms,
    Whose tall old trunks had each a grassy mound,
35 So rich for us, we counted them as realms
    With varied products: here were earth-nuts found,

    And here the Lady-fingers in deep shade;
    Here sloping toward the Moat the rushes grew,
    The large to split for pith, the small to braid;
40 While over all the dark rooks cawing flew,

    And made a happy strange solemnity,
    A deep-toned chant from life unknown to me.

IV.
    Our meadow-path had memorable spots:
    One where it bridged a tiny rivulet,
45 Deep hid by tangled blue Forget-me-nots;
    And all along the waving grasses met

    My little palm, or nodded to my cheek,
    When flowers with upturned faces gazing drew
    My wonder downward, seeming all to speak
50 With eyes of souls that dumbly heard and knew.

Then came the copse, where wild things rushed unseen,
And black-scathed grass betrayed the past abode
Of mystic gypsies, who still lurked between
Me and each hidden distance of the road.

55   A gypsy once had startled me at play,
Blotting with her dark smile my sunny day.

V.

Thus rambling we were schooled in deepest lore,
And learned the meanings that give words a soul,
The fear, the love, the primal passionate store,
60   Whose shaping impulses make manhood whole.

Those hours were seed to all my after good;
My infant gladness, through eye, ear, and touch,
Took easily as warmth a various food
To nourish the sweet skill of loving much.

65   For who in age shall roam the earth and find
Reasons for loving that will strike out love
With sudden rod from the hard year-pressed mind?
Were reasons sown as thick as stars above,

"'Tis love must see them, as the eye sees light:
70   Day is but Number to the darkened sight."

VI.

Our brown canal was endless to my thought;
And on its banks I sat in dreamy peace,
Unknowing how the good I loved was wrought,
Untroubled by the fear that it would cease.

75   Slowly the barges floated into view
Rounding a grassy hill to me sublime
With some Unknown beyond it, whither flew
The parting cuckoo toward a fresh spring time.

The wide-arched bridge, the scented elder-flowers,
80   The wondrous watery rings that died too soon,
The echoes of the quarry, the still hours
With white robe sweeping-on the shadeless noon,

Were but my growing self, are part of me,
My present Past, my root of piety.

VII.

85   Those long days measured by my little feet
Had chronicles which yield me many a text;
Where irony still finds an image meet
Of full-grown judgments in this world perplext.

One day my brother left me in high charge,
90   To mind the rod, while he went seeking bait,
And bade me, when I saw a nearing barge,
Snatch out the line lest he should come too late.

Proud of the task, I watched with all my might
For one whole minute, till my eyes grew wide,
95   Till sky and earth took on a strange new light
And seemed a dream-world floating on some tide--

A fair pavilioned boat for me alone
Bearing me onward through the vast unknown.

VIII.

But sudden came the barge's pitch-black prow,
100   Nearer and angrier came my brother's cry,
And all my soul was quivering fear, when lo!
Upon the imperilled line, suspended high,

A silver perch! My guilt that won the prey,
Now turned to merit, had a guerdon rich
105   Of songs and praises, and made merry play,

Until my triumph reached its highest pitch

When all at home were told the wondrous feat,
And how the little sister had fished well.
In secret, though my fortune tasted sweet,
110   I wondered why this happiness befell.

"The little lass had luck," the gardener said:
And so I learned, luck was with glory wed.

IX.
We had the self-same world enlarged for each
By loving difference of girl and boy:
115   The fruit that hung on high beyond my reach
He plucked for me, and oft he must employ

A measuring glance to guide my tiny shoe
Where lay firm stepping-stones, or call to mind
"This thing I like my sister may not do,
120   For she is little, and I must be kind."

Thus boyish Will the nobler mastery learned
Where inward vision over impulse reigns,
Widening its life with separate life discerned,
A Like unlike, a Self that self restrains.

125   His years with others must the sweeter be
For those brief days he spent in loving me.

X.
His sorrow was my sorrow, and his joy
Sent little leaps and laughs through all my frame;
My doll seemed lifeless and no girlish toy
130   Had any reason when my brother came.

I knelt with him at marbles, marked his fling
Cut the ringed stem and make the apple drop,

Or watched him winding close the spiral string
That looped the orbits of the humming top.

135 Grasped by such fellowship my vagrant thought
Ceased with dream-fruit dream-wishes to fulfil;
My aëry-picturing fantasy was taught
Subjection to the harder, truer skill

That seeks with deeds to grave a thought-tracked line,
140 And by "What is," "What will be" to define.

XI.
School parted us; we never found again
That childish world where our two spirits mingled
Like scents from varying roses that remain
One sweetness, nor can evermore be singled.

145 Yet the twin habit of that early time
Lingered for long about the heart and tongue:
We had been natives of one happy clime
And its dear accent to our utterance clung.

Till the dire years whose awful name is Change
150 Had grasped our souls still yearning in divorce,
And pitiless shaped them in two forms that range
Two elements which sever their life's course.

But were another childhood-world my share,
I would be born a little sister there."

STRADIVARIUS

George Eliot

<pre>
 1   Your soul was lifted by the wings today
      Hearing the master of the violin:
      You praised him, praised the great Sabastian too
      Who made that fine Chaconne; but did you think
 5   Of old Antonio Stradivari?--him
      Who a good century and a half ago
      Put his true work in that brown instrument
      And by the nice adjustment of its frame
      Gave it responsive life, continuous
10   With the master's finger-tips and perfected
      Like them by delicate rectitude of use.
      Not Bach alone, helped by fine precedent
      Of genius along before, nor Joachim
      Who holds the strain afresh incorporate
15   By inward hearing and notation strict
      Of nerve and muscle, made our joy to-day:
      Another soul was living in the air
      And swaying it to tru deliverance
      Of high invention and responsive skill:—
      That plain white-aproned man, who stood at work
20   Patient and accurate full fourscore years,
      Cherished his sight and touch by temperance,
      And since keen sense is love of perfectness
      Made perfect violins, the needed paths
      For inspiration and high mastery.

25   No simpler man than he; he never cried,
      "Why was I born to this monotonous task
      Of making violins?" or flung them down
      To suit with hurling act well-hurled curse
      At labor on such perishable stuff.
30   Hence neighbors in Cremona held him dull,
</pre>

Called him a slave, a mill-horse, a machine,
Begged hom to tell his motives or to lend
A few gold pieces to a loftier mind.
Yet he had pithy words full fed by fact;
35 For fact, well-trusted, reasons and persuades,
Is gnomic, cutting, or ironical,
Draws tears, or is a tocsin to arouse—
Can hold all figures of the orator
In one plain sentence; has her pause too—
Eloquent silence at the chasm abrupt
40 Where knowledge ceases. Thus Antonio
Made answers as Fact willed, and made them strong

Naldo, a painter of eclectic school,
Knowing all tricks of style at thirty-one,
45 And weary of them, while Antonio
At sixty-nine wrought placidly his best,
Making the violin you heard today—
Naldo would tease him oft to tell his aims.
"Perhaps thou hast some pleasant vice to feed-
The love of louis d'ors in heaps of four,
50 Each violin a heap—I've naught to blame;
My vices waste such heaps. But then, why work
With painful nicety?"

Antonio then:
55 "I like the gold—well, yes—but not for meals.
And as my stomach, so my eye and hand,
And inward sense that works along with both,
Have hunger that can never feed on coin.
Who draws a line and satisfies his soul,
Making it crooked where it should be straight?
60 Antonio Stradivari has an eye
That winces at false work and loves the true."
Then Naldo: "'Tis a petty kind of fame
At best, that comes of making violins;
And saves no masses, either. Thou wilt go

To purgatory none the less."

But he:
65 "'Twere purgatory here to make them ill;
And for my fame—when any master holds
'Twixt chin and hand a violin of mine,
He will be glad that Stradivari lived,
Made violins, and made them of the best.
70 The masters only know whose work is good:
They will choose mine, and while God gives them skill
I give them instruments to play upon,
God choosing me to help him.

"What! Were God
75 at fault for violins, thou absent?"

"Yes;
He were at fault for Stradivari's work."

80 "Why, many hold Giuseppe's violins
As good as thine."

"May be: they are different.
His quality declines: he spoils his hand
85 With over-drinking. But were his the best,
He could not work for two. My work is mine,
And, heresy or not, if my hand slacked
I should rob God—since his is fullest good—
Leaving a blank instead of violins.
90 I say, not God himself can make man's best
Without best men to help him.

'Tis God gives skill,
But not without men's hands: he could not make
95 Antonio Stradivari's violins
Without Antonio. Get thee to thy easel."

TWO LOVERS

George Eliot

1 Two lovers by a moss-grown spring:
 They leaned soft cheeks together there,
 Mingled the dark and sunny hair,
 And heard the wooing thrushes sing.
5 O budding time!
 O love's blest prime!

 Two wedded from the portal stept:
 The bells made happy carolings,
 The air was soft as fanning wings,
10 White petals on the pathway slept.
 O pure-eyed bride!
 O tender pride!

 Two faces o'er a cradle bent:
 Two hands above the head were locked:
15 These pressed each other while they rocked,
 Those watched a life that love had sent.
 O solemn hour!
 O hidden power!

 Two parents by the evening fire:
20 The red light fell about their knees
 On heads that rose by slow degrees
 Like buds upon the lily spire.
 O patient life!
 O tender strife!

25 The two still sat together there,
 The red light shone about their knees;
 But all the heads by slow degrees
 Had gone and left that lonely pair.

O voyage fast!
30   O vanished past!

The red light shone upon the floor
And made the space between them wide;
They drew their chairs up side by side,
Their pale cheeks joined, and said, "Once more!"
35   O memories!
O past that is!

ARION

George Eliot

1   Arion, whose melodic soul
Taught the dithyramb to roll
Like forest fires, and sing
Olympian suffering,
5   Had carried his diviner lore
From Corinth to the sister shore
Where Greece could largelier be,
Branching o'er Italy.
Then weighted with his glorious name
10   And bags of gold, aboard he came
'Mid harsh seafaring men
To Corinth bound again.
The sailors eyed the bags and thought:
"The gold is good, the man is nought —
15   And who shall track the wave
That opens for his grave?"
With brawny arms and cruel eyes
They press around him where he lies
In sleep beside his lyre,

20 Hearing the Muses quire.
He waked and saw this wolf-faced Death
Breaking the dream that filled his breath
With inspiration strong
Of yet unchanted song.

25 "Take, take my gold and let me live!"
He prayed, as kings do when they give
Their all with royal will,
Holding born kingship still.
To rob the living they refuse,

30 One death or other he must choose,
Either the watery pall
Or wounds and burial.
"My solemn robe then let me don,
Give me high space to stand upon,

35 That dying I may pour
A song unsung before."
It pleased them well to grant this prayer,
To hear for nought how it might fare
With men who paid their gold

40 For what a poet sold.
In flowing stole, his eyes aglow
With inward fire, he neared the prow
And took his god-like stand,
The cithara in hand.

45 The wolfish men all shrank aloof,
And feared this singer might be proof
Against their murderous power,
After his lyric hour.
But he, in liberty of song,

50 Fearless of death or other wrong,
With full spondaic toll
Poured forth his mighty soul:
Poured forth the strain his dream had taught,
A nome with lofty passion fraught

55 Such as makes battles won
On fields of Marathon.

The last long vowels trembled then
As awe within those wolfish men:
They said, with mutual stare,
60   Some god was present there.
But lo! Arion leaped on high
Ready, his descant done, to die;
Not asking, " Is it well? "
Like a pierced eagle fell.

O MAY I JOIN THE CHOIR INVISIBLE

George Eliot

1   O May I join the choir invisible
Of those immortal dead who live again
In minds made better by their presence: live
In pulses stirr'd to generosity,
5   In deeds of daring rectitude, in scorn
For miserable aims that end with self,
In thoughts sublime that pierce the night like stars,
And with their mild persistence urge man's search
To vaster issues.
10   So to live is heaven:
To make undying music in the world,
Breathing as beauteous order that controls
With growing sway the growing life of man.
So we inherit that sweet purity
15   For which we struggled, fail'd, and agoniz'd
With widening retrospect that bred despair.

Rebellious flesh that would not be subdued,
A vicious parent shaming still its child,
Poor anxious penitence, is quick dissolv'd;
20 Its discords, quench'd by meeting harmonies,
Die in the large and charitable air.
And all our rarer, better, truer self,
That sobb'd religiously in yearning song,
That watch'd to ease the burthen of the world,
25 Laboriously tracing what must be,
And what may yet be better,—saw within
A worthier image for the sanctuary,
And shap'd it forth before the multitude,
Divinely human, raising worship so
30 To higher reverence more mix'd with love,—
That better self shall live till human Time
Shall fold its eyelids, and the human sky
Be gather'd like a scroll within the tomb Unread forever.
        This is life to come,
35 Which martyr'd men have made more glorious
For us who strive to follow. May I reach
That purest heaven, be to other souls
The cup of strength in some great agony,
Enkindle generous ardor, feed pure love,
40 Beget the smiles that have no cruelty,
Be the sweet presence of a good diffus'd,
And in diffusion ever more intense!
So shall I join the choir invisible
Whose music is the gladness of the world.

45

50

BRIGHT, O BRIGHT FEDALMA

George Eliot

1   Maiden crowned with glossy blackness,
       Lithe as panther forest-roaming,
       Long-armed Naiad when she dances
       On a stream of ether floating,
5   Bright, o bright Fedalma!

       Form all curves like softness drifted,
       Wave-kissed marble roundly dimpling,
       Far-off music slowly wingèd,
       Gently rising, gently sinking,
10   Bright, o bright Fedalma!

       Pure as rain-tear on a rose-leaf,
       Cloud high born in noonday spotless
       Sudden perfect like the dew-bead,
       Gem of earth and sky begotten,
15   Bright, o bright Fedalma!

       Beauty has no mortal father,
       Holy light her form engendered,
       Out of tremor yearning, gladness,
       Presage sweet, and joy remembered,
20   Child of light! Child of light!
       Child of light, Fedalma!

SWEET SPRINGTIME

George Eliot

1   It was in the prime
       Of the sweet springtime
       In the linnet's throat
       Trembled the love note,
5   And the love-stirred air
       Thrilled the blossoms there.
       Little shadows danced,
       Each a tiny elf
       Happy in large light
10   And the thinnest self.

       It was but a minute
       In a far-off spring,
       But each gentle thing,
       Sweetly wooing linnet,
15   Soft thrilled hawthorn tree,
       Happy shadowy elf,
       With the thinnest self,
       Live on still in me.
       It was in the prime
20   Of the past springtime!

MATTHEW ARNOLD (1822-1888)

Arnold was a writer of poetry and critical essays. His "Dover Beach" captures the experience that many Victorians were feeling in the age of Darwin and his theory of evolution. Despite his own defense of Christianity, Arnold wrote of his struggles with faith. Arnold worked as a government school inspector, which allowed him to travel across England and the Continent. From 1857 to 1867, he was Professor of Poetry at Oxford University—the first professor to lecture in English instead of Latin. Arnold's first two poetry collections *The Strayed Reveller and Other Poems* (1849) and *Empedocles on Etna* (1852) were published pseudonymously; *Poems: A New Edition* (1853) was the first Arnold published under his own name. He is credited with helping to establish literary criticism as an art form. Arnold is remembered almost as much for his controversial agenda for high culture delineated in his series of essays, *Culture and Anarchy* (1869), as he is for his poetry.

TO A FRIEND

Matthew Arnold

1   Who prop, thou ask'st in these bad days, my mind?--
He much, the old man, who, clearest-souled of men,
Saw The Wide Prospect, and the Asian Fen,
And Tmolus hill, and Smyrna bay, though blind.

5   Much he, whose friendship I not long since won,
That halting slave, who in Nicopolis
Taught Arrian, when Vespasian's brutal son
Cleared Rome of what most shamed him. But be his

My special thanks, whose even-balanced soul,
10   From first youth tested up to extreme old age,
Business could not make dull, nor passion wild;

Who saw life steadily, and saw it whole;
The mellow glory of the Attic stage,
Singer of sweet Colonus, and its child.

THE FORSAKEN MERMAN

Matthew Arnold

1   Come, dear children, let us away;
Down and away below!
Now my brothers call from the bay,
Now the great winds shoreward blow,
5   Now the salt tides seaward flow;
Now the wild white horses play,
Champ and chafe and toss in the spray.
Children dear, let us away!
This way, this way!
10   Call her once before you go—
Call once yet!
In a voice that she will know:
"Margaret! Margaret!"
Children's voices should be dear
15   (Call once more) to a mother's ear;

Children's voices, wild with pain—
Surely she will come again!
Call her once and come away;
This way, this way!
20   "Mother dear, we cannot stay!
The wild white horses foam and fret."
Margaret! Margaret!

Come, dear children, come away down;
Call no more!
25   One last look at the white-wall'd town
And the little grey church on the windy shore,
Then come down!
She will not come though you call all day;
Come away, come away!

30   Children dear, was it yesterday
        We heard the sweet bells over the bay?
        In the caverns where we lay,
        Through the surf and through the swell,
        The far-off sound of a silver bell?
35   Sand-strewn caverns, cool and deep,
        Where the winds are all asleep;
        Where the spent lights quiver and gleam,
        Where the salt weed sways in the stream,
        Where the sea-beasts, ranged all round,
40   Feed in the ooze of their pasture-ground;
        Where the sea-snakes coil and twine,
        Dry their mail and bask in the brine;
        Where great whales come sailing by,
        Sail and sail, with unshut eye,
45   Round the world for ever and aye?
        When did music come this way?
        Children dear, was it yesterday?

        Children dear, was it yesterday
        (Call yet once) that she went away?
50   Once she sate with you and me,
        On a red gold throne in the heart of the sea,
        And the youngest sate on her knee.
        She comb'd its bright hair, and she tended it well,
        When down swung the sound of a far-off bell.
55   She sigh'd, she look'd up through the clear green sea;
        She said: "I must go, to my kinsfolk pray
        In the little grey church on the shore to-day.
        'T will be Easter-time in the world—ah me!
        And I lose my poor soul, Merman! here with thee."
60   I said: "Go up, dear heart, through the waves;
        Say thy prayer, and come back to the kind sea-caves!"
        She smiled, she went up through the surf in the bay.
        Children dear, was it yesterday?

        Children dear, were we long alone?

65   "The sea grows stormy, the little ones moan;
      Long prayers," I said, "in the world they say;
      Come!" I said; and we rose through the surf in the bay.
      We went up the beach, by the sandy down
      Where the sea-stocks bloom, to the white-wall'd town;
70   Through the narrow paved streets, where all was still,
      To the little grey church on the windy hill.
      From the church came a murmur of folk at their prayers,
      But we stood without in the cold blowing airs.
      We climb'd on the graves, on the stones worn with rains,
75   And we gazed up the aisle through the small leaded panes.
      She sate by the pillar; we saw her clear:
      "Margaret, hist! come quick, we are here!
      Dear heart," I said, "we are long alone;
      The sea grows stormy, the little ones moan."
80   But, ah, she gave me never a look,
      For her eyes were seal'd to the holy book!
      Loud prays the priest; shut stands the door.
      Come away, children, call no more!
      Come away, come down, call no more!

85   Down, down, down!
      Down to the depths of the sea!
      She sits at her wheel in the humming town,
      Singing most joyfully.
      Hark what she sings: "O joy, O joy,
90   For the humming street, and the child with its toy!
      For the priest, and the bell, and the holy well;
      For the wheel where I spun,
      And the blessed light of the sun!"
      And so she sings her fill,
95   Singing most joyfully,
      Till the spindle drops from her hand,
      And the whizzing wheel stands still.
      She steals to the window, and looks at the sand,
      And over the sand at the sea;
100   And her eyes are set in a stare;

And anon there breaks a sigh,
And anon there drops a tear,
From a sorrow-clouded eye,
And a heart sorrow-laden,
105   A long, long sigh;
For the cold strange eyes of a little Mermaiden
And the gleam of her golden hair.

Come away, away children
Come children, come down!
110   The hoarse wind blows coldly;
Lights shine in the town.
She will start from her slumber
When gusts shake the door;
She will hear the winds howling,
115   Will hear the waves roar.
We shall see, while above us
The waves roar and whirl,
A ceiling of amber,
A pavement of pearl.
120   Singing: "Here came a mortal,
But faithless was she!
And alone dwell for ever
The kings of the sea."

But, children, at midnight,
125   When soft the winds blow,
When clear falls the moonlight,
When spring-tides are low;
When sweet airs come seaward
From heaths starr'd with broom,
130   And high rocks throw mildly
On the blanch'd sands a gloom;
Up the still, glistening beaches,
Up the creeks we will hie,
Over banks of bright seaweed
135   The ebb-tide leaves dry.

We will gaze, from the sand-hills,
At the white, sleeping town;
At the church on the hill-side—
And then come back down.
140   Singing: "There dwells a loved one,
But cruel is she!
She left lonely for ever
The kings of the sea."

LINES WRITTEN IN KENSINGTON GARDENS

Matthew Arnold

1   In this lone, open glade I lie,
Screen'd by deep boughs on either hand;
And at its end, to stay the eye,
Those black-crown'd, red-boled pine-trees stand!

5   Birds here make song, each bird has his,
Across the girdling city's hum.
How green under the boughs it is!
How thick the tremulous sheep-cries come!

Sometimes a child will cross the glade
10   To take his nurse his broken toy;
Sometimes a thrush flit overhead
Deep in her unknown day's employ.

Here at my feet what wonders pass,
What endless, active life is here!
15   What blowing daisies, fragrant grass!
An air-stirr'd forest, fresh and clear.

Scarce fresher is the mountain-sod
Where the tired angler lies, stretch'd out,
And, eased of basket and of rod,
20 Counts his day's spoil, the spotted trout.

In the huge world, which roars hard by,
Be others happy if they can!
But in my helpless cradle I
Was breathed on by the rural Pan.

25 I, on men's impious uproar hurl'd,
Think often, as I hear them rave,
That peace has left the upper world
And now keeps only in the grave.

Yet here is peace for ever new!
30 When I who watch them am away,
Still all things in this glade go through
The changes of their quiet day.

Then to their happy rest they pass!
The flowers upclose, the birds are fed,
35 The night comes down upon the grass,
The child sleeps warmly in his bed.

Calm soul of all things! make it mine
To feel, amid the city's jar,
That there abides a peace of thine,
40 Man did not make, and cannot mar.

The will to neither strive nor cry,
The power to feel with others give!
Calm, calm me more! nor let me die
Before I have begun to live.

THE BURIED LIFE

Matthew Arnold

1 Light flows our war of mocking words, and yet,
 Behold, with tears mine eyes are wet!
 I feel a nameless sadness o'er me roll.
 Yes, yes, we know that we can jest,
5 We know, we know that we can smile!
 But there's a something in this breast,
 To which thy light words bring no rest,
 And thy gay smiles no anodyne.
 Give me thy hand, and hush awhile,
10 And turn those limpid eyes on mine,
 And let me read there, love! thy inmost soul.

 Alas! is even love too weak
 To unlock the heart, and let it speak?
 Are even lovers powerless to reveal
15 To one another what indeed they feel?
 I knew the mass of men conceal'd
 Their thoughts, for fear that if reveal'd
 They would by other men be met
 With blank indifference, or with blame reproved;
20 I knew they lived and moved
 Trick'd in disguises, alien to the rest
 Of men, and alien to themselves—and yet
 The same heart beats in every human breast!
 But we, my love!—doth a like spell benumb
25 Our hearts, our voices?—must we too be dumb?

 Ah! well for us, if even we,
 Even for a moment, can get free
 Our heart, and have our lips unchain'd;
 For that which seals them hath been deep-ordain'd!

30   Fate, which foresaw
       How frivolous a baby man would be—
       By what distractions he would be possess'd,
       How he would pour himself in every strife,
       And well-nigh change his own identity—
35   That it might keep from his capricious play
       His genuine self, and force him to obey
       Even in his own despite his being's law,
       Bade through the deep recesses of our breast
       The unregarded river of our life
40   Pursue with indiscernible flow its way;
       And that we should not see
       The buried stream, and seem to be
       Eddying at large in blind uncertainty,
       Though driving on with it eternally.

45   But often, in the world's most crowded streets,
       But often, in the din of strife,
       There rises an unspeakable desire
       After the knowledge of our buried life;
       A thirst to spend our fire and restless force
50   In tracking out our true, original course;
       A longing to inquire
       Into the mystery of this heart which beats
       So wild, so deep in us—to know
       Whence our lives come and where they go.
55   And many a man in his own breast then delves,
       But deep enough, alas! none ever mines.
       And we have been on many thousand lines,
       And we have shown, on each, spirit and power;
       But hardly have we, for one little hour,
60   Been on our own line, have we been ourselves—
       Hardly had skill to utter one of all
       The nameless feelings that course through our breast,
       But they course on for ever unexpress'd.
       And long we try in vain to speak and act
65   Our hidden self, and what we say and do

Is eloquent, is well—but 't is not true!
And then we will no more be rack'd
With inward striving, and demand
Of all the thousand nothings of the hour
70 Their stupefying power;
Ah yes, and they benumb us at our call!
Yet still, from time to time, vague and forlorn,
From the soul's subterranean depth upborne
As from an infinitely distant land,
75 Come airs, and floating echoes, and convey
A melancholy into all our day.

Only—but this is rare—
When a belovèd hand is laid in ours,
When, jaded with the rush and glare
80 Of the interminable hours,
Our eyes can in another's eyes read clear,
When our world-deafen'd ear
Is by the tones of a loved voice caress'd—
A bolt is shot back somewhere in our breast,
85 And a lost pulse of feeling stirs again.
The eye sinks inward, and the heart lies plain,
And what we mean, we say, and what we would, we know.
A man becomes aware of his life's flow,
And hears its winding murmur; and he sees
90 The meadows where it glides, the sun, the breeze.

And there arrives a lull in the hot race
Wherein he doth for ever chase
That flying and elusive shadow, rest.
An air of coolness plays upon his face,
95 And an unwonted calm pervades his breast.
And then he thinks he knows
The hills where his life rose,
And the sea where it goes.

ISOLATION: TO MARGUERITE

Matthew Arnold

1 We were apart; yet, day by day,
 I bade my heart more constant be.
 I bade it keep the world away,
 And grow a home for only thee;
5 Nor fear'd but thy love likewise grew,
 Like mine, each day, more tried, more true.

 The fault was grave! I might have known,
 What far too soon, alas! I learn'd—
 The heart can bind itself alone,
10 And faith may oft be unreturn'd.
 Self-sway'd our feelings ebb and swell—
 Thou lov'st no more;—Farewell! Farewell!

 Farewell!—and thou, thou lonely heart,
 Which never yet without remorse
15 Even for a moment didst depart
 From thy remote and spherèd course
 To haunt the place where passions reign—
 Back to thy solitude again!

 Back! with the conscious thrill of shame
20 Which Luna felt, that summer-night,
 Flash through her pure immortal frame,
 When she forsook the starry height
 To hang over Endymion's sleep
 Upon the pine-grown Latmian steep.

25 Yet she, chaste queen, had never proved
 How vain a thing is mortal love,
 Wandering in Heaven, far removed.
 But thou hast long had place to prove

This truth—to prove, and make thine own:
30 "Thou hast been, shalt be, art, alone."
Or, if not quite alone, yet they
Which touch thee are unmating things—
Ocean and clouds and night and day;
Lorn autumns and triumphant springs;
35 And life, and others' joy and pain,
And love, if love, of happier men.

Of happier men—for they, at least,
Have dream'd two human hearts might blend
In one, and were through faith released
40 From isolation without end
Prolong'd; nor knew, although not less
Alone than thou, their loneliness.

THE SCHOLAR-GIPSY

Matthew Arnold

1   Go, for they call you, shepherd, from the hill;
Go, shepherd, and untie the wattled cotes!
No longer leave thy wistful flock unfed,
Nor let thy bawling fellows rack their throats,
5   Nor the cropp'd herbage shoot another head.
But when the fields are still,
And the tired men and dogs all gone to rest,
And only the white sheep are sometimes seen
Cross and recross the strips of moon-blanch'd green.
10   Come, shepherd, and again begin the quest!
Here, where the reaper was at work of late—
In this high field's dark corner, where he leaves
His coat, his basket, and his earthen cruse,
And in the sun all morning binds the sheaves,
15   Then here, at noon, comes back his stores to use—
Here will I sit and wait,
While to my ear from uplands far away
The bleating of the folded flocks is borne,
With distant cries of reapers in the corn—
20   All the live murmur of a summer's day.

Screen'd is this nook o'er the high, half-reap'd field,
And here till sun-down, shepherd! will I be.
Through the thick corn the scarlet poppies peep,
And round green roots and yellowing stalks I see
25   Pale pink convolvulus in tendrils creep;
And air-swept lindens yield
Their scent, and rustle down their perfumed showers
Of bloom on the bent grass where I am laid,
And bower me from the August sun with shade;
30   And the eye travels down to Oxford's towers.

And near me on the grass lies Glanvil's book—
Come, let me read the oft-read tale again!
The story of the Oxford scholar poor,
Of pregnant parts and quick inventive brain,
35   Who, tired of knocking at preferment's door,
One summer-morn forsook
His friends, and went to learn the gipsy-lore,
And roam'd the world with that wild brotherhood,
And came, as most men deem'd, to little good,
40   But came to Oxford and his friends no more.

But once, years after, in the country-lanes,
Two scholars, whom at college erst he knew,
Met him, and of his way of life enquired;
Whereat he answer'd, that the gipsy-crew,
45   His mates, had arts to rule as they desired
The workings of men's brains,
And they can bind them to what thoughts they will.
"And I," he said, "the secret of their art,
When fully learn'd, will to the world impart;
50   But it needs heaven-sent moments for this skill."

This said, he left them, and return'd no more.—
But rumours hung about the country-side,
That the lost Scholar long was seen to stray,
Seen by rare glimpses, pensive and tongue-tied,
55   In hat of antique shape, and cloak of grey,
The same the gipsies wore.
Shepherds had met him on the Hurst in spring;
At some lone alehouse in the Berkshire moors,
On the warm ingle-bench, the smock-frock'd boors
60   Had found him seated at their entering,

But, 'mid their drink and clatter, he would fly.
And I myself seem half to know thy looks,
And put the shepherds, wanderer! on thy trace;
And boys who in lone wheatfields scare the rooks

65   I ask if thou hast pass'd their quiet place;
Or in my boat I lie
Moor'd to the cool bank in the summer-heats,
'Mid wide grass meadows which the sunshine fills,
And watch the warm, green-muffled Cumner hills,
70   And wonder if thou haunt'st their shy retreats.

For most, I know, thou lov'st retired ground!
Thee at the ferry Oxford riders blithe,
Returning home on summer-nights, have met
Crossing the stripling Thames at Bab-lock-hithe,
75   Trailing in the cool stream thy fingers wet,
As the punt's rope chops round;
And leaning backward in a pensive dream,
And fostering in thy lap a heap of flowers
Pluck'd in shy fields and distant Wychwood bowers,
80   And thine eyes resting on the moonlit stream.

And then they land, and thou art seen no more!—
Maidens, who from the distant hamlets come
To dance around the Fyfield elm in May,
Oft through the darkening fields have seen thee roam,
85   Or cross a stile into the public way.
Oft thou hast given them store
Of flowers—the frail-leaf'd, white anemony,
Dark bluebells drench'd with dews of summer eves,
And purple orchises with spotted leaves—
90   But none hath words she can report of thee.

And, above Godstow Bridge, when hay-time's here
In June, and many a scythe in sunshine flames,
Men who through those wide fields of breezy grass
Where black-wing'd swallows haunt the glittering Thames,
95   To bathe in the abandon'd lasher pass,
Have often pass'd thee near
Sitting upon the river bank o'ergrown;
Mark'd thine outlandish garb, thy figure spare,

Thy dark vague eyes, and soft abstracted air—
100   But, when they came from bathing, thou wast gone!

At some lone homestead in the Cumner hills,
Where at her open door the housewife darns,
Thou hast been seen, or hanging on a gate
To watch the threshers in the mossy barns.
105   Children, who early range these slopes and late
For cresses from the rills,
Have known thee eyeing, all an April-day,
The springing pasture and the feeding kine;
And mark'd thee, when the stars come out and shine,
110   Through the long dewy grass move slow away.

In autumn, on the skirts of Bagley Wood—
Where most the gipsies by the turf-edged way
Pitch their smoked tents, and every bush you see
With scarlet patches tagg'd and shreds of grey,
115   Above the forest-ground called Thessaly—
The blackbird, picking food,
Sees thee, nor stops his meal, nor fears at all;
So often has he known thee past him stray,
Rapt, twirling in thy hand a wither'd spray,
120   And waiting for the spark from heaven to fall.

And once, in winter, on the causeway chill
Where home through flooded fields foot-travellers go,
Have I not pass'd thee on the wooden bridge,
Wrapt in thy cloak and battling with the snow,
125   Thy face tow'rd Hinksey and its wintry ridge?
And thou has climb'd the hill,
And gain'd the white brow of the Cumner range;
Turn'd once to watch, while thick the snowflakes fall,
The line of festal light in Christ-Church hall—
130   Then sought thy straw in some sequester'd grange.

But what—I dream! Two hundred years are flown

Since first thy story ran through Oxford halls,
And the grave Glanvil did the tale inscribe
That thou wert wander'd from the studious walls
135 To learn strange arts, and join a gipsy-tribe;
And thou from earth art gone
Long since, and in some quiet churchyard laid—
Some country-nook, where o'er thy unknown grave
Tall grasses and white flowering nettles wave,
140 Under a dark, red-fruited yew-tree's shade.

—No, no, thou hast not felt the lapse of hours!
For what wears out the life of mortal men?
'Tis that from change to change their being rolls;
'Tis that repeated shocks, again, again,
145 Exhaust the energy of strongest souls
And numb the elastic powers.
Till having used our nerves with bliss and teen,
And tired upon a thousand schemes our wit,
To the just-pausing Genius we remit
150 Our worn-out life, and are—what we have been.

Thou hast not lived, why should'st thou perish, so?
Thou hadst one aim, one business, one desire;
Else wert thou long since number'd with the dead!
Else hadst thou spent, like other men, thy fire!
155 The generations of thy peers are fled,
And we ourselves shall go;
But thou possessest an immortal lot,
And we imagine thee exempt from age
And living as thou liv'st on Glanvil's page,
160 Because thou hadst—what we, alas! have not.

For early didst thou leave the world, with powers
Fresh, undiverted to the world without,
Firm to their mark, not spent on other things;
Free from the sick fatigue, the languid doubt,
165 Which much to have tried, in much been baffled, brings.

O life unlike to ours!
Who fluctuate idly without term or scope,
Of whom each strives, nor knows for what he strives,
And each half lives a hundred different lives;
170   Who wait like thee, but not, like thee, in hope.

Thou waitest for the spark from heaven! and we,
Light half-believers of our casual creeds,
Who never deeply felt, nor clearly will'd,
Whose insight never has borne fruit in deeds,
175   Whose vague resolves never have been fulfill'd;
For whom each year we see
Breeds new beginnings, disappointments new;
Who hesitate and falter life away,
And lose to-morrow the ground won to-day—
180   Ah! do not we, wanderer! await it too?

Yes, we await it!—but it still delays,
And then we suffer! and amongst us one,
Who most has suffer'd, takes dejectedly
His seat upon the intellectual throne;
185   And all his store of sad experience he
Lays bare of wretched days;
Tells us his misery's birth and growth and signs,
And how the dying spark of hope was fed,
And how the breast was soothed, and how the head,
190   And all his hourly varied anodynes.

This for our wisest! and we others pine,
And wish the long unhappy dream would end,
And waive all claim to bliss, and try to bear;
With close-lipp'd patience for our only friend,
195   Sad patience, too near neighbour to despair—
But none has hope like thine!
Thou through the fields and through the woods dost stray,
Roaming the country-side, a truant boy,
Nursing thy project in unclouded joy,

200 And every doubt long blown by time away.

O born in days when wits were fresh and clear,
And life ran gaily as the sparkling Thames;
Before this strange disease of modern life,
With its sick hurry, its divided aims,
205 Its heads o'ertax'd, its palsied hearts, was rife—
Fly hence, our contact fear!
Still fly, plunge deeper in the bowering wood!
Averse, as Dido did with gesture stern
From her false friend's approach in Hades turn,
210 Wave us away, and keep thy solitude!

Still nursing the unconquerable hope,
Still clutching the inviolable shade,
With a free, onward impulse brushing through,
By night, the silver'd branches of the glade—
215 Far on the forest-skirts, where none pursue,
On some mild pastoral slope
Emerge, and resting on the moonlit pales
Freshen thy flowers as in former years
With dew, or listen with enchanted ears,
220 From the dark tingles, to the nightingales!

But fly our paths, our feverish contact fly!
For strong the infection of our mental strife,
Which, though it gives no bliss, yet spoils for rest;
And we should win thee from thy own fair life,
225 Like us distracted, and like us unblest.
Soon, soon thy cheer would die,
Thy hopes grow timorous, and unfix'd thy powers,
And thy clear aims be cross and shifting made;
And then thy glad perennial youth would fade,
230 Fade and grow old at last, and die like ours.

Then fly our greetings, fly our speech and smiles!
—As some grave Tyrian trader, from the sea,

Descried at sunrise an emerging prow
Lifting the cool-hair'd creepers stealthily,
235   The fringes of a southward-facing brow
Among the Ægæan Isles;
And saw the merry Grecian coaster come,
Freighted with amber grapes, and Chian wine,
Green, bursting figs, and tunnies steep'd in brine—
240   And knew the intruders on his ancient home,

The young light-hearted masters of the waves—
And snatch'd his rudder, and shook out more sail;
And day and night held on indignantly
O'er the blue Midland waters with the gale,
245   Betwixt the Syrtes and soft Sicily,
To where the Atlantic raves
Outside the western straits; and unbent sails
There, where down cloudy cliffs, through sheets of foam,
Shy traffickers, the dark Iberians come;
250   And on the beach undid his corded bales.

THE LAST WORD

Matthew Arnold

1   Creep into thy narrow bed,
    Creep, and let no more be said!
    Vain thy onset! all stands fast.
    Thou thyself must break at last.

5   Let the long contention cease!
    Geese are swans, and swans are geese.
    Let them have it how they will!
    Thou art tired: best be still.

    They out-talked thee, hissed thee, tore thee?
10   Better men fared thus before thee;
    Fired their ringing shot and passed,
    Hotly charged - and sank at last.

    Charge once more, then, and be dumb!
    Let the victors, when they come,
15   When the forts of folly fall,
    Find thy body by the wall!

DOVER BEACH

Matthew Arnold

1   The sea is calm tonight.
The tide is full, the moon lies fair
Upon the straits; on the French coast the light
Gleams and is gone; the cliffs of England stand,
5   Glimmering and vast, out in the tranquil bay.
Come to the window, sweet is the night-air!
Only, from the long line of spray
Where the sea meets the moon-blanched land,
Listen! you hear the grating roar
10   Of pebbles which the waves draw back, and fling,
At their return, up the high strand,
Begin, and cease, and then again begin,
With tremulous cadence slow, and bring
The eternal note of sadness in.

15   Sophocles long ago
Heard it on the Ægean, and it brought
Into his mind the turbid ebb and flow
Of human misery; we
Find also in the sound a thought,
20   Hearing it by this distant northern sea.

The Sea of Faith
Was once, too, at the full, and round earth's shore
Lay like the folds of a bright girdle furled.
But now I only hear
25   Its melancholy, long, withdrawing roar,
Retreating, to the breath
Of the night-wind, down the vast edges drear
And naked shingles of the world.

Ah, love, let us be true
30   To one another! for the world, which seems
To lie before us like a land of dreams,
So various, so beautiful, so new,
Hath really neither joy, nor love, nor light,
Nor certitude, nor peace, nor help for pain;
35   And we are here as on a darkling plain
Swept with confused alarms of struggle and flight,
Where ignorant armies clash by night.

GEORGE MEREDITH (1828-1909)

Meredith was the son of a poor tailor, but with his mother's dowry, he was able to attend private schools. He began writing poetry in his 20s, and though his first collection, *Poems* (1851), didn't do well, he persevered. After studying in Germany for two years, Arnold returned to England and worked for an attorney for five years. In 1849, he married Mary Nicholls (a successful cookbook author), and they had a son in 1853. They had a difficult marriage, and she left him five years later, in 1858. Many of Arnold's poems, especially *Modern Love*, reflect this complex relationship. In 1864, he married Marie Vulliamy and had two children with her. Meredith was a highly productive Victorian author; altogether he wrote nineteen novels and thirteen poetry collections.

LOVE IN THE VALLEY

George Meredith

1   Under yonder beech-tree single on the green-sward,
Couched with her arms behind her golden head,
Knees and tresses folded to slip and ripple idly,
Lies my young love sleeping in the shade.
5   Had I the heart to slide an arm beneath her,
Press her parting lips as her waist I gather slow,
Waking in amazement she could not but embrace me:
Then would she hold me and never let me go?

Shy as the squirrel and wayward as the swallow,
10   Swift as the swallow along the river's light
Circleting the surface to meet his mirrored winglets,
Fleeter she seems in her stay than in her flight.
Shy as the squirrel that leaps among the pine-tops,
Wayward as the swallow overhead at set of sun,
15   She whom I love is hard to catch and conquer,
Hard, but O the glory of the winning were she won!

When her mother tends her before the laughing mirror,
Tying up her laces, looping up her hair,
Often she thinks, were this wild thing wedded,
20   More love should I have, and much less care.
When her mother tends her before the lighted mirror,
Loosening her laces, combing down her curls,
Often she thinks, were this wild thing wedded,
I should miss but one for many boys and girls.

25   Heartless she is as the shadow in the meadows
Flying to the hills on a blue and breezy noon.
No, she is athirst and drinking up her wonder:
Earth to her is young as the slip of the new moon.
Deals she an unkindness, 'tis but her rapid measure,

30   Even as in a dance; and her smile can heal no less:
Like the swinging May-cloud that pelts the flowers with hailstones
Off a sunny border, she was made to bruise and bless.
Lovely are the curves of the white owl sweeping
Wavy in the dusk lit by one large star.
35   Lone on the fir-branch, his rattle-note unvaried,
Brooding o'er the gloom, spins the brown eve-jar.
Darker grows the valley, more and more forgetting:
So were it with me if forgetting could be willed.
Tell the grassy hollow that holds the bubbling well-spring,
40   Tell it to forget the source that keeps it filled.

Stepping down the hill with her fair companions,
Arm in arm, all against the raying West
Boldly she sings, to the merry tune she marches,
Brave in her shape, and sweeter unpossessed.
45   Sweeter, for she is what my heart first awaking
Whispered the world was; morning light is she.
Love that so desires would fain keep her changeless;
Fain would fling the net, and fain have her free.

Happy happy time, when the white star hovers
50   Low over dim fields fresh with bloomy dew,
Near the face of dawn, that draws athwart the darkness,
Threading it with colour, as yewberries the yew.
Thicker crowd the shades while the grave East deepens
Glowing, and with crimson a long cloud swells.
55   Maiden still the morn is; and strange she is, and secret;
Strange her eyes; her cheeks are cold as cold sea-shells.

Sunrays, leaning on our southern hills and lighting
Wild cloud-mountains that drag the hills along,
Oft ends the day of your shifting brilliant laughter
60   Chill as a dull face frowning on a song.
Ay, but shows the South-West a ripple-feathered bosom
Blown to silver while the clouds are shaken and ascend
Scaling the mid-heavens as they stream, there comes a sunset

Rich, deep like love in beauty without end.

65   When at dawn she sighs, and like an infant to the window
      Turns grave eyes craving light, released from dreams,
      Beautiful she looks, like a white water-lily
      Bursting out of bud in havens of the streams.
      When from bed she rises clothed from neck to ankle
70   In her long nightgown sweet as boughs of May,
      Beautiful she looks, like a tall garden lily
      Pure from the night, and splendid for the day.

      Mother of the dews, dark eye-lashed twilight,
      Low-lidded twilight, o'er the valley's brim,
75   Rounding on thy breast sings the dew-delighted skylark,
      Clear as though the dewdrops had their voice in him.
      Hidden where the rose-flush drinks the rayless planet,
      Fountain-full he pours the spraying fountain-showers.
      Let me hear her laughter, I would have her ever
80   Cool as dew in twilight, the lark above the flowers.

      All the girls are out with their baskets for the primrose;
      Up lanes, woods through, they troop in joyful bands.
      My sweet leads: she knows not why, but now she totters,
      Eyes the bent anemones, and hangs her hands.
85   Such a look will tell that the violets are peeping,
      Coming the rose: and unaware a cry
      Springs in her bosom for odours and for colour,
      Covert and the nightingale; she knows not why.

      Kerchiefed head and chin she darts between her tulips,
90   Streaming like a willow grey in arrowy rain:
      Some bend beaten cheek to gravel, and their angel
      She will be; she lifts them, and on she speeds again.
      Black the driving raincloud breasts the iron gateway:
      She is forth to cheer a neighbour lacking mirth.
95   So when sky and grass met rolling dumb for thunder
      Saw I once a white dove, sole light of earth.

Prim little scholars are the flowers of her garden,
Trained to stand in rows, and asking if they please.
I might love them well but for loving more the wild ones:
100   O my wild ones! they tell me more than these.
You, my wild one, you tell of honied field-rose,
Violet, blushing eglantine in life; and even as they,
They by the wayside are earnest of your goodness,
You are of life's, on the banks that line the way.
105   Peering at her chamber the white crowns the red rose,
Jasmine winds the porch with stars two and three.
Parted is the window; she sleeps; the starry jasmine
Breathes a falling breath that carries thoughts of me.
Sweeter unpossessed, have I said of her my sweetest?
110   Not while she sleeps: while she sleeps the jasmine breathes,
Luring her to love; she sleeps; the starry jasmine
Bears me to her pillow under white rose-wreaths.

Yellow with birdfoot-trefoil are the grass-glades;
Yellow with cinquefoil of the dew-grey leaf;
115   Yellow with stonecrop; the moss-mounds are yellow;
Blue-necked the wheat sways, yellowing to the sheaf:
Green-yellow bursts from the copse the laughing yaffle;
Sharp as a sickle is the edge of shade and shine:
Earth in her heart laughs looking at the heavens,
120   Thinking of the harvest: I look and think of mine.

This I may know: her dressing and undressing
Such a change of light shows as when the skies in sport
Shift from cloud to moonlight; or edging over thunder
Slips a ray of sun; or sweeping into port
125   White sails furl; or on the ocean borders
White sails lean along the waves leaping green.
Visions of her shower before me, but from eyesight
Guarded she would be like the sun were she seen.

Front door and back of the mossed old farmhouse
130   Open with the morn, and in a breezy link
Freshly sparkles garden to stripe-shadowed orchard,
Green across a rill where on sand the minnows wink.
Busy in the grass the early sun of summer
Swarms, and the blackbird's mellow fluting notes
135   Call my darling up with round and roguish challenge:
Quaintest, richest carol of all the singing throats!

Cool was the woodside; cool as her white dairy
Keeping sweet the cream-pan; and there the boys from school,
Cricketing below, rushed brown and red with sunshine;
140   O the dark translucence of the deep-eyed cool!
Spying from the farm, herself she fetched a pitcher
Full of milk, and tilted for each in turn the beak.
Then a little fellow, mouth up and on tiptoe,
Said, "I will kiss you": she laughed and leaned her cheek.

145   Doves of the fir-wood walling high our red roof
Through the long noon coo, crooning through the coo.
Loose droop the leaves, and down the sleepy roadway
Sometimes pipes a chaffinch; loose droops the blue.
Cows flap a slow tail knee-deep in the river,
150   Breathless, given up to sun and gnat and fly.
Nowhere is she seen; and if I see her nowhere,
Lightning may come, straight rains and tiger sky.

O the golden sheaf, the rustling treasure-armful!
O the nutbrown tresses nodding interlaced!
155   O the treasure-tresses one another over
Nodding! O the girdle slack about the waist!
Slain are the poppies that shot their random scarlet
Quick amid the wheatears: wound about the waist,
Gathered, see these brides of Earth one blush of ripeness!
160   O the nutbrown tresses nodding interlaced!

Large and smoky red the sun's cold disk drops,
Clipped by naked hills, on violet shaded snow:
Eastward large and still lights up a bower of moonrise,
Whence at her leisure steps the moon aglow.
165   Nightlong on black print-branches our beech-tree
Gazes in this whiteness: nightlong could I.
Here may life on death or death on life be painted.
Let me clasp her soul to know she cannot die!

Gossips count her faults; they scour a narrow chamber
170   Where there is no window, read not heaven or her.
"When she was a tiny," one aged woman quavers,
Plucks at my heart and leads me by the ear.
Faults she had once as she learnt to run and tumbled:
Faults of feature some see, beauty not complete.
175   Yet, good gossips, beauty that makes holy
Earth and air, may have faults from head to feet.
Hither she comes; she comes to me; she lingers,
Deepens her brown eyebrows, while in new surprise
High rise the lashes in wonder of a stranger;
180   Yet am I the light and living of her eyes.
Something friends have told her fills her heart to brimming,
Nets her in her blushes, and wounds her, and tames.—
Sure of her haven, O like a dove alighting,
Arms up, she dropped: our souls were in our names.

185   Soon will she lie like a white-frost sunrise.
Yellow oats and brown wheat, barley pale as rye,
Long since your sheaves have yielded to the thresher,
Felt the girdle loosened, seen the tresses fly.
Soon will she lie like a blood-red sunset.
190   Swift with the to-morrow, green-winged Spring!
Sing from the South-West, bring her back the truants,
Nightingale and swallow, song and dipping wing.

Soft new beech-leaves, up to beamy April
Spreading bough on bough a primrose mountain, you,

195   Lucid in the moon, raise lilies to the skyfields,
    Youngest green transfused in silver shining through:
    Fairer than the lily, than the wild white cherry:
    Fair as in image my seraph love appears
    Borne to me by dreams when dawn is at my eyelids:
200   Fair as in the flesh she swims to me on tears.

    Could I find a place to be alone with heaven,
    I would speak my heart out: heaven is my need.
    Every woodland tree is flushing like the dog-wood,
    Flashing like the whitebeam, swaying like the reed.
205   Flushing like the dog-wood crimson in October;
    Streaming like the flag-reed South-West blown;
    Flashing as in gusts the sudden-lighted white beam:
    All seem to know what is for heaven alone.

LUCIFER IN STARLIGHT

George Meredith

1   On a starred night Prince Lucifer uprose.
    Tired of his dark dominion swung the fiend
    Above the rolling ball in cloud part screened,
    Where sinners hugged their spectre of repose.
5   Poor prey to his hot fit of pride were those.
    And now upon his western wing he leaned,
    Now his huge bulk o'er Afric's sands careened,
    Now the black planet shadowed Arctic snows.
    Soaring through wider zones that pricked his scars
10   With memory of the old revolt from Awe,
    He reached a middle height, and at the stars,
    Which are the brain of heaven, he looked, and sank.
    Around the ancient track marched, rank on rank,
    The army of unalterable law.

THE WOODS OF WESTERMAIN

George Meredith

I

1 Enter these enchanted woods,
 You who dare.
 Nothing harms beneath the leaves
 More than waves a swimmer cleaves.
5 Toss your heart up with the lark,
 Foot at peace with mouse and worm,
 Fair you fare.
 Only at a dread of dark
 Quaver, and they quit their form:
10 Thousand eyeballs under hoods
 Have you by the hair.
 Enter these enchanted woods,
 You who dare.

II

 Here the snake across your path
15 Stretches in his golden bath:
 Mossy-footed squirrels leap
 Soft as winnowing plumes of Sleep:
 Yaffles on a chuckle skim
 Low to laugh from branches dim:
20 Up the pine, where sits the star,
 Rattles deep the moth-winged jar.
 Each has business of his own;
 But should you distrust a tone,
 Then beware.
25 Shudder all the haunted roods,
 All the eyeballs under hoods
 Shroud you in their glare.

Enter these enchanted woods,
You who dare.

III

30   Open hither, open hence,
Scarce a bramble weaves a fence,
Where the strawberry runs red,
With white star-flower overhead;
Cumbered by dry twig and cone,
35   Shredded husks of seedlings flown,
Mine of mole and spotted flint:
Of dire wizardry no hint,
Save mayhap the print that shows
Hasty outward-tripping toes,
40   Heels to terror on the mould.
These, the woods of Westermain,
Are as others to behold,
Rich of wreathing sun and rain;
Foliage lustreful around
45   Shadowed leagues of slumbering sound.
Wavy tree-tops, yellow whins,
Shelter eager minikins,
Myriads, free to peck and pipe:
Would you better? would you worse?
50   You with them may gather ripe
Pleasures flowing not from purse.
Quick and far as Colour flies
Taking the delighted eyes,
You of any well that springs
55   May unfold the heaven of things;
Have it homely and within,
And thereof its likeness win,
Will you so in soul's desire:
This do sages grant t' the lyre.
60   This is being bird and more,
More than glad musician this;

Granaries you will have a store
Past the world of woe and bliss;
Sharing still its bliss and woe;
65   Harnessed to its hungers, no.
On the throne Success usurps,
You shall seat the joy you feel
Where a race of water chirps,
Twisting hues of flourished steel:
70   Or where light is caught in hoop
Up a clearing's leafy rise,
Where the crossing deerherds troop
Classic splendours, knightly dyes.
Or, where old-eyed oxen chew
75   Speculation with the cud,
Read their pool of vision through,
Back to hours when mind was mud;
Nigh the knot, which did untwine
Timelessly to drowsy suns;
80   Seeing Earth a slimy spine,
Heaven a space for winging tons.
Farther, deeper, may you read,
Have you sight for things afield,
Where peeps she, the Nurse of seed,
85   Cloaked, but in the peep revealed;
Showing a kind face and sweet:
Look you with the soul you see't.
Glory narrowing to grace,
Grace to glory magnified,
90   Following that will you embrace
Close in arms or aery wide.
Banished is the white Foam-born
Not from here, nor under ban
Phoebus lyrist, Phoebe's horn,
95   Pipings of the reedy Pan.
Loved of Earth of old they were,
Loving did interpret her;
And the sterner worship bars

None whom Song has made her stars.
100 You have seen the huntress moon
Radiantly facing dawn,
Dusky meads between them strewn
Glimmering like downy awn:
Argent Westward glows the hunt,
105 East the blush about to climb;
One another fair they front,
Transient, yet outshine the time;
Even as dewlight off the rose
In the mind a jewel sows.
110 Thus opposing grandeurs live
Here if Beauty be their dower:
Doth she of her spirit give,
Fleetingness will spare her flower.
This is in the tune we play,
115 Which no spring of strength would quell;
In subduing does not slay;
Guides the channel, guards the well:
Tempered holds the young blood-heat,
Yet through measured grave accord,
120 Hears the heart of wildness beat
Like a centaur's hoof on sward.
Drink the sense the notes infuse,
You a larger self will find:
Sweetest fellowship ensues
125 With the creatures of your kind.
Ay, and Love, if Love it be
Flaming over I and ME,
Love meet they who do not shove
Cravings in the van of Love.
130 Courtly dames are here to woo,
Knowing love if it be true.
Reverence the blossom-shoot
Fervently, they are the fruit.
Mark them stepping, hear them talk,
135 Goddess, is no myth inane,

You will say of those who walk
In the woods of Westermain.
Waters that from throat and thigh
Dart the sun his arrows back;
140   Leaves that on a woodland sigh
Chat of secret things no lack;
Shadowy branch-leaves, waters clear,
Bare or veiled they move sincere;
Not by slavish terrors tripped
145   Being anew in nature dipped,
Growths of what they step on, these;
With the roots the grace of trees.
Casket-breasts they give, nor hide,
For a tyrant's flattered pride,
150   Mind, which nourished not by light,
Lurks the shuffling trickster sprite:
Whereof are strange tales to tell;
Some in blood writ, tombed in bell.
Here the ancient battle ends,
155   Joining two astonished friends,
Who the kiss can give and take
With more warmth than in that world
Where the tiger claws the snake,
Snake her tiger clasps infurled,
160   And the issue of their fight
People lands in snarling plight.
Here her splendid beast she leads
Silken-leashed and decked with weeds
Wild as he, but breathing faint
165   Sweetness of unfelt constraint.
Love, the great volcano, flings
Fires of lower Earth to sky;
Love, the sole permitted, sings
Sovereignly of ME and I.
170   Bowers he has of sacred shade,
Spaces of superb parade,
Voiceful . . . But bring you a note

Wrangling, howsoe'er remote,
Discords out of discord spin
175   Round and round derisive din:
Sudden will a pallor pant
Chill at screeches miscreant;
Owls or spectres, thick they flee;
Nightmare upon horror broods;
180   Hooded laughter, monkish glee,
Gaps the vital air.
Enter these enchanted woods
You who dare.

IV

You must love the light so well
185   That no darkness will seem fell.
Love it so you could accost
Fellowly a livid ghost.
Whish! the phantom wisps away,
Owns him smoke to cocks of day.
190   In your breast the light must burn
Fed of you, like corn in quern
Ever plumping while the wheel
Speeds the mill and drains the meal.
Light to light sees little strange,
195   Only features heavenly new;
Then you touch the nerve of Change,
Then of Earth you have the clue;
Then her two-sexed meanings melt
Through you, wed the thought and felt.
200   Sameness locks no scurfy pond
Here for Custom, crazy-fond:
Change is on the wing to bud
Rose in brain from rose in blood.
Wisdom throbbing shall you see
205   Central in complexity;
From her pasture 'mid the beasts

Rise to her ethereal feasts,
Not, though lightnings track your wit
Starward, scorning them you quit:
210 For be sure the bravest wing
Preens it in our common spring,
Thence along the vault to soar,
You with others, gathering more,
Glad of more, till you reject
215 Your proud title of elect,
Perilous even here while few
Roam the arched greenwood with you.
Heed that snare.
Muffled by his cavern-cowl
220 Squats the scaly Dragon-fowl,
Who was lord ere light you drank,
And lest blood of knightly rank
Stream, let not your fair princess
Stray: he holds the leagues in stress,
225 Watches keenly there.
Oft has he been riven; slain
Is no force in Westermain.
Wait, and we shall forge him curbs,
Put his fangs to uses, tame,
230 Teach him, quick as cunning herbs,
How to cure him sick and lame.
Much restricted, much enringed,
Much he frets, the hooked and winged,
Never known to spare.
235 'Tis enough: the name of Sage
Hits no thing in nature, nought;
Man the least, save when grave Age
From yon Dragon guards his thought.
Eye him when you hearken dumb
240 To what words from Wisdom come.
When she says how few are by
Listening to her, eye his eye.
Self, his name declare.

Him shall Change, transforming late,
245 Wonderously renovate.
Hug himself the creature may:
What he hugs is loathed decay.
Crying, slip thy scales, and slough!
Change will strip his armour off;
250 Make of him who was all maw,
Inly only thrilling-shrewd,
Such a servant as none saw
Through his days of dragonhood.
Days when growling o'er his bone,
255 Sharpened he for mine and thine;
Sensitive within alone;
Scaly as the bark of pine.
Change, the strongest son of Life,
Has the Spirit here to wife.
260 Lo, their young of vivid breed,
Bear the lights that onward speed,
Threading thickets, mounting glades,
Up the verdurous colonnades,
Round the fluttered curves, and down,
265 Out of sight of Earth's blue crown,
Whither, in her central space,
Spouts the Fount and Lure o' the chase.
Fount unresting, Lure divine!
There meet all: too late look most.
270 Fire in water hued as wine,
Springs amid a shadowy host,
Circled: one close-headed mob,
Breathless, scanning divers heaps,
Where a Heart begins to throb,
275 Where it ceases, slow, with leaps.
And 'tis very strange, 'tis said,
How you spy in each of them
Semblance of that Dragon red,
As the oak in bracken-stem.
280 And, 'tis said, how each and each:

Which commences, which subsides:
First my Dragon! doth beseech
Her who food for all provides.
And she answers with no sign;
285   Utters neither yea nor nay;
Fires the water hued as wine;
Kneads another spark in clay.
Terror is about her hid;
Silence of the thunders locked;
290   Lightnings lining the shut lid;
Fixity on quaking rocked.
Lo, you look at Flow and Drought
Interflashed and interwrought:
Ended is begun, begun
295   Ended, quick as torrents run.
Young Impulsion spouts to sink;
Luridness and lustre link;
'Tis your come and go of breath;
Mirrored pants the Life, the Death;
300   Each of either reaped and sown:
Rosiest rosy wanes to crone.
See you so? your senses drift;
'Tis a shuttle weaving swift.
Look with spirit past the sense,
305   Spirit shines in permanence.
That is She, the view of whom
Is the dust within the tomb,
Is the inner blush above,
Look to loathe, or look to love;
310   Think her Lump, or know her Flame;
Dread her scourge, or read her aim;
Shoot your hungers from their nerve;
Or, in her example, serve.
Some have found her sitting grave;
315   Laughing, some; or, browed with sweat,
Hurling dust of fool and knave
In a hissing smithy's jet.

More it were not well to speak;
Burn to see, you need but seek.
320 Once beheld she gives the key
Airing every doorway, she.
Little can you stop or steer
Ere of her you are the seer.
On the surface she will witch,
325 Rendering Beauty yours, but gaze
Under, and the soul is rich
Past computing, past amaze.
Then is courage that endures
Even her awful tremble yours.
330 Then, the reflex of that Fount
Spied below, will Reason mount
Lordly and a quenchless force,
Lighting Pain to its mad source,
Scaring Fear till Fear escapes,
335 Shot through all its phantom shapes.
Then your spirit will perceive
Fleshly seed of fleshly sins;
Where the passions interweave,
How the serpent tangle spins
340 Of the sense of Earth misprised,
Brainlessly unrecognized;
She being Spirit in her clods,
Footway to the God of Gods.
Then for you are pleasures pure,
345 Sureties as the stars are sure:
Not the wanton beckoning flags
Which, of flattery and delight,
Wax to the grim Habit-Hags
Riding souls of men to night:
350 Pleasures that through blood run sane,
Quickening spirit from the brain.
Each of each in sequent birth,
Blood and brain and spirit, three,
(Say the deepest gnomes of Earth),

355 Join for true felicity.
Are they parted, then expect
Some one sailing will be wrecked:
Separate hunting are they sped,
Scan the morsel coveted.
360 Earth that Triad is: she hides
Joy from him who that divides;
Showers it when the three are one
Glassing her in union.
Earth your haven, Earth your helm,
365 You command a double realm;
Labouring here to pay your debt,
Till your little sun shall set;
Leaving her the future task:
Loving her too well to ask.
370 Eglantine that climbs the yew,
She her darkest wreathes for those
Knowing her the Ever-new,
And themselves the kin o' the rose.
Life, the chisel, axe and sword,
375 Wield who have her depths explored:
Life, the dream, shall be their robe
Large as air about the globe;
Life, the question, hear its cry
Echoed with concordant Why;
380 Life, the small self-dragon ramped,
Thrill for service to be stamped.
Ay, and over every height
Life for them shall wave a wand:
That, the last, where sits affright,
385 Homely shows the stream beyond.
Love the light and be its lynx,
You will track her and attain;
Read her as no cruel Sphinx
In the woods of Westermain,
390 Daily fresh the woods are ranged;
Glooms which otherwhere appal,

Sounded: here, their worths exchanged
Urban joins with pastoral:
Little lost, save what may drop
395   Husk-like, and the mind preserves.
Natural overgrowths they lop,
Yet from nature neither swerves,
Trained or savage: for this cause:
Of our Earth they ply the laws,
400   Have in Earth their feeding root,
Mind of man and bent of brute.
Hear that song; both wild and ruled.
Hear it: is it wail or mirth?
Ordered, bubbled, quite unschooled?
405   None, and all: it springs of Earth.
O but hear it! 'tis the mind;
Mind that with deep Earth unites,
Round the solid trunk to wind
Rings of clasping parasites.
410   Music have you there to feed
Simplest and most soaring need.
Free to wind, and in desire
Winding, they to her attached
Feel the trunk a spring of fire,
415   And ascend to heights unmatched,
Whence the tidal world is viewed
As a sea of windy wheat,
Momently black, barren, rude;
Golden-brown, for harvest meet,
420   Dragon-reaped from folly-sown;
Bride-like to the sickle-blade:
Quick it varies, while the moan,
Moan of a sad creature strayed,
Chiefly is its voice. So flesh
425   Conjures tempest-flails to thresh
Good from worthless. Some clear lamps
Light it; more of dead marsh-damps.
Monster is it still, and blind,

Fit but to be led by Pain.

430 Glance we at the paths behind,
Fruitful sight has Westermain.
There we laboured, and in turn
Forward our blown lamps discern,
As you see on the dark deep

435 Far the loftier billows leap,
Foam for beacon bear.
Hither, hither, if you will,
Drink instruction, or instil,
Run the woods like vernal sap,

440 Crying, hail to luminousness!
But have care.
In yourself may lurk the trap:
On conditions they caress.
Here you meet the light invoked

450 Here is never secret cloaked.
Doubt you with the monster's fry
All his orbit may exclude;
Are you of the stiff, the dry,
Cursing the not understood;

455 Grasp you with the monster's claws;
Govern with his truncheon-saws;
Hate, the shadow of a grain;
You are lost in Westermain:
Earthward swoops a vulture sun,

460 Nighted upon carrion:
Straightway venom wine-cups shout
Toasts to One whose eyes are out:
Flowers along the reeling floor
Drip henbane and hellebore:

465 Beauty, of her tresses shorn,
Shrieks as nature's maniac:
Hideousness on hoof and horn
Tumbles, yapping in her track:
Haggard Wisdom, stately once,

470 Leers fantastical and trips:

Allegory drums the sconce,
Impiousness nibblenips.
Imp that dances, imp that flits,
Imp o' the demon-growing girl,
475   Maddest! whirl with imp o' the pits
Round you, and with them you whirl
Fast where pours the fountain-rout
Out of Him whose eyes are out:
Multitudes on multitudes,
480   Drenched in wallowing devilry:
And you ask where you may be,
In what reek of a lair
Given to bones and ogre-broods:
And they yell you Where.
485   Enter these enchanted woods,
You who dare.

DANTE GABRIEL ROSSETTI (1828-1882)

Originally Italian expatriates, the Rossettis were an artistic family. Dante's father had been exiled from Italy for writing poetry in support of Napoleon; his oldest sister was a novelist; his younger brother was an editor and memoirist; and his youngest sister (Christina) became a poet as well. Dante himself was also a painter. With his siblings and friends, he formed the Pre-Raphaelite Brotherhood of artists. He met and married the beautiful Elizabeth Eleanor Siddal in 1850. She committed suicide after losing a child in 1862. He buried a manuscript of poems with her body, and seven years later he had her grave opened so that he could retrieve his only copy. Jane Burden Morris then became his muse and lover. Dante suffered from anxiety, paranoia, and various phobias throughout his life, and suffered from mental breakdowns. He was only fifty-four when he died of blood poisoning from uric acid.

THE BLESSED DAMOZEL

Dante Gabriel Rossetti

1   The blessed damozel lean'd out
From the gold bar of Heaven;
Her eyes were deeper than the depth
Of waters still'd at even;
5   She had three lilies in her hand,
And the stars in her hair were seven.

Her robe, ungirt from clasp to hem,
No wrought flowers did adorn,
But a white rose of Mary's gift,
10   For service meetly worn;
Her hair that lay along her back
Was yellow like ripe corn.

Her seem'd she scarce had been a day
One of God's choristers;
15   The wonder was not yet quite gone
From that still look of hers;
Albeit, to them she left, her day
Had counted as ten years.

(To one, it is ten years of years.
20   ...Yet now, and in this place,
Surely she lean'd o'er me—her hair
Fell all about my face....
Nothing: the autumn-fall of leaves.
The whole year sets apace.)

25   It was the rampart of God's house
That she was standing on;
By God built over the sheer depth
The which is Space begun;

So high, that looking downward thence
30   She scarce could see the sun.

It lies in Heaven, across the flood
Of ether, as a bridge.
Beneath, the tides of day and night
With flame and darkness ridge
35   The void, as low as where this earth
Spins like a fretful midge.

Around her, lovers, newly met
'Mid deathless love's acclaims,
Spoke evermore among themselves
40   Their heart-remember'd names;
And the souls mounting up to God
Went by her like thin flames.

And still she bow'd herself and stoop'd
Out of the circling charm;
45   Until her bosom must have made
The bar she lean'd on warm,
And the lilies lay as if asleep
Along her bended arm.

From the fix'd place of Heaven she saw
50   Time like a pulse shake fierce
Through all the worlds. Her gaze still strove
Within the gulf to pierce
Its path; and now she spoke as when
The stars sang in their spheres.

55   The sun was gone now; the curl'd moon
Was like a little feather
Fluttering far down the gulf; and now
She spoke through the still weather.
Her voice was like the voice the stars
60   Had when they sang together.

(Ah sweet! Even now, in that bird's song,
Strove not her accents there,
Fain to be hearken'd? When those bells
Possess'd the mid-day air,
65   Strove not her steps to reach my side
Down all the echoing stair?)

"I wish that he were come to me,
For he will come," she said.
"Have I not pray'd in Heaven?—on earth,
70   Lord, Lord, has he not pray'd?
Are not two prayers a perfect strength?
And shall I feel afraid?

"When round his head the aureole clings,
And he is cloth'd in white,
75   I'll take his hand and go with him
To the deep wells of light;
As unto a stream we will step down,
And bathe there in God's sight.

"We two will stand beside that shrine,
80   Occult, withheld, untrod,
Whose lamps are stirr'd continually
With prayer sent up to God;
And see our old prayers, granted, melt
Each like a little cloud.

85   "We two will lie i' the shadow of
That living mystic tree
Within whose secret growth the Dove
Is sometimes felt to be,
While every leaf that His plumes touch
90   Saith His Name audibly.

"And I myself will teach to him,

I myself, lying so,
The songs I sing here; which his voice
Shall pause in, hush'd and slow,
95   And find some knowledge at each pause,
Or some new thing to know."

(Alas! We two, we two, thou say'st!
Yea, one wast thou with me
That once of old. But shall God lift
100   To endless unity
The soul whose likeness with thy soul
Was but its love for thee?)

"We two," she said, "will seek the groves
Where the lady Mary is,
105   With her five handmaidens, whose names
Are five sweet symphonies,
Cecily, Gertrude, Magdalen,
Margaret and Rosalys.

"Circlewise sit they, with bound locks
110   And foreheads garlanded;
Into the fine cloth white like flame
Weaving the golden thread,
To fashion the birth-robes for them
Who are just born, being dead.

115   "He shall fear, haply, and be dumb:
Then will I lay my cheek
To his, and tell about our love,
Not once abash'd or weak:
And the dear Mother will approve
120   My pride, and let me speak.

"Herself shall bring us, hand in hand,
To Him round whom all souls
Kneel, the clear-rang'd unnumber'd heads

Bow'd with their aureoles:
125 And angels meeting us shall sing
To their citherns and citoles.

"There will I ask of Christ the Lord
Thus much for him and me:—
Only to live as once on earth
130 With Love,—only to be,
As then awhile, for ever now
Together, I and he."

She gaz'd and listen'd and then said,
Less sad of speech than mild,—
135 "All this is when he comes." She ceas'd.
The light thrill'd towards her, fill'd
With angels in strong level flight.
Her eyes pray'd, and she smil'd.

(I saw her smile.) But soon their path
140 Was vague in distant spheres:
And then she cast her arms along
The golden barriers,
And laid her face between her hands,
And wept. (I heard her tears.)

MY SISTER'S SLEEP

Dante Gabriel Rossetti

1   She fell asleep on Christmas Eve:
At length the long-ungranted shade
Of weary eyelids overweigh'd
The pain nought else might yet relieve.

5   Our mother, who had lean'd all day
Over the bed from chime to chime,
Then rais'd herself for the first time,
And as she sat her down, did pray.

Her little work-table was spread
10   With work to finish. For the glare
Made by her candle, she had care
To work some distance from the bed.

Without, there was a cold moon up,
Of winter radiance sheer and thin;
15   The hollow halo it was in
Was like an icy crystal cup.

Through the small room, with subtle sound
Of flame, by vents the fireshine drove
And redden'd. In its dim alcove
20   The mirror shed a clearness round.

I had been sitting up some nights,
And my tired mind felt weak and blank;
Like a sharp strengthening wine it drank
The stillness and the broken lights.

25   Twelve struck. That sound, by dwindling years
Heard in each hour, crept off; and then
The ruffled silence spread again,
Like water that a pebble stirs.

Our mother rose from where she sat:
30 Her needles, as she laid them down,
Met lightly, and her silken gown
Settled: no other noise than that.

"Glory unto the Newly Born!"
So, as said angels, she did say;
35 Because we were in Christmas Day,
Though it would still be long till morn.

Just then in the room over us
There was a pushing back of chairs,
As some who had sat unawares
40 So late, now heard the hour, and rose.

With anxious softly-stepping haste
Our mother went where Margaret lay,
Fearing the sounds o'erhead—should they
Have broken her long watch'd-for rest!

45 She stoop'd an instant, calm, and turn'd;
But suddenly turn'd back again;
And all her features seem'd in pain
With woe, and her eyes gaz'd and yearn'd.

For my part, I but hid my face,
50 And held my breath, and spoke no word:
There was none spoken; but I heard
The silence for a little space.

Our mother bow'd herself and wept:
And both my arms fell, and I said,
55 "God knows I knew that she was dead."
And there, all white, my sister slept.

Then kneeling, upon Christmas morn
A little after twelve o'clock
We said, ere the first quarter struck,
60 "Christ's blessing on the newly born!"

SOUL'S BEAUTY

Dante Gabriel Rossetti

1   Under the arch of Life, where love and death,
Terror and mystery, guard her shrine, I saw
Beauty enthroned; and though her gaze struck awe,
I drew it in as simply as my breath.
5   Hers are the eyes which, over and beneath,
The sky and sea bend on thee,—which can draw,
By sea or sky or woman, to one law,
The allotted bondman of her palm and wreath.

This is that Lady Beauty, in whose praise
10   Thy voice and hand shake still,—long known to thee
By flying hair and fluttering hem,—the beat
Following her daily of thy heart and feet,
How passionately and irretrievably,
In what fond flight, how many ways and days!

BODY'S BEAUTY

Dante Gabriel Rossetti

1   Of Adam's first wife, Lilith, it is told
(The witch he loved before the gift of Eve,)
That, ere the snake's, her sweet tongue could deceive,
And her enchanted hair was the first gold.
5   And still she sits, young while the earth is old,
And, subtly of herself contemplative,
Draws men to watch the bright web she can weave,
Till heart and body and life are in its hold.
The rose and poppy are her flowers; for where
10   Is he not found, O Lilith, whom shed scent
And soft-shed kisses and soft sleep shall snare?
Lo! as that youth's eyes burned at thine, so went
Thy spell through him, and left his straight neck bent
And round his heart one strangling golden hair.

NUPTIAL SLEEP

Dante Gabriel Rossetti

1   At length their long kiss severed, with sweet smart:
    And as the last slow sudden drops are shed
    From sparkling eaves when all the storm has fled,
    So singly flagged the pulses of each heart.
5   Their bosoms sundered, with the opening start
    Of married flowers to either side outspread
    From the knit stem; yet still their mouths, burnt red,
    Fawned on each other where they lay apart.

    Sleep sank them lower than the tide of dreams,
10   And their dreams watched them sink, and slid away.
    Slowly their souls swam up again, through gleams
    Of watered light and dull drowned waifs of day;
    Till from some wonder of new woods and streams
    He woke, and wondered more: for there she lay.

THE WOODSPURGE

Dante Gabriel Rossetti

1   The wind flapp'd loose, the wind was still,
    Shaken out dead from tree and hill:
    I had walk'd on at the wind's will,—
    I sat now, for the wind was still.

5   Between my knees my forehead was,—
    My lips, drawn in, said not Alas!
    My hair was over in the grass,
    My naked ears heard the day pass.

    My eyes, wide open, had the run
10   Of some ten weeds to fix upon;
    Among those few, out of the sun,
    The woodspurge flower'd, three cups in one.

    From perfect grief there need not be
    Wisdom or even memory:
15   One thing then learnt remains to me,—
    The woodspurge has a cup of three.

PENUMBRA

Dante Gabriel Rossetti

1   I did not look upon her eyes,
     (Though scarcely seen, with no surprise,
     'Mid many eyes a single look,)
     Because they should not gaze rebuke,
5   At night, from stars in sky and brook.

     I did not take her by the hand,
     (Though little was to understand
     From touch of hand all friends might take,)
     Because it should not prove a flake
10   Burnt in my palm to boil and ache.

     I did not listen to her voice,
     (Though none had noted, where at choice
     All might rejoice in listening,)
     Because no such a thing should cling
15   In the wood's moan at evening.

     I did not cross her shadow once,
     (Though from the hollow west the sun's
     Last shadow runs along so far,)
     Because in June it should not bar
20   My ways, at noon when fevers are.

     They told me she was sad that day,
     (Though wherefore tell what love's soothsay,
     Sooner than they, did register?)
     And my heart leapt and wept to her,
25   And yet I did not speak nor stir.

     So shall the tongues of the sea's foam
     (Though many voices therewith come
     From drowned hope's home to cry to me,)
     Bewail one hour the more, when sea
30   And wind are one with memory.

THE SEA LIMITS

from House of Life
Dante Gabriel Rossetti

1   Consider the sea's listless chime;
    Time's self it is, made audible -
    The murmur of the earth's own shell.
    Secret continuance sublime
5   Is the sea's end: our sight may pass
    No furlong further. Since time was,
    This sound hath told the lapse of time.

    No quiet, which is death's -it hath
    The mournfulness of ancient life,
10   Enduring always at dull strife.
    As the world's heart of rest and wrath,
    Its painful pulse is in the sands.
    Last utterly, the whole sky stands
    Grey and not known, along its path.

THE SONNET

Dante Gabriel Rossetti

1   A Sonnet is a moment's monument,—
      Memorial from the Soul's eternity
      To one dead deathless hour. Look that it be,
      Whether for lustral rite or dire portent,
5   Of its own intricate fulness reverent:
      Carve it in ivory or in ebony,
      As Day or Night prevail; and let Time see
      Its flowering crest impearled and orient.

      A Sonnet is a coin: its face reveals
10   The soul,--its converse, to what Power 'tis due:—
      Whether for tribute to the august appeals
      Of Life, or dower in Love's high retinue
      It serve; or, 'mid the dark wharf's cavernous breath,
      In Charon's palm it pay the toll to Death.

3: LOVE'S TESTAMENT

from House of Life
Dante Gabriel Rossetti

1   O thou who at Love's hour ecstatically
        Unto my heart dost ever more present,
        Clothed with his fire, thy heart his testament;
        Whom I have neared and felt thy breath to be
5   The inmost incense of his sanctuary;
        Who without speech hast owned him, and, intent
        Upon his will, thy life with mine hast blent,
        And murmured, "I am thine, thou'rt one with me!"

      O what from thee the grace, to me the prize,
10   And what to Love the glory,—when the whole
        Of the deep stair thou tread'st to the dim shoal
        And weary water of the place of sighs,
        And there dost work deliverance, as thine eyes
        Draw up my prisoned spirit to thy soul!

4: LOVESIGHT

from House of Life
Dante Gabriel Rossetti

1   When do I see thee most, beloved one?
      When in the light the spirits of mine eyes
      Before thy face, their altar, solemnize
      The worship of that Love through thee made known?
5   Or when in the dusk hours (we two alone)
      Close-kissed and eloquent of still replies
      Thy twilight-hidden glimmering visage lies,
      And my soul only sees thy soul its own?

      O love, my love! if I no more should see
10   Thyself, nor on the earth the shadow of thee,
      Nor image of thine eyes in any spring,—
      How then should sound upon Life's darkening slope
      The ground-whirl of the perished leaves of Hope,
      The wind of Death's imperishable wing?

11: THE LOVE-LETTER

from House of Life
Dante Gabriel Rossetti

1   Warmed by her hand and shadowed by her hair
As close she leaned and poured her heart through thee,
Whereof the articulate throbs accompany
The smooth black stream that makes thy whiteness fair,—
5   Sweet fluttering sheet, even of her breath aware,—
Oh let thy silent song disclose to me
That soul wherewith her lips and eyes agree
Like married music in Love's answering air.

Fain had I watched her when, at some fond thought,
10   Her bosom to the writing closelier press'd,
And her breast's secrets peered into her breast;
When, through eyes raised an instant, her soul sought
My soul, and from the sudden confluence caught
The words that made her love the loveliest.

19: SILENT NOON

from House of Life
Dante Gabriel Rossetti

1   Your hands lie open in the long fresh grass,—
The finger-points look through like rosy blooms:
Your eyes smile peace. The pasture gleams and glooms
'Neath billowing skies that scatter and amass.
5   All round our nest, far as the eye can pass,
Are golden kingcup-fields with silver edge
Where the cow-parsley skirts the hawthorn-hedge.
'Tis visible silence, still as the hour-glass.

Deep in the sun-searched growths the dragon-fly
10   Hangs like a blue thread loosened from the sky:—
So this wing'd hour is dropt to us from above.
Oh! clasp we to our hearts, for deathless dower,
This close-companioned inarticulate hour
When twofold silence was the song of love.

22: HEART'S HAVEN

from House of Life
Dante Gabriel Rossetti

1   Sometimes she is a child within mine arms,
Cowering beneath dark wing that love must chase,—
With still tears showering and averted face,
Inexplicably filled with faint alarms:
5   And oft from mine own spirit's hurtling harms
I crave the refuge of her deep embrace,—
Against all ills the fortified strong place
And sweet reserve of sovereign counter-charms.

And Love, our light at night and shade at noon,
10   Lulls us to rest with songs, and turns away
All shafts of shelterless tumultuous day.
Like the moon's growth, his face gleams through his tune;
And as soft waters warble to the moon,
Our answering spirits chime one roundelay.

27: HEART'S COMPASS

from House of Life
Dante Gabriel Rossetti

1   Sometimes thou seem'st not as thyself alone,
But as the meaning of all things that are;
A breathless wonder, shadowing forth afar
Some heavenly solstice hushed and halcyon;
5   Whose unstirred lips are music's visible tone;
Whose eyes the sun-gate of the soul unbar,
Being of its furthest fires oracular;—
The evident heart of all life sown and mown.

Even such Love is; and is not thy name Love?
10   Yea, by thy hand the Love-god rends apart
All gathering clouds of Night's ambiguous art;
Flings them far down, and sets thine eyes above;
And simply, as some gage of flower or glove,
Stakes with a smile the world against thy heart.

36: LIFE-IN-LOVE

from House of Life
Dante Gabriel Rossetti

1   Not in thy body is thy life at all
But in this lady's lips and hands and eyes;
Through these she yields thee life that vivifies
What else were sorrow's servant and death's thrall.
5   Look on thyself without her, and recall
The waste remembrance and forlorn surmise
That lived but in a dead-drawn breath of sighs
O'er vanished hours and hours eventual.

Even so much life hath the poor tress of hair
10   Which, stored apart, is all love hath to show
For heart-beats and for fire-heats long ago;
Even so much life endures unknown, even where,
'Mid change the changeless night environeth,
Lies all that golden hair undimmed in death.

41: THROUGH DEATH TO LOVE

from House of Life
Dante Gabriel Rossetti

1   Like labour-laden moonclouds faint to flee
From winds that sweep the winter-bitten wold,—
Like multiform circumfluence manifold
Of night's flood-tide,—like terrors that agree
5   Of hoarse-tongued fire and inarticulate sea,—
Even such, within some glass dimmed by our breath,
Our hearts discern wild images of Death,
Shadows and shoals that edge eternity.

Howbeit athwart Death's imminent shade doth soar
10   One Power, than flow of stream or flight of dove
Sweeter to glide around, to brood above.
Tell me, my heart,—what angel-greeted door
Or threshold of wing-winnowed threshing-floor
Hath guest fire-fledged as thine, whose lord is Love?

43: LOVE AND HOPE

from House of Life
Dante Gabriel Rossetti

1   Bless love and hope. Full many a withered year
    Whirled past us, eddying to its chill doomsday;
    And clasped together where the blown leaves lay,
    We long have knelt and wept full many a tear.
5   Yet lo! one hour at last, the Spring's compeer,
    Flutes softly to us from some green byeway:
    Those years, those tears are dead, but only they—
    Bless love and hope, true soul; for we are here.

    Cling heart to heart; nor of this hour demand
10   Whether in very truth, when we are dead,
    Our hearts shall wake to know Love's golden head
    Sole sunshine of the imperishable land;
    Or but discern, through night's unfeatured scope,
    Scorn-fired at length the illusive eyes of Hope.

48: DEATH-IN-LOVE

from House of Life
Dante Gabriel Rossetti

1   There came an image in Life's retinue
That had Love's wings and bore his gonfalon;
Fair was the web, and nobly wrought thereon,
O soul-sequestered face, thy form and hue!
5   Bewildering sounds, such as spring wakens to,
Shook in its folds; and through my heart its power
Sped trackless as the immemorable hour
When birth's dark portal groaned and all was new.

But a veiled woman followed, and she caught
10   The banner 'round its staff, to furl and cling—
Then plucked a feather from the bearer's wing
And held it to his lips that stirred it not,
And said to me, "Behold, there is no breath;
I and this Love are one, and I am Death."

49: WILLOWWOOD 1

from House of Life
Dante Gabriel Rossetti

1   I sat with Love upon a woodside well,
    Leaning across the water, I and he;
    Nor ever did he speak nor looked at me,
    But touched his lute wherein was audible
5   The certain secret thing he had to tell:
    Only our mirrored eyes met silently
    In the low wave; and that sound came to be
    The passionate voice I knew; and my tears fell.

    And at their fall, his eyes beneath grew hers;
10   And with his foot and with his wing-feathers
    He swept the spring that watered my heart's drouth.
    Then the dark ripples spread to waving hair,
    And as I stooped, her own lips rising there
    Bubbled with brimming kisses at my mouth.

50: WILLOWWOOD 2

from House of Life
Dante Gabriel Rossetti

1   And now Love sang: but his was such a song,
    So meshed with half-remembrance hard to free,
    As souls disused in death's sterility
    May sing when the new birthday tarries long.
5   And I was made aware of a dumb throng
    That stood aloof, one form by every tree,
    All mournful forms, for each was I or she,
    The shades of those our days that had no tongue.

    They looked on us, and knew us and were known;
10 While fast together, alive from the abyss,
    Clung the soul-wrung implacable close kiss;
    And pity of self through all made broken moan
    Which said, 'For once, for once, for once alone!'
    And still Love sang, and what he sang was this:—

51: WILLOWWOOD 3

from House of Life
Dante Gabriel Rossetti

1   'O ye, all ye that walk in Willowwood,
       That walk with hollow faces burning white;
       What fathom-depth of soul-struck widowhood,
       What long, what longer hours, one lifelong night,
5   Ere ye again, who so in vain have wooed
       Your last hope lost, who so in vain invite
       Your lips to that their unforgotten food,
       Ere ye, ere ye again shall see the light!

       Alas! the bitter banks in Willowwood,
10   With tear-spurge wan, with blood-wort burning red:
       Alas! if ever such a pillow could
       Steep deep the soul in sleep till she were dead,
       Better all life forget her than this thing,
       That Willowwood should hold her wandering!'

52: WILLOWWOOD 4

from House of Life
Dante Gabriel Rossetti

1   So sang he: and as meeting rose and rose
     Together cling through the wind's wellaway
     Nor change at once, yet near the end of day
     The leaves drop loosened where the heart-stain glows,—
5   So when the song died did the kiss unclose;
     And her face fell back drowned, and was as grey
     As its grey eyes; and if it ever may
     Meet mine again I know not if Love knows.

     Only I know that I leaned low and drank
10   A long draught from the water where she sank,
     Her breath and all her tears and all her soul:
     And as I leaned, I know I felt Love's face
     Pressed on my neck with moan of pity and grace,
     Till both our heads were in his aureole.

53: WITHOUT HER

from House of Life
Dante Gabriel Rossetti

1   What of her glass without her? The blank gray
      There where the pool is blind of the moon's face.
      Her dress without her? The tossed empty space
Of cloud-rack whence the moon has passed away.
5   Her paths without her? Day's appointed sway
      Usurped by desolate night. Her pillowed place
      Without her? Tears, ah me! for love's good grace,
And cold forgetfulness of night or day.

What of the heart without her? Nay, poor heart,
10   Of thee what word remains ere speech be still?
      A wayfarer by barren ways and chill,
Steep ways and weary, without her thou art,
Where the long cloud, the long wood's counterpart,
      Sheds doubled darkness up the labouring hill.

66: THE HEART OF THE NIGHT

from House of Life
Dante Gabriel Rossetti

1   From child to youth; from youth to arduous man;
    From lethargy to fever of the heart;
    Prom faithful life to dream-dowered days apart;
    From trust to doubt; from doubt to brink of ban;—
5   Thus much of change in one swift cycle ran
    Till now. Alas, the soul!—how soon must she
    Accept her primal immortality,—
    The flesh resume its dust whence it began?

    O Lord of work and peace! O Lord of life!
10   O Lord, the awful Lord of will! though late,
    Even yet renew this soul with duteous breath:
    That when the peace is garnered in from strife,
    The work retrieved, the will regenerate,
    This soul may see thy face, O Lord of death

71: THE CHOICE 1

from House of Life
Dante Gabriel Rossetti

1   Eat thou and drink; to-morrow thou shalt die.
Surely the earth, that's wise being very old,
Needs not our help. Then loose me, love, and hold
Thy sultry hair up from my face; that I
5   May pour for thee this golden wine, brim-high,
Till round the glass thy fingers glow like gold.
We'll drown all hours: thy song, while hours are toll'd,
Shall leap, as fountains veil the changing sky.

Now kiss, and think that there are really those,
10   My own high-bosom'd beauty, who increase
Vain gold, vain lore, and yet might choose our way!
Through many years they toil; then on a day
They die not,—for their life was death,—but cease;
And round their narrow lips the mould falls close.

72: THE CHOICE 2

from House of Life
Dante Gabriel Rossetti

1 Watch thou and fear; to-morrow thou shalt die.
Or art thou sure thou shalt have time for death?
Is not the day which God's word promiseth
To come man knows not when? In yonder sky,
5 Now while we speak, the sun speeds forth: can I
Or thou assure him of his goal? God's breath
Even at this moment haply quickeneth
The air to a flame; till spirits, always nigh

Though screen'd and hid, shall walk tha daylight here.
10 And dost thou prate of all that man shall do?
Canst thou, who hast but plagues, presume to be
Glad in his gladness that comes after thee?
Will his strength slay thy worm in Hell? Go to:
Cover thy countenance, and watch, and fear.

73: THE CHOICE 3

from House of Life
Dante Gabriel Rossetti

1   Think thou and act; to-morrow thou shalt die
Outstretch'd in the sun's warmth upon the shore,
Thou say'st: "Man's measur'd path is all gone o'er:
Up all his years, steeply, with strain and sigh,
5   Man clomb until he touch'd the truth; and I,
Even I, am he whom it was destin'd for."
How should this be? Art thou then so much more
Than they who sow'd, that thou shouldst reap thereby?

Nay, come up hither. From this wave-wash'd mound
10   Unto the furthest flood-brim look with me;
Then reach on with thy thought till it be drown'd.
Miles and miles distant though the last line be,
And though thy soul sail leagues and leagues beyond,—
Still, leagues beyond those leagues, there is more sea.

97: A SUPERSCRIPTION

from House of Life
Dante Gabriel Rossetti

1   Look in my face; my name is Might-have-been;
I am also called No-more, Too-late, Farewell;
Unto thine ear I hold the dead-sea shell
Cast up thy Life's foam-fretted feet between;
5   Unto thine eyes the glass where that is seen
Which had Life's form and Love's, but by my spell
Is now a shaken shadow intolerable,
Of ultimate things unuttered the frail screen.

Mark me, how still I am! But should there dart
10   One moment through thy soul the soft surprise
Of that winged Peace which lulls the breath of sighs,
Then shalt thou see me smile, and turn apart
Thy visage to mine ambush at thy heart
Sleepless with cold commemorative eyes.

CHRISTINA ROSSETTI (1830-1894)

Christina Rossetti was the youngest child of the talented Rossetti family. She was known to have a fiery temper in her youth. For example, once after getting angry with her mother, she stabbed herself in the arm with scissors. While caring for her ailing father in 1845, she became ill. Her diagnosis varied from mental illness ("religious mania") to a heart condition. She began to publish her poems from the age of seventeen, some of which were published in her brother's Pre-Raphaelite periodical. Christian Rossetti was briefly engaged to James Collinson. She insisted that he convert from Catholicism to the Church of England before she would agree to marry him, and then broke off the engagement when he converted back to Catholicism. With her mother, Rossetti attempted to run a school; after it failed, she was supported financially by her brothers for the rest of her life. Her illnesses continued to plague her. She suffered from Grave's Disease, a rare thyroid condition, and in 1892, she was diagnosed with breast cancer. Although she underwent a mastectomy, the cancer returned and she succumbed to it in 1894.

A TRIAD

Christina Rossetti

1   Three sang of love together: one with lips
Crimson, with cheeks and bosom in a glow,
Flushed to the yellow hair and finger-tips;
And one there sang who soft and smooth as snow
5   Bloomed like a tinted hyacinth at a show;
And one was blue with famine after love,
Who like a harpstring snapped rang harsh and low
The burden of what those were singing of.
One shamed herself in love; one temperately
10   Grew gross in soulless love, a sluggish wife;
One famished died for love. Thus two of three
Took death for love and won him after strife;
One droned in sweetness like a fattened bee:
All on the threshold, yet all short of life.

A BIRTHDAY

Christina Rossetti

1   My heart is like a singing bird
          Whose nest is in a water'd shoot;
    My heart is like an apple-tree
          Whose boughs are bent with thickset fruit;
5   My heart is like a rainbow shell
          That paddles in a halcyon sea;
    My heart is gladder than all these
          Because my love is come to me.

    Raise me a dais of silk and down;
10   Hang it with vair and purple dyes;
    Carve it in doves and pomegranates,
          And peacocks with a hundred eyes;
    Work it in gold and silver grapes,
          In leaves and silver fleurs-de-lys;
15   Because the birthday of my life
          Is come, my love is come to me.

REMEMBER

Christina Rossetti

1   Remember me when I am gone away,
        Gone far away into the silent land;
        When you can no more hold me by the hand,
Nor I half turn to go yet turning stay.
5   Remember me when no more day by day
        You tell me of our future that you plann'd:
        Only remember me; you understand
It will be late to counsel then or pray.
Yet if you should forget me for a while
10   And afterwards remember, do not grieve:
        For if the darkness and corruption leave
        A vestige of the thoughts that once I had,
Better by far you should forget and smile
        Than that you should remember and be sad.

AFTER DEATH

Christina Rossetti

1   The curtains were half drawn, the floor was swept
         And strewn with rushes, rosemary and may
         Lay thick upon the bed on which I lay,
         Where through the lattice ivy-shadows crept.
5   He leaned above me, thinking that I slept
         And could not hear him; but I heard him say,
         'Poor child, poor child': and as he turned away
         Came a deep silence, and I knew he wept.
         He did not touch the shroud, or raise the fold
10   That hid my face, or take my hand in his,
         Or ruffle the smooth pillows for my head:
         He did not love me living; but once dead
         He pitied me; and very sweet it is
         To know he still is warm though I am cold.

AN APPLE GATHERING

Christina Rossetti

1   I plucked pink blossoms from mine apple-tree
       And wore them all that evening in my hair:
     Then in due season when I went to see
       I found no apples there.

5   With dangling basket all along the grass
       As I had come I went the selfsame track:
     My neighbours mocked me while they saw me pass
       So empty-handed back.

     Lilian and Lilias smiled in trudging by,
10   Their heaped-up basket teased me like a jeer;
     Sweet-voiced they sang beneath the sunset sky,
       Their mother's home was near.

     Plump Gertrude passed me with her basket full,
       A stronger hand than hers helped it along;
15   A voice talked with her through the shadows cool
       More sweet to me than song.

     Ah Willie, Willie, was my love less worth
       Than apples with their green leaves piled above?
     I counted rosiest apples on the earth
20   Of far less worth than love.

     So once it was with me you stooped to talk
       Laughing and listening in this very lane:
     To think that by this way we used to walk
       We shall not walk again!

25   I let me neighbours pass me, ones and twos
       And groups; the latest said the night grew chill,
     And hastened: but I loitered, while the dews
       Fell fast I loitered still.

WINTER: MY SECRET

Christina Rossetti

1   I tell my secret? No indeed, not I;
     Perhaps some day, who knows?
     But not today; it froze, and blows and snows,
     And you're too curious: fie!
5   You want to hear it? well:
     Only, my secret's mine, and I won't tell.

     Or, after all, perhaps there's none:
     Suppose there is no secret after all,
     But only just my fun.
10   Today's a nipping day, a biting day;
     In which one wants a shawl,
     A veil, a cloak, and other wraps:
     I cannot ope to everyone who taps,
     And let the draughts come whistling thro' my hall;
15   Come bounding and surrounding me,
     Come buffeting, astounding me,
     Nipping and clipping thro' my wraps and all.
     I wear my mask for warmth: who ever shows
     His nose to Russian snows
20   To be pecked at by every wind that blows?
     You would not peck? I thank you for good will,
     Believe, but leave the truth untested still.

     Spring's an expansive time: yet I don't trust
     March with its peck of dust,
25   Nor April with its rainbow-crowned brief showers,
     Nor even May, whose flowers
     One frost may wither thro' the sunless hours.

Perhaps some languid summer day,
When drowsy birds sing less and less,
30   And golden fruit is ripening to excess,
If there's not too much sun nor too much cloud,
And the warm wind is neither still nor loud,
Perhaps my secret I may say,
Or you may guess.

NO, THANK YOU, JOHN

Christina Rossetti

1   I never said I loved you, John:
Why will you tease me day by day,
And wax a weariness to think upon
With always "do" and "pray"?

5   You Know I never loved you, John;
No fault of mine made me your toast:
Why will you haunt me with a face as wan
As shows an hour-old ghost?

I dare say Meg or Moll would take
10   Pity upon you, if you'd ask:
And pray don't remain single for my sake
Who can't perform the task.

I have no heart?-Perhaps I have not;
But then you're mad to take offence
15   That don't give you what I have not got:
Use your common sense.

Let bygones be bygones:
Don't call me false, who owed not to be true:
I'd rather answer "No" to fifty Johns
20   Than answer "Yes" to you.

Let's mar our plesant days no more,
Song-birds of passage, days of youth:
Catch at today, forget the days before:
I'll wink at your untruth.

25   Let us strike hands as hearty friends;
No more, no less; and friendship's good:
Only don't keep in veiw ulterior ends, And points not understood

In open treaty. Rise above
Quibbles and shuffling off and on:
30   Here's friendship for you if you like; but love,-
No, thank you, John.

SONG

Christina Rossetti

1   When I am dead, my dearest,
       Sing no sad songs for me;
    Plant thou no roses at my head,
       Nor shady cypress tree:
5   Be the green grass above me
       With showers and dewdrops wet;
    And if thou wilt, remember,
       And if thou wilt, forget.

    I shall not see the shadows,
10   I shall not feel the rain;
    I shall not hear the nightingale
       Sing on, as if in pain:
    And dreaming through the twilight
       That doth not rise nor set,
15   Haply I may remember,
       And haply may forget.

SHE SAT AND SANG ALWAYS

Christina Rossetti

1   She sat and sang always
By the green margin of a stream,
Watching the fishes leap and play
Beneath the glad sunbeam.

5   I sat and wept alway
Beneath the moon's most shadowy beam,
Watching the blossoms of the May
Weep leaves into the stream.

I wept for memory;
10   She sang for hope that is so fair:
My tears were swallowed by the sea;
Her songs died in the air.

A PORTRAIT

Christina Rossetti

I

1   She gave up beauty in her tender youth,
     Gave all her hope and joy and pleasant ways;
     She covered up her eyes lest they should gaze
     On vanity, and chose the bitter truth.
5   Harsh towards herself, towards others full of ruth,
     Servant of servants, little known to praise,
     Long prayers and fasts trenched on her nights and days:
     She schooled herself to sights and sounds uncouth
     That with the poor and stricken she might make
10   A home, until the least of all sufficed
     Her wants; her own self learned she to forsake,
     Counting all earthly gain but hurt and loss.
     So with calm will she chose and bore the cross
     And hated all for love of Jesus Christ.

II

15   They knelt in silent anguish by her bed,
     And could not weep; but calmly there she lay.
     All pain had left her; and the sun's last ray
     Shone through upon her; warming into red
     The shady curtains. In her heart she said:
     'Heaven opens; I leave these and go away;
     The Bridegroom calls,—shall the Bride seek to stay?'
20   Then low upon her breast she bowed her head.
     O lily flower, O gem of priceless worth,
     O dove with patient voice and patient eyes,
     O fruitful vine amid a land of dearth,
     O maid replete with loving purities,
25   Thou bowedst down thy head with friends on earth
     To raise it with the saints in Paradise.

COBWEBS

Christina Rossetti

1   It is a land with neither night nor day,
Nor heat nor cold, nor any wind, nor rain,
Nor hills nor valleys; but one even plain
Stretches thro' long unbroken miles away:
5   While thro' the sluggish air a twilight grey
Broodeth; no moons or seasons wax and wane,
No ebb and flow are there among the main,
No bud-time no leaf-falling there for aye,
No ripple on the sea, no shifting sand,
10   No beat of wings to stir the stagnant space,
No pulse of life thro' all the loveless lands:
And loveless sea: no trace of days before,
No guarded home, no time-worn restingplace
No future hope no fear forevermore.

IN AN ARTIST'S STUDIO

Christina Rossetti

1   One face looks out from all his canvases,
    One selfsame figure sits or walks or leans:
    We found her hidden just behind those screens,
    That mirror gave back all her loveliness.
5   A queen in opal or in ruby dress,
    A nameless girl in freshest summer-greens,
    A saint, an angel—every canvas means
    The same one meaning, neither more nor less.
    He feeds upon her face by day and night,
10   And she with true kind eyes looks back on him,
    Fair as the moon and joyful as the light:
    Not wan with waiting, not with sorrow dim;
    Not as she is, but was when hope shone bright;
    Not as she is, but as she fills his dream.

LATER LIFE: SONNET 17

Christina Rossetti

1   Something this foggy day, a something which
    Is neither of this fog nor of today,
    Has set me dreaming of the winds that play
    Past certain cliffs, along one certain beach,
5   And turn the topmost edge of waves to spray:
    Ah pleasant pebbly strand so far away,
    So out of reach while quite within my reach,
    As out of reach as India or Cathay!

I am sick of where I am and where I am not,
10   I am sick of foresight and of memory,
I am sick of all I have and all I see,
I am sick of self, and there is nothing new;
Oh weary impatient patience of my lot!
Thus with myself: how fares it, Friends, with you?

SLEEPING AT LAST

Christina Rossetti

1   Sleeping at last, the trouble and tumult over,
Sleeping at last, the struggle and horror past,
Cold and white, out of sight of friend and of lover,
Sleeping at last.

5   No more a tired heart downcast or overcast,
No more pangs that wring or shifting fears that hover,
Sleeping at last in a dreamless sleep locked fast.

Fast asleep. Singing birds in their leafy cover
Cannot wake her, nor shake her the gusty blast.
10   Under the purple thyme and the purple clover
Sleeping at last.

PROMISES LIKE PIE CRUST

Christina Rossetti

1   Promise me no promises,
    So will I not promise you:
    Keep we both our liberties,
    Never false and never true:
5   Let us hold the die uncast,
    Free to come as free to go:
    For I cannot know your past,
    And of mine what can you know?

    You, so warm, may once have been
10   Warmer towards another one:
    I, so cold, may once have seen
    Sunlight, once have felt the sun:
    Who shall show us if it was
    Thus indeed in time of old?
15   Fades the image from the glass,
    And the fortune is not told.

    If you promised, you might grieve
    For lost liberty again:
    If I promised, I believe
20   I should fret to break the chain.
    Let us be the friends we were,
    Nothing more but nothing less:
    Many thrive on frugal fare
    Who would perish of excess.

OSCAR WILDE (1854-1900)

Oscar Wilde is Victorian author who is known primarily for his nine plays and his novel, *A Picture of Dorian Gray*. Wilde's poetry, however, is currently experiencing a revival of critical and popular interest. Wilde's father was a surgeon, and his mother was a poet and Irish revolutionary. He attended Trinity College, Dublin, and Magdalen College, Oxford. After settling in London, Wilde published his first book, *Poems*, in 1881. Wilde became very well known not only for his writing but also for his personal "dandy" style and extroverted personality. His lecture tour in the US brought him wealth and fame. He worked as editor of the fashion magazine *Women's World*. In 1884, Wilde married Constance Lloyd and the couple had two sons, but he also had affairs with men, most notoriously with Lord Alfred Douglas. In 1895, when Douglas's father called Wilde a "sodomite," Wilde tried to sue for libel, but after he lost his suit, the evidence was used to charge and convict him with sodomy. He was sentenced to two years of hard labor at Reading Gaol. It broke his spirit, and after Wilde was released from prison, he wandered Europe under a false name and died bankrupt, possibly from alcoholism, in a Parisian hotel.

IMPRESSIONS

Oscar Wilde

I. Les Silhouettes

1   The sea is flecked with bars of grey,
    The dull dead wind is out of tune,
    And like a withered leaf the moon
Is blown across the stormy bay.

5   Etched clear upon the pallid sand
    Lies the black boat: a sailor boy
    Clambers aboard in careless joy
With laughing face and gleaming hand.

    And overhead the curlews cry,
10   Where through the dusky upland grass
    The young brown-throated reapers pass,
Like silhouettes against the sky.

II. La Fuite de la Lune

    To outer senses there is peace,
    A dreamy peace on either hand
15   Deep silence in the shadowy land,
Deep silence where the shadows cease.

    Save for a cry that echoes shrill
    From some lone bird disconsolate;
    A corncrake calling to its mate;
20 The answer from the misty hill.

    And suddenly the moon withdraws
    Her sickle from the lightening skies,
    And to her sombre cavern flies,
Wrapped in a veil of yellow gauze.

HER VOICE

Oscar Wilde

1   The wild bee reels from bough to bough
    With his furry coat and his gauzy wing.
    Now in a lily-cup, and now
    Setting a jacinth bell a-swing,
5   In his wandering;
    Sit closer love: it was here I trow
    I made that vow,

    Swore that two lives should be like one
    As long as the sea-gull loved the sea,
10   As long as the sunflower sought the sun,—
    It shall be, I said, for eternity
    'Twixt you and me!
    Dear friend, those times are over and done,
    Love's web is spun.

15   Look upward where the poplar trees
    Sway and sway in the summer air,
    Here in the valley never a breeze
    Scatters the thistledown, but there
    Great winds blow fair
20   From the mighty murmuring mystical seas,
    And the wave-lashed leas.

    Look upward where the white gull screams,
    What does it see that we do not see?
    Is that a star? or the lamp that gleams
25   On some outward voyaging argosy,—
    Ah! can it be
    We have lived our lives in a land of dreams!
    How sad it seems.

Sweet, there is nothing left to say
30   But this, that love is never lost,
Keen winter stabs the breasts of May
Whose crimson roses burst his frost,
Ships tempest-tossed
Will find a harbour in some bay,
35   And so we may.

And there is nothing left to do
But to kiss once again, and part,
Nay, there is nothing we should rue,
I have my beauty,—you your Art,
40   Nay, do not start,
One world was not enough for two
Like me and you.

E TENEBIS

Oscar Wilde

1   Come down, O Christ, and help me! reach thy hand,
     For I am drowning in a stormier sea
     Than Simon on thy lake of Galilee:
     The wine of life is spilt upon the sand,
5   My heart is as some famine-murdered land,
     Whence all good things have perished utterly,
     And well I know my soul in Hell must lie
     If I this night before God's throne should stand.
     'He sleeps perchance, or rideth to the chase,
10   Like Baal, when his prophets howled that name
     From morn to noon on Carmel's smitten height.'
     Nay, peace, I shall behold before the night,
     The feet of brass, the robe more white than flame,
     The wounded hands, the weary human face.

ENDYMION

Oscar Wilde

1   The apple trees are hung with gold,
And birds are loud in Arcady,
The sheep lie bleating in the fold,
The wild goat runs across the wold,
5   But yesterday his love he told,
I know he will come back to me.
O rising moon! O Lady moon!
Be you my lover's sentinel,
You cannot choose but know him well,
10   For he is shod with purple shoon,
You cannot choose but know my love,
For he a shepherd's crook doth bear,
And he is soft as any dove,
And brown and curly is his hair.

15   The turtle now has ceased to call
Upon her crimson-footed groom,
The grey wolf prowls about the stall,
The lily's singing seneschal
Sleeps in the lily-bell, and all
20   The violet hills are lost in gloom.
O risen moon! O holy moon!
Stand on the top of Helice,
And if my own true love you see,
Ah! if you see the purple shoon,
25   The hazel crook, the lad's brown hair,
The goat-skin wrapped about his arm,
Tell him that I am waiting where
The rushlight glimmers in the Farm.

The falling dew is cold and chill,
30 And no bird sings in Arcady,
The little fauns have left the hill,
Even the tired daffodil
Has closed its gilded doors, and still
My lover comes not back to me.
35 False moon! False moon! O waning moon!
Where is my own true lover gone,
Where are the lips vermilion,
The shepherd's crook, the purple shoon?
Why spread that silver pavilion,
40 Why wear that veil of drifting mist?
Ah! thou hast young Endymion,
Thou hast the lips that should be kissed!

AMOR INTELLECTUALIS

Oscar Wilde

1 Oft have we trod the vales of Castaly
And heard sweet notes of sylvan music blown
From antique reeds to common folk unknown:
And often launched our bark upon that sea
5 Which the nine Muses hold in empery,
And ploughed free furrows through the wave and foam,
Nor spread reluctant sail for more safe home
Till we had freighted well our argosy.
Of which despoilèd treasures these remain,
10 Sordello's passion, and the honied line
Of young Endymion, lordly Tamburlaine
Driving his pampered jades, and more than these,
The seven-fold vision of the Florentine,
And grave-browed Milton's solemn harmonies.

AVA MARIA PLENA GRATIA

Oscar Wilde

1   Was this His coming! I had hoped to see
A scene of wondrous glory, as was told
Of some great God who in a rain of gold
Broke open bars and fell on Danae:
5   Or a dread vision as when Semele
Sickening for love and unappeased desire
Prayed to see God's clear body, and the fire
Caught her white limbs and slew her utterly:
With such glad dreams I sought this holy place,
10   And now with wondering eyes and heart I stand
Before this supreme mystery of Love:
A kneeling girl with passionless pale face,
An angel with a lily in his hand,
And over both with outstretched wings the Dove.

GARDEN OF EROS

Oscar Wilde

1   It is full summer now, the heart of June,
    Not yet the sun-burnt reapers are a-stir
    Upon the upland meadow where too soon
    Rich autumn time, the season's usurer,
5   Will lend his hoarded gold to all the trees,
    And see his treasure scattered by the wild and spendthrift breeze.

    Too soon indeed! yet here the daffodil,
    That love-child of the Spring, has lingered on
    To vex the rose with jealousy, and still
10   The harebell spreads her azure pavilion,
    And like a strayed and wandering reveller
    Abandoned of its brothers, whom long since June's messenger

    The missel-thrush has frighted from the glade,
    One pale narcissus loiters fearfully
15   Close to a shadowy nook, where half afraid
    Of their own loveliness some violets lie
    That will not look the gold sun in the face
    For fear of too much splendour,--ah! methinks it is a place

    Which should be trodden by Persephone
20   When wearied of the flowerless fields of Dis!
    Or danced on by the lads of Arcady!
    The hidden secret of eternal bliss
    Known to the Grecian here a man might find,
    Ah! you and I may find it now if Love and Sleep be kind.

25   There are the flowers which mourning Herakles
    Strewed on the tomb of Hylas, columbine,
    Its white doves all a-flutter where the breeze
    Kissed them too harshly, the small celandine,

That yellow-kirtled chorister of eve,
30 And lilac lady's-smock,--but let them bloom alone, and leave

Yon spired holly-hock red-crocketed
To sway its silent chimes, else must the bee,
Its little bellringer, go seek instead
Some other pleasaunce; the anemone
35 That weeps at daybreak, like a silly girl
Before her love, and hardly lets the butterflies unfurl

Their painted wings beside it,--bid it pine
In pale virginity; the winter snow
Will suit it better than those lips of thine
40 Whose fires would but scorch it, rather go
And pluck that amorous flower which blooms alone,
Fed by the pander wind with dust of kisses not its own.

The trumpet-mouths of red convolvulus
So dear to maidens, creamy meadow-sweet
45 Whiter than Juno's throat and odorous
As all Arabia, hyacinths the feet
Of Huntress Dian would be loth to mar
For any dappled fawn,--pluck these, and those fond flowers which are

Fairer than what Queen Venus trod upon
50 Beneath the pines of Ida, eucharis,
That morning star which does not dread the sun,
And budding marjoram which but to kiss
Would sweeten Cytheræa's lips and make
Adonis jealous,--these for thy head,--and for thy girdle take

55 Yon curving spray of purple clematis
Whose gorgeous dye outflames the Tyrian King,
And fox-gloves with their nodding chalices,
But that one narciss which the startled Spring
Let from her kirtle fall when first she heard
60 In her own woods the wild tempestuous song of summer's bird,

Ah! leave it for a subtle memory
Of those sweet tremulous days of rain and sun,
When April laughed between her tears to see
The early primrose with shy footsteps run
65 From the gnarled oak-tree roots till all the wold,
Spite of its brown and trampled leaves, grew bright with shim-
mering gold.

Nay, pluck it too, it is not half so sweet
As thou thyself, my soul's idolatry!
70 And when thou art a-wearied at thy feet
Shall oxlips weave their brightest tapestry,
For thee the woodbine shall forget its pride
And vail its tangled whorls, and thou shalt walk on daisies pied.

And I will cut a reed by yonder spring
75 And make the wood-gods jealous, and old Pan
Wonder what young intruder dares to sing
In these still haunts, where never foot of man
Should tread at evening, lest he chance to spy
The marble limbs of Artemis and all her company.

80 And I will tell thee why the jacinth wears
Such dread embroidery of dolorous moan,
And why the hapless nightingale forbears
To sing her song at noon, but weeps alone
When the fleet swallow sleeps, and rich men feast,
85 And why the laurel trembles when she sees the lightening east.

And I will sing how sad Proserpina
Unto a grave and gloomy Lord was wed,
And lure the silver-breasted Helena
Back from the lotus meadows of the dead,
90 So shalt thou see that awful loveliness
For which two mighty Hosts met fearfuly in war's abyss!

And then I 'll pipe to thee that Grecian tale
How Cynthia loves the lad Endymion,
And hidden in a grey and misty veil

95   Hies to the cliffs of Latmos once the Sun
        Leaps from his ocean bed in fruitless chase
        Of those pale flying feet which fade away in his embrace.

        And if my flute can breathe sweet melody,
        We may behold Her face who long ago
100   Dwelt among men by the Ægean sea,
        And whose sad house with pillaged portico
        And friezeless wall and columns toppled down
        Looms o'er the ruins of that fair and violet-cinctured town.

        Spirit of Beauty! tarry still a-while,
105   They are not dead, thine ancient votaries,
        Some few there are to whom thy radiant smile
        Is better than a thousand victories,
        Though all the nobly slain of Waterloo
        Rise up in wrath against them! tarry still, there are a few.

110   Who for thy sake would give their manlihood
        And consecrate their being, I at least
        Have done so, made thy lips my daily food,
        And in thy temples found a goodlier feast
        Than this starved age can give me, spite of all
115   Its new-found creeds so sceptical and so dogmatical.

        Here not Cephissos, not Ilissos flows,
        The woods of white Colonos are not here,
        On our bleak hills the olive never blows,
        No simple priest conducts his lowing steer
120   Up the steep marble way, nor through the town
        Do laughing maidens bear to thee the crocus-flowered gown.

        Yet tarry! for the boy who loved thee best,
        Whose very name should be a memory
125   To make thee linger, sleeps in silent rest
        Beneath the Roman walls, and melody
        Still mourns her sweetest lyre, none can play
        The lute of Adonais, with his lips Song passed away.

Nay, when Keats died the Muses still had left
130   One silver voice to sing his threnody,
But ah! too soon of it we were bereft
When on that riven night and stormy sea
Panthea claimed her singer as her own,
And slew the mouth that praised her; since which time we walk alone,

135   Save for that fiery heart, that morning star
Of re-arisen England, whose clear eye
Saw from our tottering throne and waste of war
The grand Greek limbs of young Democracy
Rise mightily like Hesperus and bring
The great Republic! him at least thy love hath taught to sing,
140

And he hath been with thee at Thessaly,
And seen white Atalanta fleet of foot
In passionless and fierce virginity
Hunting the tuskéd boar, his honied lute
Hath pierced the cavern of the hollow hill,
145   And Venus laughs to know one knee will bow before her still.

And he hath kissed the lips of Proserpine,
And sung the Galilæan's requiem,
That wounded forehead dashed with blood and wine
150   He hath discrowned, the Ancient Gods in him
Have found their last, most ardent worshipper,
And the new Sign grows grey and dim before its conqueror.

Spirit of Beauty! tarry with us still,
It is not quenched the torch of poesy,
155   The star that shook above the Eastern hill
Holds unassailed its argent armoury
From all the gathering gloom and fretful fight--
O tarry with us still! for through the long and common night,

Morris, our sweet and simple Chaucer's child,
160   Dear heritor of Spenser's tuneful reed,

With soft and sylvan pipe has oft beguiled
The weary soul of man in troublous need,
And from the far and flowerless fields of ice
Has brought fair flowers meet to make an earthly paradise.

165   We know them all, Gudrun the strong men's bride,
Aslaug and Olafson we know them all,
How giant Grettir fought and Sigurd died,
And what enchantment held the king in thrall
When lonely Brynhild wrestled with the powers
170   That war against all passion, ah! how oft through summer hours,

Long listless summer hours when the noon
Being enamoured of a damask rose
Forgets to journey westward, till the moon
The pale usurper of its tribute grows
175   From a thin sickle to a silver shield
And chides its loitering car--how oft, in some cool grassy field

Far from the cricket-ground and noisy eight,
At Bagley, where the rustling bluebells come
Almost before the blackbird finds a mate
180   And overstay the swallow, and the hum
Of many murmuring bees flits through the leaves,
Have I lain poring on the dreamy tales his fancy weaves,

And through their unreal woes and mimic pain
Wept for myself, and so was purified,
185   And in their simple mirth grew glad again;
For as I sailed upon that pictured tide
The strength and splendour of the storm was mine
Without the storm's red ruin, for the singer is divine,

The little laugh of water falling down
190   Is not so musical, the clammy gold
Close hoarded in the tiny waxen town
Has less of sweetness in it, and the old
Half-withered reeds that waved in Arcady
Touched by his lips break forth again to fresher harmony.

195   Spirit of Beauty tarry yet a-while!
      Although the cheating merchants of the mart
      With iron roads profane our lovely isle,
      And break on whirling wheels the limbs of Art,
      Ay! though the crowded factories beget
200   The blind-worm Ignorance that slays the soul, O tarry yet!

      For One at least there is,--He bears his name
      From Dante and the seraph Gabriel,--
      Whose double laurels burn with deathless flame
      To light thine altar; He too loves thee well,
205   Who saw old Merlin lured in Vivien's snare,
      And the white feet of angels coming down the golden stair,

      Loves thee so well, that all the World for him
      A gorgeous-coloured vestiture must wear,
      And Sorrow take a purple diadem,
210   Or else be no more Sorrow, and Despair
      Gild its own thorns, and Pain, like Adon, be
      Even in anguish beautiful;--such is the empery

      Which Painters hold, and such the heritage
      This gentle solemn Spirit doth possess,
215   Being a better mirror of his age
      In all his pity, love, and weariness,
      Than those who can but copy common things,
      And leave the Soul unpainted with its mighty questionings.

      But they are few, and all romance has flown,
220   And men can prophesy about the sun,
      And lecture on his arrows--how, alone,
      Through a waste void the soulless atoms run,
      How from each tree its weeping nymph has fled,
      And that no more 'mid English reeds a Naïad shows her head.

225   Methinks these new Actæons boast too soon
      That they have spied on beauty; what if we
      Have analyzed the rainbow, robbed the moon

Of her most ancient, chastest mystery,
Shall I, the last Endymion, lose all hope
230 Because rude eyes peer at my mistress through a telescope!

What profit if this scientific age
Burst through our gates with all its retinue
Of modern miracles! Can it assuage
One lover's breaking heart? what can it do
235 To make one life more beautiful, one day
More god-like in its period? but now the Age of Clay

Returns in horrid cycle, and the earth
Hath borne again a noisy progeny
Of ignorant Titans, whose ungodly birth
240 Hurls them against the august hierarchy
Which sat upon Olympus, to the Dust
They have appealed, and to that barren arbiter they must

Repair for judgment, let them, if they can,
From Natural Warfare and insensate Chance,
245 Create the new Ideal rule for man!
Methinks that was not my inheritance;
For I was nurtured otherwise, my soul
Passes from higher heights of life to a more supreme goal.

Lo! while we spake the earth did turn away
250 Her visage from the God, and Hecate's boat
Rose silver-laden, till the jealous day
Blew all its torches out: I did not note
The waning hours, to young Endymions
Time's palsied fingers count in vain his rosary of suns!--

255 Mark how the yellow iris wearily
Leans back its throat, as though it would be kissed
By its false chamberer, the dragon-fly,
Who, like a blue vein on a girl's white wrist,
Sleeps on that snowy primrose of the night,
260 Which 'gins to flush with crimson shame, and die beneath the light.

Come let us go, against the pallid shield
Of the wan sky the almond blossoms gleam,
The corn-crake nested in the unmown field
Answers its mate, across the misty stream
265   On fitful wing the startled curlews fly,
And in his sedgy bed the lark, for joy that Day is nigh,

Scatters the pearléd dew from off the grass,
In tremulous ecstasy to greet the sun,
Who soon in gilded panoply will pass
270   Forth from yon orange-curtained pavilion
Hung in the burning east, see, the red rim
O'ertops the expectant hills! it is the God! for love of him

Already the shrill lark is out of sight,
Flooding with waves of song this silent dell,--
275   Ah! there is something more in that bird's flight
Than could be tested in a crucible!--
But the air freshens, let us go,--why soon
The woodmen will be here; how we have lived this night of June!

TO MILTON

Oscar Wilde

1   Milton! I think thy spirit hath passed away
From these white cliffs, and high-embattled towers;
This gorgeous fiery-coloured world of ours
Seems fallen into ashes dull and grey,
5   And the age changed unto a mimic play
Wherein we waste our else too-crowded hours:
For all our pomp and pageantry and powers
We are but fit to delve the common clay,
Seeing this little isle on which we stand,
10   This England, this sea-lion of the sea,
By ignorant demagogues is held in fee,
Who love her not: Dear God! is this the land
Which bare a triple empire in her hand
When Cromwell spake the word Democracy!

THE HARLOT'S HOUSE

Oscar Wilde

1   We caught the tread of dancing feet,
We loitered down the moonlit street,
And stopped beneath the harlot's house.

Inside, above the din and fray,
5   We heard the loud musicians play
The 'Treues Liebes Herz' of Strauss.

Like strange mechanical grotesques,
Making fantastic arabesques,
The shadows raced across the blind.

10   We watched the ghostly dancers spin
To sound of horn and violin,
Like black leaves wheeling in the wind.

Like wire-pulled automatons,
Slim silhouetted skeletons
15   Went sidling through the slow quadrille,

Then took each other by the hand,
And danced a stately saraband;
Their laughter echoed thin and shrill.

Sometimes a clockwork puppet pressed
20   A phantom lover to her breast,
Sometimes they seemed to try to sing.

Sometimes a horrible marionette
Came out, and smoked its cigarette
Upon the steps like a live thing.

Then, turning to my love, I said,
'The dead are dancing with the dead,
The dust is whirling with the dust.'

But she--she heard the violin,
And left my side, and entered in:
Love passed into the house of lust.

Then suddenly the tune went false,
The dancers wearied of the waltz,
The shadows ceased to wheel and whirl.

And down the long and silent street,
The dawn, with silver-sandalled feet,
Crept like a frightened girl.

HOUSE OF JUDGEMENT

Oscar Wilde

And there was silence in the House of Judgment, and the Man came naked before God.

And God opened the Book of the Life of the Man.

And God said to the Man, 'Thy life hath been evil, and thou hast shown cruelty to those who were in need of succour, and to those who lacked help thou hast been bitter and hard of heart. The poor called to thee and thou didst not hearken, and thine ears were closed to the cry of My afflicted. The inheritance of the fatherless thou didst take unto thyself, and thou didst send the foxes into the vineyard of thy neighbour's field. Thou didst take the bread of the children and give it to the dogs to eat, and My lepers who lived in the marshes, and were at peace and praised Me, thou didst drive forth on to the highways, and on Mine earth out of which I made thee thou didst spill innocent blood.'

And the Man made answer and said, 'Even so did I.'

And again God opened the Book of the Life of the Man.

And God said to the Man, 'Thy life hath been evil, and the Beauty I have shown thou hast sought for, and the Good I have hidden thou didst pass by. The walls of thy chamber were painted with images, and from the bed of thine abominations thou didst rise up to the sound of flutes. Thou didst build seven altars to the sins I have suffered, and didst eat of the thing that may not be eaten, and the purple of thy raiment was broidered with the three signs of shame. Thine idols were neither of gold nor of silver that endure, but of flesh that dieth. Thou didst stain their hair with perfumes and put pomegranates in their hands. Thou didst stain their feet with saffron and spread carpets before them. With antimony thou didst stain their eyelids and their bodies thou didst smear with myrrh. Thou didst bow thyself to the ground before them, and the thrones of thine idols were set in the sun. Thou didst show to the sun thy shame and to the moon thy madness.'

And the Man made answer and said, 'Even so did I.'

And a third time God opened the Book of the Life of the Man.

And God said to the Man, 'Evil hath been thy life, and with evil didst thou requite good, and with wrongdoing kindness. The hands that fed thee thou didst wound, and the breasts that gave thee suck thou didst despise. He who came to thee with water went away thirsting, and the outlawed men who hid thee in their tents at night thou didst betray before dawn. Thine enemy who spared thee thou didst snare in an am bush, and the friend who walked with thee thou didst sell for a price, and to those who brought thee Love thou didst ever give Lust in thy turn.'

And the Man made answer and said, 'Even so did I.'

And God closed the Book of the Life of the Man, and said, 'Surely I will send thee into Hell. Even into Hell will I send thee.'

And the Man cried out, 'Thou canst not.'

And God said to the Man, 'Wherefore can I not send thee to Hell, and for what reason?'

'Because in Hell have I always lived,' answered the Man.

And there was silence in the House of Judgment.

And after a space God spake, and said to the Man, 'Seeing that I may not send thee into Hell, surely I will send thee unto Heaven. Even unto Heaven will I send thee.'

And the Man cried out, 'Thou canst not.'

And God said to the Man, 'Wherefore can I not send thee unto Heaven, and for what reason?'

'Because never, and in no place, have I been able to imagine it,' answered the Man.

And there was silence in the House of Judgment.

THE DISCIPLE

Oscar Wilde

When Narcissus died the pool of his pleasure changed from a cup of sweet waters into a cup of salt tears, and the Oreads came weeping through the woodland that they might sing to the pool and give it comfort.

And when they saw that the pool had changed from a cup of sweet waters into a cup of salt tears, they loosened the green tresses of their hair and cried to the pool and said, 'We do not wonder that you should mourn in this manner for Narcissus, so beautiful was he.'

'But was Narcissus beautiful?' said the pool.

'Who should know that better than you?' answered the Oreads. 'Us did he ever pass by, but you he sought for, and would lie on your banks and look down at you, and in the mirror of your waters he would mirror his own beauty.'

And the pool answered, 'But I loved Narcissus because, as he lay on my banks and looked down at me, in the mirror of his eyes I saw ever my own beauty mirrored.'

THE ARTIST

Oscar Wilde

One evening there came into his soul the desire to fashion an image of The Pleasure that abideth for a Moment. And he went forth into the world to look for bronze. For he could only think in bronze.

But all the bronze of the whole world had disappeared, nor anywhere in the whole world was there any bronze to be found, save only the bronze of the image of The Sorrow that endureth for Ever.

Now this image he had himself, and with his own hands, fashioned, and had set it on the tomb of the one thing he had loved in life. On the tomb of the dead thing he had most loved had he set this image of his own fashioning, that it might serve as a sign of the love of man that dieth not, and a symbol of the sorrow of man that endureth for ever. And in the whole world there was no other bronze save the bronze of this image.

And he took the image he had fashioned, and set it in a great furnace, and gave it to the fire.

And out of the bronze of the image of The Sorrow that endureth for Ever he fashioned an image of The Pleasure that abideth for a Moment.

THE MASTER

Oscar Wilde

Now when the darkness came over the earth Joseph of Arimathea, having lighted a torch of pinewood, passed down from the hill into the valley. For he had business in his own home.

And kneeling on the flint stones of the Valley of Desolation he saw a young man who was naked and weeping. His hair was the colour of honey, and his body was as a white flower, but he had wounded his body with thorns and on his hair had he set ashes as a crown.

And he who had great possessions said to the young man who was naked and weeping, 'I do not wonder that your sorrow is so great, for surely He was a just man.'

And the young man answered, 'It is not for Him that I am weeping, but for myself. I too have changed water into wine, and I have healed the leper and given sight to the blind. I have walked upon the waters, and from the dwellers in the tombs I have cast out devils. I have fed the hungry in the desert where there was no food, and I have raised the dead from their narrow houses, and at my bidding, and before a great multitude, of people, a barren fig-tree withered away. All things that this man has done I have done also. And yet they have not crucified me.'

THE BALLAD OF THE READING GAOL

Oscar Wilde

I

1   He did not wear his scarlet coat,
       For blood and wine are red,
     And blood and wine were on his hands
       When they found him with the dead,
5   The poor dead woman whom he loved,
       And murdered in her bed.

     He walked amongst the Trial Men
       In a suit of shabby grey;
     A cricket cap was on his head,
10   And his step seemed light and gay;
     But I never saw a man who looked
       So wistfully at the day.

     I never saw a man who looked
       With such a wistful eye
15   Upon that little tent of blue
       Which prisoners call the sky,
     And at every drifting cloud that went
       With sails of silver by.

     I walked, with other souls in pain,
20   Within another ring,
     And was wondering if the man had done
       A great or little thing,
     When a voice behind me whispered low,
       "That fellow's got to swing."

25   Dear Christ! the very prison walls

Suddenly seemed to reel,
And the sky above my head became
  Like a casque of scorching steel;
And, though I was a soul in pain,
30   My pain I could not feel.

I only knew what hunted thought
  Quickened his step, and why
He looked upon the garish day
  With such a wistful eye;
35 The man had killed the thing he loved
  And so he had to die.

Yet each man kills the thing he loves
  By each let this be heard,
Some do it with a bitter look,
40   Some with a flattering word,
The coward does it with a kiss,
  The brave man with a sword!

Some kill their love when they are young,
  And some when they are old;
45 Some strangle with the hands of Lust,
  Some with the hands of Gold:
The kindest use a knife, because
  The dead so soon grow cold.

Some love too little, some too long,
50   Some sell, and others buy;
Some do the deed with many tears,
  And some without a sigh:
For each man kills the thing he loves,
  Yet each man does not die.

55 He does not die a death of shame
  On a day of dark disgrace,
Nor have a noose about his neck,

Nor a cloth upon his face,
Nor drop feet foremost through the floor
60   Into an empty place

He does not sit with silent men
    Who watch him night and day;
Who watch him when he tries to weep,
    And when he tries to pray;
65   Who watch him lest himself should rob
    The prison of its prey.

He does not wake at dawn to see
    Dread figures throng his room,
The shivering Chaplain robed in white,
70   The Sheriff stern with gloom,
And the Governor all in shiny black,
    With the yellow face of Doom.

He does not rise in piteous haste
    To put on convict-clothes,
75 While some coarse-mouthed Doctor gloats, and notes
    Each new and nerve-twitched pose,
Fingering a watch whose little ticks
    Are like horrible hammer-blows.

He does not know that sickening thirst
80   That sands one's throat, before
The hangman with his gardener's gloves
    Slips through the padded door,
And binds one with three leathern thongs,
    That the throat may thirst no more.

85   He does not bend his head to hear
    The Burial Office read,
Nor, while the terror of his soul
    Tells him he is not dead,
Cross his own coffin, as he moves

90   Into the hideous shed.

He does not stare upon the air
  Through a little roof of glass;
He does not pray with lips of clay
  For his agony to pass;
95   Nor feel upon his shuddering cheek
  The kiss of Caiaphas.

II

Six weeks our guardsman walked the yard,
  In a suit of shabby grey:
His cricket cap was on his head,
100   And his step seemed light and gay,
But I never saw a man who looked
  So wistfully at the day.

I never saw a man who looked
  With such a wistful eye
105 Upon that little tent of blue
  Which prisoners call the sky,
And at every wandering cloud that trailed
  Its raveled fleeces by.

He did not wring his hands, as do
110   Those witless men who dare
To try to rear the changeling Hope
  In the cave of black Despair:
He only looked upon the sun,
  And drank the morning air.

115 He did not wring his hands nor weep,
  Nor did he peek or pine,
But he drank the air as though it held
  Some healthful anodyne;

With open mouth he drank the sun
120   As though it had been wine!

And I and all the souls in pain,
   Who tramped the other ring,
Forgot if we ourselves had done
   A great or little thing,
125   And watched with gaze of dull amaze
   The man who had to swing.

And strange it was to see him pass
   With a step so light and gay,
And strange it was to see him look
130   So wistfully at the day,
And strange it was to think that he
   Had such a debt to pay.

For oak and elm have pleasant leaves
   That in the spring-time shoot:
135   But grim to see is the gallows-tree,
   With its adder-bitten root,
And, green or dry, a man must die
   Before it bears its fruit!

The loftiest place is that seat of grace
140   For which all worldlings try:
But who would stand in hempen band
   Upon a scaffold high,
And through a murderer's collar take
   His last look at the sky?

145   It is sweet to dance to violins
   When Love and Life are fair:
To dance to flutes, to dance to lutes
   Is delicate and rare:
But it is not sweet with nimble feet
150   To dance upon the air!

So with curious eyes and sick surmise
  We watched him day by day,
And wondered if each one of us
  Would end the self-same way,
155   For none can tell to what red Hell
  His sightless soul may stray.

At last the dead man walked no more
  Amongst the Trial Men,
And I knew that he was standing up
160   In the black dock's dreadful pen,
And that never would I see his face
  In God's sweet world again.

Like two doomed ships that pass in storm
  We had crossed each other's way:
165   But we made no sign, we said no word,
  We had no word to say;
For we did not meet in the holy night,
  But in the shameful day.

A prison wall was round us both,
170   Two outcast men were we:
The world had thrust us from its heart,
  And God from out His care:
And the iron gin that waits for Sin
  Had caught us in its snare.

III

175   In Debtors' Yard the stones are hard,
  And the dripping wall is high,
So it was there he took the air
  Beneath the leaden sky,
And by each side a Warder walked,

180   For fear the man might die.

        Or else he sat with those who watched
          His anguish night and day;
        Who watched him when he rose to weep,
          And when he crouched to pray;
185   Who watched him lest himself should rob
          Their scaffold of its prey.

        The Governor was strong upon
          The Regulations Act:
        The Doctor said that Death was but
190   A scientific fact:
        And twice a day the Chaplain called
          And left a little tract.

        And twice a day he smoked his pipe,
          And drank his quart of beer:
195   His soul was resolute, and held
          No hiding-place for fear;
        He often said that he was glad
          The hangman's hands were near.

        But why he said so strange a thing
200   No Warder dared to ask:
        For he to whom a watcher's doom
          Is given as his task,
        Must set a lock upon his lips,
          And make his face a mask.

205   Or else he might be moved, and try
          To comfort or console:
        And what should Human Pity do
          Pent up in Murderers' Hole?
        What word of grace in such a place
210   Could help a brother's soul?

With slouch and swing around the ring
   We trod the Fool's Parade!
We did not care: we knew we were
   The Devil's Own Brigade:
215 And shaven head and feet of lead
   Make a merry masquerade.

We tore the tarry rope to shreds
   With blunt and bleeding nails;
We rubbed the doors, and scrubbed the floors,
220 And cleaned the shining rails:
And, rank by rank, we soaped the plank,
   And clattered with the pails.

We sewed the sacks, we broke the stones,
   We turned the dusty drill:
225 We banged the tins, and bawled the hymns,
   And sweated on the mill:
But in the heart of every man
   Terror was lying still.

So still it lay that every day
230 Crawled like a weed-clogged wave:
And we forgot the bitter lot
   That waits for fool and knave,
Till once, as we tramped in from work,
   We passed an open grave.

235 With yawning mouth the yellow hole
   Gaped for a living thing;
The very mud cried out for blood
   To the thirsty asphalte ring:
And we knew that ere one dawn grew fair
240 Some prisoner had to swing.

Right in we went, with soul intent
   On Death and Dread and Doom:

The hangman, with his little bag,
  Went shuffling through the gloom
245 And each man trembled as he crept
  Into his numbered tomb.

That night the empty corridors
  Were full of forms of Fear,
And up and down the iron town
250 Stole feet we could not hear,
And through the bars that hide the stars
  White faces seemed to peer.

He lay as one who lies and dreams
  In a pleasant meadow-land,
255 The watcher watched him as he slept,
  And could not understand
How one could sleep so sweet a sleep
  With a hangman close at hand?

But there is no sleep when men must weep
260 Who never yet have wept:
So we—the fool, the fraud, the knave—
  That endless vigil kept,
And through each brain on hands of pain
  Another's terror crept.

265 Alas! it is a fearful thing
  To feel another's guilt!
For, right within, the sword of Sin
  Pierced to its poisoned hilt,
And as molten lead were the tears we shed
270 For the blood we had not spilt.

The Warders with their shoes of felt
  Crept by each padlocked door,
And peeped and saw, with eyes of awe,
  Grey figures on the floor,

275   And wondered why men knelt to pray
      Who never prayed before.

    All through the night we knelt and prayed,
      Mad mourners of a corpse!
    The troubled plumes of midnight were
280   The plumes upon a hearse:
    And bitter wine upon a sponge
      Was the savior of Remorse.

    The cock crew, the red cock crew,
      But never came the day:
285   And crooked shape of Terror crouched,
      In the corners where we lay:
    And each evil sprite that walks by night
      Before us seemed to play.

    They glided past, they glided fast,
290   Like travelers through a mist:
    They mocked the moon in a rigadoon
      Of delicate turn and twist,
    And with formal pace and loathsome grace
      The phantoms kept their tryst.

295   With mop and mow, we saw them go,
      Slim shadows hand in hand:
    About, about, in ghostly rout
      They trod a saraband:
    And the damned grotesques made arabesques,
300   Like the wind upon the sand!

    With the pirouettes of marionettes,
      They tripped on pointed tread:
    But with flutes of Fear they filled the ear,
      As their grisly masque they led,
305   And loud they sang, and loud they sang,
      For they sang to wake the dead.

"Oho!" they cried, "The world is wide,
  But fettered limbs go lame!
And once, or twice, to throw the dice
310   Is a gentlemanly game,
But he does not win who plays with Sin
  In the secret House of Shame."

No things of air these antics were
  That frolicked with such glee:
315 To men whose lives were held in gyves,
  And whose feet might not go free,
Ah! wounds of Christ! they were living things,
  Most terrible to see.

Around, around, they waltzed and wound;
320   Some wheeled in smirking pairs:
With the mincing step of demirep
  Some sidled up the stairs:
And with subtle sneer, and fawning leer,
  Each helped us at our prayers.

325 The morning wind began to moan,
  But still the night went on:
Through its giant loom the web of gloom
  Crept till each thread was spun:
And, as we prayed, we grew afraid
330   Of the Justice of the Sun.

The moaning wind went wandering round
  The weeping prison-wall:
Till like a wheel of turning-steel
  We felt the minutes crawl:
335 O moaning wind! what had we done
  To have such a seneschal?

At last I saw the shadowed bars

Like a lattice wrought in lead,
Move right across the whitewashed wall
340   That faced my three-plank bed,
And I knew that somewhere in the world
    God's dreadful dawn was red.

At six o'clock we cleaned our cells,
    At seven all was still,
345   But the sough and swing of a mighty wing
    The prison seemed to fill,
For the Lord of Death with icy breath
    Had entered in to kill.

He did not pass in purple pomp,
350   Nor ride a moon-white steed.
Three yards of cord and a sliding board
    Are all the gallows' need:
So with rope of shame the Herald came
    To do the secret deed.

355   We were as men who through a fen
    Of filthy darkness grope:
We did not dare to breathe a prayer,
    Or give our anguish scope:
Something was dead in each of us,
360   And what was dead was Hope.

For Man's grim Justice goes its way,
    And will not swerve aside:
It slays the weak, it slays the strong,
    It has a deadly stride:
365   With iron heel it slays the strong,
    The monstrous parricide!

We waited for the stroke of eight:
    Each tongue was thick with thirst:
For the stroke of eight is the stroke of Fate

370   That makes a man accursed,
      And Fate will use a running noose
        For the best man and the worst.

      We had no other thing to do,
        Save to wait for the sign to come:
375   So, like things of stone in a valley lone,
        Quiet we sat and dumb:
      But each man's heart beat thick and quick
        Like a madman on a drum!

      With sudden shock the prison-clock
380   Smote on the shivering air,
      And from all the gaol rose up a wail
        Of impotent despair,
      Like the sound that frightened marshes hear
        From a leper in his lair.

385   And as one sees most fearful things
        In the crystal of a dream,
      We saw the greasy hempen rope
        Hooked to the blackened beam,
      And heard the prayer the hangman's snare
390   Strangled into a scream.

      And all the woe that moved him so
        That he gave that bitter cry,
      And the wild regrets, and the bloody sweats,
        None knew so well as I:
395   For he who lives more lives than one
        More deaths than one must die.

IV

      There is no chapel on the day
        On which they hang a man:
      The Chaplain's heart is far too sick,

Or his face is far too wan,
400   Or there is that written in his eyes
    Which none should look upon.

So they kept us close till nigh on noon,
    And then they rang the bell,
And the Warders with their jingling keys
405   Opened each listening cell,
And down the iron stair we tramped,
    Each from his separate Hell.

Out into God's sweet air we went,
    But not in wonted way,
410   For this man's face was white with fear,
    And that man's face was grey,
And I never saw sad men who looked
    So wistfully at the day.

I never saw sad men who looked
415   With such a wistful eye
Upon that little tent of blue
    We prisoners called the sky,
And at every careless cloud that passed
    In happy freedom by.

420   But there were those amongst us all
    Who walked with downcast head,
And knew that, had each got his due,
    They should have died instead:
He had but killed a thing that lived
425   Whilst they had killed the dead.

For he who sins a second time
    Wakes a dead soul to pain,
And draws it from its spotted shroud,
    And makes it bleed again,
430   And makes it bleed great gouts of blood

And makes it bleed in vain!

Like ape or clown, in monstrous garb
  With crooked arrows starred,
Silently we went round and round
435   The slippery asphalte yard;
Silently we went round and round,
  And no man spoke a word.

Silently we went round and round,
  And through each hollow mind
440 The memory of dreadful things
    Rushed like a dreadful wind,
And Horror stalked before each man,
  And terror crept behind.

The Warders strutted up and down,
445   And kept their herd of brutes,
Their uniforms were spick and span,
  And they wore their Sunday suits,
But we knew the work they had been at
  By the quicklime on their boots.

450 For where a grave had opened wide,
    There was no grave at all:
Only a stretch of mud and sand
  By the hideous prison-wall,
And a little heap of burning lime,
455   That the man should have his pall.

For he has a pall, this wretched man,
  Such as few men can claim:
Deep down below a prison-yard,
  Naked for greater shame,
460 He lies, with fetters on each foot,
  Wrapt in a sheet of flame!

And all the while the burning lime
  Eats flesh and bone away,
It eats the brittle bone by night,
465   And the soft flesh by the day,
It eats the flesh and bones by turns,
  But it eats the heart alway.

For three long years they will not sow
  Or root or seedling there:
470 For three long years the unblessed spot
  Will sterile be and bare,
And look upon the wondering sky
  With unreproachful stare.

They think a murderer's heart would taint
475   Each simple seed they sow.
It is not true! God's kindly earth
  Is kindlier than men know,
And the red rose would but blow more red,
  The white rose whiter blow.

480 Out of his mouth a red, red rose!
  Out of his heart a white!
For who can say by what strange way,
  Christ brings his will to light,
Since the barren staff the pilgrim bore
485   Bloomed in the great Pope's sight?

But neither milk-white rose nor red
  May bloom in prison air;
The shard, the pebble, and the flint,
  Are what they give us there:
490 For flowers have been known to heal
  A common man's despair.

So never will wine-red rose or white,
  Petal by petal, fall

On that stretch of mud and sand that lies
495   By the hideous prison-wall,
To tell the men who tramp the yard
   That God's Son died for all.

Yet though the hideous prison-wall
   Still hems him round and round,
500   And a spirit man not walk by night
   That is with fetters bound,
And a spirit may not weep that lies
   In such unholy ground,

He is at peace—this wretched man—
505   At peace, or will be soon:
There is no thing to make him mad,
   Nor does Terror walk at noon,
For the lampless Earth in which he lies
   Has neither Sun nor Moon.

510   They hanged him as a beast is hanged:
   They did not even toll
A reguiem that might have brought
   Rest to his startled soul,
But hurriedly they took him out,
515   And hid him in a hole.

They stripped him of his canvas clothes,
   And gave him to the flies;
They mocked the swollen purple throat
   And the stark and staring eyes:
520   And with laughter loud they heaped the shroud
   In which their convict lies.

The Chaplain would not kneel to pray
   By his dishonored grave:
Nor mark it with that blessed Cross
525   That Christ for sinners gave,

Because the man was one of those
    Whom Christ came down to save.

Yet all is well; he has but passed
    To Life's appointed bourne:
530   And alien tears will fill for him
      Pity's long-broken urn,
For his mourner will be outcast men,
    And outcasts always mourn.

    V

I know not whether Laws be right,
535   Or whether Laws be wrong;
All that we know who lie in gaol
    Is that the wall is strong;
And that each day is like a year,
    A year whose days are long.

540   But this I know, that every Law
    That men have made for Man,
Since first Man took his brother's life,
    And the sad world began,
But straws the wheat and saves the chaff
545   With a most evil fan.

This too I know—and wise it were
    If each could know the same—
That every prison that men build
    Is built with bricks of shame,
550   And bound with bars lest Christ should see
    How men their brothers maim.

With bars they blur the gracious moon,
    And blind the goodly sun:
And they do well to hide their Hell,
555   For in it things are done

That Son of God nor son of Man
  Ever should look upon!

The vilest deeds like poison weeds
  Bloom well in prison-air:
560 It is only what is good in Man
  That wastes and withers there:
Pale Anguish keeps the heavy gate,
  And the Warder is Despair

For they starve the little frightened child
565   Till it weeps both night and day:
And they scourge the weak, and flog the fool,
  And gibe the old and grey,
And some grow mad, and all grow bad,
  And none a word may say.

570 Each narrow cell in which we dwell
  Is foul and dark latrine,
And the fetid breath of living Death
  Chokes up each grated screen,
And all, but Lust, is turned to dust
575   In Humanity's machine.

The brackish water that we drink
  Creeps with a loathsome slime,
And the bitter bread they weigh in scales
  Is full of chalk and lime,
580 And Sleep will not lie down, but walks
  Wild-eyed and cries to Time.

But though lean Hunger and green Thirst
  Like asp with adder fight,
We have little care of prison fare,
585   For what chills and kills outright
Is that every stone one lifts by day
  Becomes one's heart by night.

With midnight always in one's heart,
    And twilight in one's cell,
590 We turn the crank, or tear the rope,
    Each in his separate Hell,
And the silence is more awful far
    Than the sound of a brazen bell.

And never a human voice comes near
595   To speak a gentle word:
And the eye that watches through the door
    Is pitiless and hard:
And by all forgot, we rot and rot,
    With soul and body marred.

600 And thus we rust Life's iron chain
    Degraded and alone:
And some men curse, and some men weep,
    And some men make no moan:
But God's eternal Laws are kind
605   And break the heart of stone.

And every human heart that breaks,
    In prison-cell or yard,
Is as that broken box that gave
    Its treasure to the Lord,
610 And filled the unclean leper's house
    With the scent of costliest nard.

Ah! happy day they whose hearts can break
    And peace of pardon win!
How else may man make straight his plan
165   And cleanse his soul from Sin?
How else but through a broken heart
    May Lord Christ enter in?

And he of the swollen purple throat.
    And the stark and staring eyes,
620 Waits for the holy hands that took
    The Thief to Paradise;
And a broken and a contrite heart
    The Lord will not despise.

The man in red who reads the Law
625 Gave him three weeks of life,
Three little weeks in which to heal
    His soul of his soul's strife,
And cleanse from every blot of blood
    The hand that held the knife.

630 And with tears of blood he cleansed the hand,
    The hand that held the steel:
For only blood can wipe out blood,
    And only tears can heal:
And the crimson stain that was of Cain
635 Became Christ's snow-white seal.

VI

In Reading gaol by Reading town
    There is a pit of shame,
And in it lies a wretched man
    Eaten by teeth of flame,
640 In burning winding-sheet he lies,
    And his grave has got no name.

And there, till Christ call forth the dead,
    In silence let him lie:
No need to waste the foolish tear,
645 Or heave the windy sigh:
The man had killed the thing he loved,
    And so he had to die.

And all men kill the thing they love,
  By all let this be heard,
650 Some do it with a bitter look,
  Some with a flattering word,
The coward does it with a kiss,

FLOWER OF LOVE

Oscar Wilde

1 Sweet, I blame you not, for mine the fault was, had I not
        been made of common clay
I had climbed the higher heights unclimbed yet,
        seen the fuller air, the larger day.

From the wildness of my wasted passion I had struck a
        better, clearer song,
Lit some lighter light of freer freedom, battled with
        some Hydra-headed wrong.

5 Had my lips been smitten into music by the kisses that
        but made them bleed,
You had walked with Bice and the angels on that
        verdant and enamelled meed.

I had trod the road which Dante treading saw the suns
        of seven circles shine,
Ay! perchance had seen the heavens opening, as they
        opened to the Florentine.

And the mighty nations would have crowned me, who

am crownless now and without name,

10   And some orient dawn had found me kneeling on the
threshold of the House of Fame.

I had sat within that marble circle where the oldest bard
is as the young,
And the pipe is ever dropping honey, and the lyre's
strings are ever strung.

Keats had lifted up his hymeneal curls from out the
poppy-seeded wine,
With ambrosial mouth had kissed my forehead, clasped
the hand of noble love in mine.

15   And at springtide, when the apple-blossoms brush the
burnished bosom of the dove,
Two young lovers lying in an orchard would have read
the story of our love;

Would have read the legend of my passion, known the
bitter secret of my heart,
Kissed as we have kissed, but never parted as we two are
fated now to part.

For the crimson flower of our life is eaten by the
cankerworm of truth,
20   And no hand can gather up the fallen withered petals of
the rose of youth.

Yet I am not sorry that I loved you -ah! what else had I
a boy to do? -
For the hungry teeth of time devour, and the
silent-footed years pursue.

Rudderless, we drift athwart a tempest, and when once
the storm of youth is past,
Without lyre, without lute or chorus, Death the silent
pilot comes at last.

25 And within the grave there is no pleasure, for the blind
      worm battens on the root,
And Desire shudders into ashes, and the tree of Passion
      bears no fruit.

Ah! what else had I to do but love you? God's own
      mother was less dear to me,
And less dear the Cytheraean rising like an argent lily
      from the sea.

I have made my choice, have lived my poems, and,
      though youth is gone in wasted days,
30 I have found the lover's crown of myrtle better than the
      poet's crown of bays.

SYMPHONY IN YELLOW

Oscar Wilde

1 An omnibus across the bridge
  Crawls like a yellow butterfly,
  And, here and there, a passer-by
  Shows like a little restless midge.

5 Big barges full of yellow hay
  Are moored against the shadowy wharf,
  And, like a yellow silken scarf,
  The thick fog hangs along the quay.

  The yellow leaves begin to fade
10 And flutter from the Temple elms,
  And at my feet the pale green Thames
  Lies like a rod of rippled jade.

MARY ELIZABETH COLERIDGE (1854-1900)

During her lifetime, Mary Elizabeth Coleridge, the great-grand-niece of Samuel Taylor Coleridge, was better known for her essays and novels. She was talented and smart, and fluent in six languages in addition to English. Coleridge taught grammar and literature to young women, first in her home, and then later at the Working Women's College. Fearing she would disgrace the family name, Coleridge published her poetry under the pseudonym "Anodos." There is no known portrait of Mary Elizabeth Coleridge, which is understandable, given her shyness and reserve about promoting herself and her writing.

[*Study of a Girl Reading*, Valentine Cameron Prinsep (1838-1904)]

THE OTHER SIDE OF A MIRROR

Mary Elizabeth Coleridge

1   I sat before my glass one day,
    And conjured up a vision bare,
    Unlike the aspects glad and gay,
    That erst were found reflected there -
5   The vision of a woman, wild
    With more than womanly despair.

    Her hair stood back on either side
    A face bereft of loveliness.
    It had no envy now to hide
10   What once no man on earth could guess.
    It formed the thorny aureole
    Of hard, unsanctified distress.

    Her lips were open - not a sound
    Came though the parted lines of red,
15   Whate'er it was, the hideous wound
    In silence and secret bled.
    No sigh relieved her speechless woe,
    She had no voice to speak her dread.

    And in her lurid eyes there shone
20   The dying flame of life's desire,
    Made mad because its hope was gone,
    And kindled at the leaping fire
    Of jealousy and fierce revenge,
    And strength that could not change nor tire.

25   Shade of a shadow in the glass,
    O set the crystal surface free!
    Pass - as the fairer visions pass -
    Nor ever more return, to be
    The ghost of a distracted hour,
30   That heard me whisper: - 'I am she!'

A MOMENT

Mary Elizabeth Coleridge

1   The clouds had made a crimson crown
Above the mountains high.
The stormy sun was going down
In a stormy sky.

5   Why did you let your eyes so rest on me,
And hold your breath between?
In all the ages this can never be
As if it had not been.

IN DISPRAISE OF THE MOON

Mary Elizabeth Coleridge

1   I would not be the Moon, the sickly thing,
To summon owls and bats upon the wing;
For when the noble Sun is gone away,
She turns his night into a pallid day.
5   She hath no air, no radiance of her own,
That world unmusical of earth and stone.
She wakes her dim, uncolored, voiceless hosts,
Ghost of the Sun, herself the sun of ghosts.
The mortal eyes that gaze too long on her
10   Of Reason's piercing ray defrauded are.
Light in itself doth feed the living brain;
That light, reflected, but makes darkness plain.

THE POISON FLOWER

Mary Elizabeth Coleridge

1   The poison flower that in my garden grew
Killed all the other flowers beside.
They withered off and died,
Because their fiery foe sucked up the dew.

5   When the sun shone, the poison flower breathed cold
And spread a chilly mist of dull disgrace.
They could not see his face,
Roses and lilies languished and grew old.

Wherefore I tore that flower up by the root,
10   And flung it on the rubbish heap to fade
Amid the havoc that itself had made.
I did not leave one shoot.

Fair is my garden as it once was fair.
Lilies and roses reign.
15   They drink the dew, they see the sun again;
But I rejoice no longer, walking there.

AN INSINCERE WISH ADDRESSED TO A BEGGAR

Mary Elizabeth Coleridge

1   We are not near enough to love,
I can but pity all your woe;
For wealth has lifted me above,
And falsehood set you down below.

5   If you were true, we still might be
Brothers in something more than name;
And were I poor, your love to me
Would make our differing bonds the same.

But golden gates between us stretch,
10   Truth opens her forbidding eyes;
You can't forget that I am rich,
Nor I that you are telling lies.

Love never comes but at love's call,
And pity asks for him in vain;
15   Because I cannot give you all,
You give me nothing back again.

And you are right with all your wrong,
For less than all is nothing too;
May Heaven beggar me ere long,
20   And Truth reveal herself to you!

MARRIAGE

Mary Elizabeth Coleridge

1   No more alone sleeping, no more alone waking,
Thy dreams divided, thy prayers in twain;
Thy merry sisters tonight forsaking,
Never shall we see, maiden, again.

5   Never shall we see thee, thine eyes glancing.
Flashing with laughter and wild in glee,
Under the mistletoe kissing and dancing,
Wantonly free.

There shall come a matron walking sedately,
10   Low-voiced, gentle, wise in reply.
Tell me, O tell me, can I love her greatly?
All for her sake must the maiden die!

AFFECTION

Mary Elizabeth Coleridge

1   The earth that made the rose,
She also is thy mother, and not I.
The flame wherewith thy maiden spirit glows
Was lighted at no hearth that I sit by.
5   I am as far below as heaven above thee.
Were I thine angel, more I could not love thee.

Bid me defend thee!
Thy danger over-human strength shall lend me,
A hand of iron and a heart of steel,
10   To strike, to wound, to slay, and not to feel.
But if you chide me,
I am a weak, defenceless child beside thee.

THE WHITE WOMEN

Mary Elizabeth Coleridge

1   Where dwell the lovely, wild white women folk,
       Mortal to man?
They never bowed their necks beneath the yoke,
They dwelt alone when the first morning broke
5   And Time began.

Taller are they than man, and very fair,
      Their cheeks are pale,
At sight of them the tiger in his lair,
The falcon hanging in the azure air,
10   The eagles quail.

The deadly shafts their nervous hands let fly
      Are stronger than our strongest—in their form
Larger, more beauteous, carved amazingly,
And when they fight, the wild white women cry
15   The war-cry of the storm.

Their words are not as ours. If man might go
      Among the waves of Ocean when they break
And hear them—hear the language of the snow
Falling on torrents—he might also know
20   The tongue they speak.

Pure are they as the light; they never sinned,
      But when the rays of the eternal fire
Kindle the West, their tresses they unbind
And fling their girdles to the Western wind,
25   Swept by desire.

Lo, maidens to the maidens then are born,

Strong children of the maidens and the breeze,
Dreams are not—in the glory of the morn,
Seen through the gates of ivory and horn—
30 More fair than these.

And none may find their dwelling. In the shade
  Primeval of the forest oaks they hide.
One of our race, lost in an awful glade,
35 Saw with his human eyes a wild white maid,
  And gazing, died.

TO MEMORY

Mary Elizabeth Coleridge

1 Strange Power, I know not what thou art,
 Murderer or mistress of my heart.
 I know I'd rather meet the blow
 Of my most unrelenting foe
5 Than live---as now I live---to be
 Slain twenty times a day by thee.

 Yet, when I would command thee hence,
 Thou mockest at the vain pretence,
 Murmuring in mine ear a song
10 Once loved, alas! forgotten long;
 And on my brow I feel a kiss
 That I would rather die than miss.

THE DESERTED HOUSE

Mary Elizabeth Coleridge

1   There's no smoke in the chimney,
    And the rain beats on the floor;
    There's no glass in the window,
    There's no wood in the door;
5   The heather grows behind the house,
    And the sand lies before.

    No hand hath trained the ivy,
    The walls are grey and bare;
    The boats upon the sea sail by,
10   Nor ever tarry there.
    No beast of the field comes nigh,
    Nor any bird of the air.

THE WITCH

Mary Elizabeth Coleridge

1   I have walked a great while over the snow,
And I am not tall nor strong.
My clothes are wet, and my teeth are set,
And the way was hard and long.
5   I have wandered over the fruitful earth,
But I never came here before.
Oh, lift me over the threshold, and let me in at the door!

The cutting wind is a cruel foe.
10   I dare not stand in the blast.
My hands are stone, and my voice a groan,
And the worst of death is past.
I am but a little maiden still,
My little white feet are sore.
15   Oh, lift me over the threshold, and let me in at the door!

Her voice was the voice that women have,
Who plead for their heart's desire.
She came—she came—and the quivering flame
Sunk and died in the fire.
20   It never was lit again on my hearth
Since I hurried across the floor,
To lift her over the threshold, and let her in at the door.

I ASK OF THEE, LOVE, NOTHING BUT RELIEF

Mary Elizabeth Coleridge

1   I ask of thee, love, nothing but relief.
Thou canst not bring the old days back again;
For I was happy then,
Not knowing heavenly joy, not knowing grief.

MY TRUE LOVE HATH MY HEART
AND I HAVE HIS

Mary Elizabeth Coleridge

1   None ever was in love with me but grief.
She wooed my from the day that I was born;
She stole my playthings first, the jealous thief,
And left me there forlorn.

5   The birds that in my garden would have sung,
She scared away with her unending moan;
She slew my lovers too when I was young,
And left me there alone.

Grief, I have cursed thee often—now at last
10 To hate thy name I am no longer free;
Caught in thy bony arms and prisoned fast,
I love no love but thee.

L'OISEAU BLEU

Mary Elizabeth Coleridge

1   The lake lay blue below the hill.
O'er it, as I looked, there flew
Across the waters, cold and still,
A bird whose wings were palest blue.

5   The sky above was blue at last,
The sky beneath me blue in blue.
A moment, ere the bird had passed,
It caught his image as he flew.

INDEX